DUE DATE	RETURN DATE	DUE DATE	RETURN DATE

THE DYNAMICS OF COMPUTING

THE
DYNAMICS
OF COMPUTING

John Leslie King
and Kenneth L. Kraemer

COLUMBIA UNIVERSITY PRESS
—New York—1985

Columbia University Press
New York   Guildford, Surrey
Copyright © 1985 Columbia University Press
All rights reserved

Printed in the United States of America

Library of Congress Cataloging in Publication Data

King, John Leslie.
  The dynamics of computing.

  Bibliography: p.
  Includes index.
  1. Municipal government—Data processing.
I. Kraemer, Kenneth L.   II. Title.
JS100.E43K56 1985   352'.00724'02854   84-15528
ISBN 0-231-05432-7

CONTENTS

TABLES AND FIGURES

Tables

FIGURES

PREFACE

This book continues the reporting of research results from studies of computing in complex organizations conducted at the Public Policy Research Organization of the University of California, Irvine. These studies, which began in 1972, are aimed at improving understanding of the ways in which computing technology and technics are adopted by, used, and managed in organizations.

The venue of most of this research has been government agencies in the United States and abroad, although additional studies have been conducted in state and federal government agencies as well as private sector organizations. The predominant focus on one organizational sector does constrain the generalizability of the research findings to some extent. However, this focus has allowed us to penetrate the confusion and complexity of the computing world organizations to greater depth than most studies allow. The findings we report here are somewhat surprising, in that they contradict the prevailing literature on the management of computing. We do not claim that the experiences of the organizations we studied are universal. But we believe they are common in many organizations in the public and private sector. We hope our findings will stimulate new and creative research into the factors that make the management of computing so challenging a task.

We owe thanks to many colleagues and friends who have helped make this work possible. Above all others, we thank Debbie Dunkle for her highly professional and unselfish work on the project. In every respect, she was a co-investigator with us, and the project would not have been what it was without her.

We are very grateful for the support of the National Science ·Foundation, and the NSF program managers who have helped and inspired us: W. Richards Adrion, Vaughn Blankenship, Charles Brownstein, Trudi Miller, Frank Scioli, and Larry Oliver. We are appreciative of the guidance and insight provided by our International Advisory Committee: Mogens Rømer of Denmark, George Gaits of the United Kingdom, Wolfgang Hartenstein of West Germany, Jacques Lefevre of France, Barry Wellar of Canada, and Hans Peter Gassman and Paul Kenneth of the Organization for Economic Cooperation and Development, Paris. Our colleagues and fellow researchers also have sustained us with new ideas, encouragement and criticism: James Danziger, Rob Kling, Nick Vitalari, and Alladi Venkatesh of U.C. Irvine; and Bill Dutton, Les Gasser, and Walt Scacchi of the University of Southern California. Our research associates Joey George and Joe Lane have been invaluable to the progress of our work. The PPRO support staff, as always, made it possible for us to actually do the work. Marti Dennis, Shirley Hoberman, Doris McBride, and Sherry Merryman provided budgetary and office management support, while Kathleen Bracy, Rosa Garza, Helen Sandoz, and Julie Takahashi typed and retyped the manuscripts without once asking why.

Finally, we thank the love and support provided by our wives, Kathleen and Norine, and our children, Matthew, Kurt and Kim.

THE DYNAMICS OF COMPUTING

CHAPTER ONE
LIVING
WITH
COMPUTING

THIS BOOK tells two stories. One is the story of computing use in a single organizational sector—city governments in ten countries—at one point in time. This story, which appears in chapters 2 through 6, concerns the relationships among organizational context for computing use, policies for computing, and the benefits and problems of computing use. The other story which is begun in this chapter and resumed in chapter 7, deals with the changes that take place over time in the use of computing in organizations. Together, these two stories form an assessment of computing *in vivo;* that is, in the living systems of real organizations.

We undertook the research that resulted in this book because of a unique opportunity to merge the findings of a national U.S. data base on the use of computing in city governments with similar data collected on cities in nine other countries. We felt the contrast between conditions in U.S. cities and cities in other countries would provide us with a chance to explore further the differences in extra- and intra-organizational environments that proved to be important in earlier analyses of computing in cities (Kraemer, Dutton, and Northrop 1981; Danziger, Dutton, Kling, and Kraemer 1982). As expected, our analyses revealed that environmental differences are important.

But our findings went beyond our expectations and revealed some surprises. In particular, our studies showed that, despite serious efforts to manage computing effectively in the cities, many problems remain. Moreover, those cities that had adopted what the conventional literature on the management of computing prescribes as "preferred" policies exhibited unusually high levels of problems with computing. These unexpected and counter-intuitive findings stimulated us to conduct further analyses and resulted in the writing of this book. What began as a project to refine the list of appropriate policies for management of computing resulted in a challenge to the prevailing expectations about the efficacy of policy in the control of computing activities. Our research raised more questions than it answered, as often happens with empirical research, but our findings should be of interest for others undertaking policy-oriented studies of the complex phenomenon of computing in organizations.

A Background for Our Research

We begin this book with an examination of the recent past and current state of computing in organizations. This will provide a setting for the analyses and interpretations that follow. In particular, this chapter suggests that the rapid growth of computing use in organizations has been accompanied by a commensurate increase in demand for the attention of policy makers and managers.[1] The evolution of effective policies for the use of computing has lagged somewhat behind the evolution of that use, and many of the prescribed policies for computing have proved to be as problematic as the issues they were designed to address. Given the highly dynamic nature of computing and the complexity of managing computing activities, the development of improved policy depends on improving our understanding of the processes that govern computing growth in organizations.

After this examination of the state of computing in organizations, we present our research model. The model, which was developed from our previous research, was a guide for our empirical analyses and will be used to explain the findings of our study. We conclude this chapter with an overview of the subsequent chapters of the book that will serve as a guide to the reader, and should expedite the telling of the two stories in the book.

THE EARLY COMPUTERS

The earliest computing devices were physical counting aids such as counting boards and the abacus, which overcame the limitations of finger counting. Later, in the seventeenth century, mechanical devices invented by Pascal and Leibniz using gears and levers with counting wheels allowed automatic addition, subtraction, division, and multiplication, and paved the way for the development of the mechanical business machines of the late eighteenth and nineteenth centuries (e.g., the calculators of Monroe, Burroughs, and others). Electromechanical analog calculators were developed to speed up calculation in the early twentieth century. The first successful digital computers (other than the analytical engine of Charles Babbage, conceived in the mid-nineteenth century but never built) appeared in the 1930s, and the first electronic digital computers in the 1940s. Data handling methods that created machine-readable records were developed in the eighteenth century by Jaquard to drive weaving looms, and the Jaquard concept was modified by Herman Hollerith in the late nineteenth century to expedite calculation of data for the U.S. Census. The marriage of automatic data handling and calculation technologies took place in the early 1900s, and these two technologies were blended together in successive development of modern digital computers. All these devices emerged to meet the generalized need for faster and more accurate data management and calculation necessitated by the growth of the modern industrial state; once introduced, these devices also contributed to that growth. Interesting histories of the development of computing can be found in Bernstein (1963), Austrian (1982), Goldstine (1972), and Moseley (1964).

THE GROWTH OF COMPUTING IN ORGANIZATIONS

Between 1950 and 1983 the number of computers used in organizations increased dramatically. The first commercial computer in the United States, the UNIVAC 1, was used by only a handful of large organizations when it was introduced in the early 1950s. Within a few years, the growth curve describing the number of computer systems installed in organizations took on exponential proportions. According to Phister, between 1955 and 1974 the total accumulated value of computing hardward in use in the United States grew from about $1 billion to more than $40 billion. The yearly investment in software grew from less than $1 billion to more than $19 billion during the same period (values are normalized for inflation: Phister 1979:6, 24). Less comprehensive statistical summaries for the period 1974–1983 show that this rapid rate of growth has been sustained, and predictions suggest that it will continue until at least 1985 (Dallota et al. 1980).

What accounts for this spectacular growth? Research on the adoption and use of innovations suggests that the growth can be accounted for by an elaboration of the economic law of supply and demand. On one hand growth is stimulated by "supply-push" forces in which producers of goods and services perceive an opportunity to sell their products and actively push them in the marketplace. Their marketing efforts are enhanced, and sometimes enabled, by technological and manufacturing advancements that improve product capabilities,[2] reduce product costs,[3] or both. On the other hand are "demand-pull" forces in the market place that stimulate the production of goods and services to meet perceived or proven needs (Roessner 1979; Tornatsky et al. 1983; Perry and Kraemer 1979). The interaction of supply and demand forces stimulate growth in use of innovations that have potential as products that will sell. An overview of supply-push and demand-pull forces operating in the acquisition of computing can be seen in figure 1.1.

The most frequently cited explanations for computing's growth have been supply-push factors of declining entry costs for computing hardware and increased capabilities of both hardware and software systems (e.g., Glaser et al. 1983). Considerably less attention has been paid to the demand-pull factors in computing growth, although there is frequently reference to a general organizational need to improve productivity by substituting automation for labor. The continual increase in computing capability multiplies the potential substitutions,

Figure 1.1 SUPPLY-PUSH AND DEMAND-PULL FORCES IN THE ACQUISITION OF COMPUTING

Supply-Push Forces	Demand-Pull Forces
Changes in technological infrastructure (e.g., improvements in technological capability, declining price/performance ratios, and improved packaging of technical components to perform useful tasks)	Endemic demand for accomplishing routine tasks (e.g., need for faster and more accurate data handling in calculating/printing, record-keeping, record searching, and analysis tasks; need for any available assistance in dealing with uncertainty in the organization's external environment)
Concerted marketing efforts of technology suppliers (e.g., advertising that creates an aura of "necessity" for acquisition, direct contacts of salespeople to potential buyers)	Institutionalized demand (e.g., needs arising from already having adopted computing, such as "keeping current" with technology and maintaining systems on which the organization has become dependent)
Long-term strategies of technology suppliers (e.g., use of selective "phase-outs" in which certain systems are dropped from maintenance support to enhance user migration to newer systems)	Affective demand (e.g., perceived needs among organizational actors to exploit the political, entertainment, and other potentials of computing not directly related to the above)

while the steady decline in entry costs for computing enhances the possible productivity gains.

This explanation might account for much of the growth of computing seen in the last three decades, even though it leaves out other factors that might be important from the supply-push perspective (e.g., concerted marketing)[4] or the demand-pull side (e.g., enchantment with computing as an entertaining technology).[5] However, it does not account for the particular pattern of computing growth that has occurred, except in the sense that there has been an increase in the amount of money organizations spend on computing. Nor does it address the question of whether computing enhances productivity, or specify the mechanisms by which such enhancements are recognized and encouraged within organizations. Most importantly, perhaps, such general explanations provide little grounds for prediction or prescription. The only prediction possible from these explanations is that computing use will grow as long as buyers perceive value in getting more computing capability and suppliers are able to produce computing capability. Nothing can be said about whether the present growth will continue, or for how long. Prescription is limited to trivial observations about the importance of making "appropriate" policies and management decisions given the changing nature of computing. Little can be said about which policies to enact and what decisions to make.

Computing is a commodity that sells well, and this explains something about *why* computing has grown. But to understand *how* computing has grown, it is necessary to examine how computing systems are adopted, used, and managed in organizations.

COMPUTING IN ORGANIZATIONAL LIFE

The adoption of computing into an organization is the first step in the growth of computing use within the organization. Concurrently with computing acquisition begins the incorporation of computing as an ongoing activity in routine organizational life. With the expansion of computing applications to more tasks, the concept of computing moves beyond the narrow application of a given machine to a given task. The system, in the formal sense of the term, becomes larger and more complex as more applications are introduced. A larger number of people become dependent on computing; the initial resource constraints on computing lose ground to mounting demands; and the overall investment in computing rises. The simple, stand-alone applications overseen by a few technicians and users give way to complex and interdependent networks of activities involving many people, many systems, many data bases, and large arrays of hardware, software, management protocols, and organizational actors (Kling and Scacchi 1982).

Using our simple supply/demand model above, the investment in computing is presumed to be offset by the benefits obtained from the use of computing in organizational life: improved efficiency and effectiveness in service delivery or production, better management, better planning, and so forth. At least it is hoped that computing will enhance the organization's ability to cope with an increasingly complex environment. Assuming that organizational managers generally make good decisions, the simple fact that computing has been allowed to grow so dramatically attests to its value to those that adopt it.[6]

On the other hand, as computing has become established as an integral part of organizational life, another side of the computing story has emerged and calls into question the beneficence of the technology in many specific instances. This observation began to appear fairly soon after computing became institutionalized by the first using organizations. Early concerns had to do with the problems of getting the technology accepted and used by those who might benefit from it. The high start-up costs resulting from the expense of computer mainframes, coupled with the alien "black box" nature of computers, seemed to make many potential users reluctant to adopt computing. Overcoming "user resistance" to computing was a serious challenge.

In time, a new concern appeared that seemed to be a consequence of the successful resolution of the "user resistance" problem. This was the problem top managers faced in trying to control the "proliferation" of computing centers in the organization. The high cost of computing activities required organizational control at the top levels to insure efficient use of this expensive resource. Unnecessary, duplicative, and wasteful uses of computing were targeted for elimination through structural reform and increased central control. Thus was born the centralization/decentralization debate about organization of computing activity that persists to this day (King 1983).

Similarly, the high costs of computer processor time spurred efforts to develop operating systems software that would make more efficient use of the computer processor, and management protocols to expedite processing of batch jobs. The successful development of time-sharing ushered in a new era of efficiency and flexibility in use of powerful processors. But it also brought about the first agonizing catharsis in data processing: the software conversion from older first- and second-generation systems to the new third-generation time-shared systems, as illustrated by the IBM 360 and its operating systems OS/360.[7] Thus emerged the endemic and costly problem of moving current systems into new technological environments without suffering serious organizational disruptions and prohibitive costs. This problem of managing the upgrades of equipment and software, like that of centralization/decentralization above, persists to this day.

Finally, the initial policy focus on computing hardware and software was slowly broadened to include concerns about the people who design, build, install, maintain, and manage computing systems. As computing systems became increasingly powerful and comparatively less expensive to acquire, their use grew rapidly in those organizations that could afford to acquire them. Systems often proliferated before the educational and training institutions could produce the people to deal with them. There soon developed a shortage of qualified and competent technical people to care for these systems, and this shortage has been an endemic feature of the computing landscape ever since. The scarcity of skilled people in a market place of high demand has bid up the price of such people; and increases in the salaries of such professionals have usually outpaced inflation. Rapid salary growth has had several serious effects. One is that salaries of computing personnel have grown more quickly than those in other job categories, causing displeasure and labor problems among other employees. Similarly, the continued scarcity of computing personnel has resulted in interorganizational piracy of these people, with attendant high levels of turnover. This is a particularly troublesome problem because these trained personnel take with them essential knowledge of built systems and their maintenance when they go.

These examples illustrate that the growth of computing use in organizations has produced at least three generic areas of concern for those who must deal with the technology in routine organizational life. The first is *control of the technology,* as illustrated by the centralization/decentralization example above. Control includes many things, but it can be summed up as determining who gets to set policy regarding computing, who implements those policies, and who determines the ways in which those policies can be changed to meet new organizational conditions. This is largely an internal organizational issue.

The second concern is the *effective and efficient exploitation of the technology,* as illustrated by the software conversion example above. Computing is technology-dependent and the technology is not stable. It is in a state of continued flux as new advancements are made, new products delivered, and old products discontinued. Knowing when and how to exploit new technology, given the costs of changeover, is not an easy task.

The third area of concern is the *problem of matching the requirements and capabilities of computers to the requirements and capabilities of people,* as illustrated above by the shortage of computing personnel. Acquiring and retaining scarce technical people is a great challenge, but it is only one of many facets of the behavioral side of computing. Others include the questions of what kinds of computer-related training to provide to users and managers, how to deploy technical personnel in the organization to facilitate both effective user exploitation of the technology and responsible management control over the technology, and determining the extent to which non-technical users are permitted to "go their own way" in acquiring and using the technology.

In short, the task of managing the evolution and use of computing in organizations is difficult and complex. The inherently complex problems of managing systems that are deeply embedded in organizational life are compounded by the shortage of skilled personnel and the rapid pace of change in the underlying technologies of computing.

THE EFFECTIVE MANAGEMENT OF COMPUTING: WHICH THINGS ARE THE RIGHT THINGS?

The growing recognition that management of computing is a difficult undertaking has been accompanied by growth in the literature containing recommendations about how to manage computing effectively. This literature on the management of computing has become a subset within several disciplines, including computer science, business administration, engineering, and public administration. An example of this growth can be seen in three sets of reprints of articles appearing between 1962 and 1976 in the *Harvard Business Review* on the subject of computers in management (Harvard 1967, 1969, 1976). A total of forty-four articles were reprinted dealing with computers and management, meaning either "computer applications in management" or "the management of computing and information systems." Of the six articles that appeared between 1961 and 1965, three were about the management problems of dealing with computing. Of the twenty-four articles that appeared between 1966 and 1970, thirteen were about management problems with computing. Of the fourteen articles on the subject that appeared between 1971 and 1976, eight were about the management of computing. In each period both the number of articles on computing and the proportion of articles on the management of computing increased.[8] This simple exploration of the literature suggests that as the use of computing has grown, so has management concern about dealing with computing in appropriate ways.

Over the past two decades the recommendations for management of computing have addressed a number of specific problem areas managers face: whether to centralize or decentralize the computing function (Price 1969; Solomon 1970; Glaser 1970; Dearden 1965; Jenkins and Santos 1982; King 1983; McKenney and McFarlan 1982); whether and how to charge organizational users for in-house computing services (Nolan 1977b; Gill and Samet 1969; Sobczak 1974; Sharpe 1969; Hootman 1969; Kreitzberg and Webb 1972; Nielsen 1968, 1970); how to organize the computing service activity (Daniel 1961; Schoderbek and Babcock 1969a; Lipperman 1968; McLean and Soden 1977); when and how to involve users and managers in system design and development (Schoderbek and Babcock 1969b; Baume 1961; Garrity 1963, Garrity and Barnes 1964; Diebold 1962; O'Toole and O'Toole 1966; Swanson 1974; Nolan 1982); how to improve software development productivity (Powers 1971; Dickson and Powers 1971; Morgan and Soden 1973; Boehm 1981; Chrysler 1978); how to control the costs of computing (Middleton 1967; Orlicky 1969; Nolan 1977a, 1979); and how to deal with new technological developments (Luing 1969; Brandon 1972; McKenney and McFarlan 1982).

These recommendations are well-intentioned prescriptions, based on the sensible insights of people with knowledge of, and experience in, the management of computing. Still, there are some characteristics of most of these recommendations that cause concern. First, very little literature on the management of computing is based on rigorous empirical research. In most cases the views of the authors are drawn from their personal experiences in a few organizations or from limited surveys of managers' attitudes about computing use and management. Such research methods do not adequately assess the behavioral realities of computing as it takes place in complex organizations. Studies based on consulting experiences of the authors are often weak because they represent only a handful of unscientifically selected organizations within a given sector (e.g., banking, insurance, manufacturing). Such studies can produce general observations common to most organizations (e.g., "be sure somebody is in charge of computing and is accountable for it"), but they cannot provide the finer background data across a large number of data sources that allows for testing of more subtle interactions (e.g., "who should be put in charge of computing, under what conditions, and for what kinds of projects"). Simple surveys of managers' perceptions about the management of computing can provide useful insights, but they cannot produce evidence that the recommendations do, in fact, yield the desired results.[9]

Second, much of the research on management of computing is too narrowly conceived to be of value in real-world situations where the broader circumstances of organizational life constrain the options of managers in important ways (Kling 1979). In some cases these broader constraints make general recommendations useless or even dysfunctional. Many recommendations for the management of computing aimed at dealing with particular computing problems fail to account for the importance of the context in which the problems occur, and the fact that under some circumstances the recommended cure can produce results that are worse than the disease.

Take, for example, the recommended use of "chargeback" policies whereby departmental users are charged for the services they receive from the organization's computing center. This policy has been recommended to encourage prudence among users in their use of computing and to encourage the computing center to provide good service for its "customers" (Nolan 1977a and b). This recommendation is simple in principle, but it can be difficult to implement. For example, if the organization requires use of the in-house computer center, the "market" characteristics of the chargeback scheme are diminished by the retention of the computer center's monopoly power. Similarly, an effective chargeback system must insure that charges are fair and users have confidence in the system, a challenge many organizations lack the expertise to meet. An inaccurate or unfair chargeback system will actually work against its purpose by distorting the resource allocation process in unpredictable ways and by obscuring the basic issue of deciding whose interests in the organization are going to be served by the limited computing resources (Danziger 1977b).[10] Many different factors affect the outcomes of mnagement decisions about computing, and these must be taken into account in order that policy recommendations make sense in given organizational settings.

Finally, and perhaps most importantly, much of the literature on the management of computing is grounded in the belief that computing is manageable in a rational manner. Computing can be dealt with by organizations, as demonstrated by the fact that many organizations do manage to get the results they desire from computing use. But at the same time, many managers find it difficult to cope with the myriad problems in complex computing environments, in which control, technology, and human factors are undergoing constant flux. There is nothing logically inconsistent about the idea that computing might be brought under organizational control. But the question remains as to whether or not control is in fact ever achieved, and, if it is achieved, whether or not it is maintained for long.

The highly rationalistic assumptions that underlie many recommendations for management of computing are appealing. They seem to make sense, given what top managers would like to see happen; that is, they are consistent with the goals of improving the efficiency and effectiveness of computing in organizations. They deal with discrete and well-circumscribed obstacles that stand in the way of achieving these goals. But as Kling and Scacchi point out, the "discrete entity" view of computing as a tool to be managed for the accomplishment of desired objectives weakens when one examines the broader context of computing as it actually takes place in organizations (Kling and Scacchi 1982). Policies promulgated under a "discrete entity" image of computing miss the subtle but powerful behavioral factors that affect the outcomes of all organizational policies and thus are less likely to be successful.

Few studies of the management of computing have addressed the basic question: Is computing manageable in a rational manner, and, if so, what aspects of computing are manageable and under what conditions? This shortcoming calls into question any effort to build a general base of "preferred" policies for the management of this complex phenomenon. The issue here is not really whether or not it is possible for organizations to put computing to useful ends. There already is a "natural demonstration" of that fact: organizations do use computing and seem to get along with it. Rather the question our research addresses is what difference do the widely prescribed policies for the management of computing make for organizations that are trying to improve the way they live with computing?

A FOCUS ON THE WORLD AS IT IS

In order to develop a more solidly grounded base for the creation of policy recommendations for the management of computing, we have attempted to overcome some of the shortcomings common to current literature on the subject. The basic concept behind the research reported here can be summarized as an effort to focus attention on the world of computing in organizations as it actually is rather than on how it should or could be. Three features characterize our research.

First, the research relied on empirical assessment of computing in organizations using established social science research methods.[11] Considerable attention has been paid to the technical issues of survey and sampling design, construction of data collection instruments, strict execution of data collection plans, and rigorous analysis of the large amount of data collected in the study. Rather than collect a limited amount of data on a wide array of organizations and industries, we focused our efforts on collecting detailed data on a single industry sector (city governments). This focus on only one sector obviously affects the generalizability of our findings, and in some cases the conclusions we draw might not directly relate to other sectors (e.g., manufacturing, construction). But we believe the conclusions may well be generalizable to other levels of government and to other service sector industries. Moreover, the choice of city government as our domain of investigation yielded important research benefits. Local governments are highly standard in comparison to other industry sectors. Despite differences among local governments from state to state and country to country, most are engaged in specific kinds of service delivery in comparable political and administrative settings. Because local governments are public entities that draw their operational funding from taxation, they also are less affected by economic changes of the kind that affect businesses (e.g., changes in the business cycle). Both of these characteristics help "stabilize" the domain of our research and, in effect, control for important environmental factors that otherwise might overwhelm our analyses. Finally, local governments are generally very open and cooperative in granting access for study, reducing the problem of participation bias in our analyses.

Second, the research reported here encompassed a much larger set of variables than do most studies of computing in organizatons. This strategy is in keeping with the view of computing as a "package" consisting of many interrelated parts, rather than simply a tool consisting of hardware and software techniques.[12] The "package" of computing could conceivably consist of too many things to be included in even a large study, and certainly not every variable one could collect data on would be worth studying. Nevertheless, we made an effort to assess a wide array of control, technical, and human factors that are thought to influence the way computing takes place in organizations.

Third, the study specifically investigated the relationships between the characteristics of organizations, the policies used to manage computing, and the benefits and problems of computing in those organizations. The research was not intended to develop new policies, but to evaluate what effect the policies that organizations now follow for managing computing have on the way computing is used and what difference it makes in the organization. Data for the research were collected in a cross-sectional manner (i.e., as a snapshot of conditions at one point in time) as opposed to a longitudinal manner (i.e., from a particular set of organizations over time), so it is not possible from these data to demonstrate the causal relationships between policies for computing and the outcomes of computing. However, policies are believed to have some effect on outcomes, and the general hypothesis behind the research is that preferred outcomes of computing are related to certain computing policies. The research was designed to build a theoretical base for future longitudinal research that will demonstrate the causal connections between policies and their outcomes.

By focusing on computing as it actally happens, it is possible to establish a baseline that sheds light on two important issues in the management of computing. The first is the question of what computing, broadly conceived, looks like *in vivo*. The second is the question of whether the policies for management of computing followed by the organizations studied are associated with outcomes of computing use in the manner predicted by existing literature on the management of computing. The ultimate goal of the research has been to ascertain whether the conventional wisdom underlying recommendations on the management of computing is validated or called into question by the actual experiences of organizations. As later chapters indicate, many aspects of the conventional wisdom are not validated by our research results.

The Research Project

This research continues a tradition of studies of computing use in public agencies carried out at the Public Policy Research Organization since 1970. The major source of data for this research was the URBIS Research Project, which was conducted between 1974 and 1979. This ´ research is more than simply an extension of the URBIS project, however. It incorporates the data from another major empirical research project conducted by the Organization for Economic Cooperation and Development between 1974 and 1978. We will briefly describe the URBIS and OECD studies to povide background on the nature of these research efforts. More extensive discussions of the projects can be found in Kraemer, Dutton, and Northrop (1981), Danziger, Dutton, Kling, and Kraemer (1982), OECD (1978), Gaits (1978), and in the appendix to this book.

THE URBIS PROJECT

The URBIS Project was the first and, to date, the only empirical study of computing use in an entire economic sector: medium and large city governments. The project, supported by a grant from the National Science Foundation, consisted of two study phases. The first phase utilized mail-out/mail-back questionnaires to conduct a survey of the nature of computing use in U.S. cities over 50,000 in population. A total of 400 cities were surveyed. The Phase 1 questionnaires collected data on a large number of variables that make up the organizational political/administrative system, computing policies, and computing environment. Additional data for the cities were collected from secondary sources, particularly the 1970 U.S. Census, to provide insight about certain extra-organizational environment variables. Data were collected from two sources for each city: the city's chief executive officer (mayor, city manager) who provided a personal assessment of the impacts of computing use on local planning, management, and service delivery; and the data processing manager(s) of each computing installation in the city, who provided data related to the computing environment and policies for management of computing.

The Phase 1 data provided a comprehensive profile of computing policies and use in cities over 50,000 in population. These data were used to provide a baseline from which a set of cities was selected for more intensive investigation in the second phase of the research. The purpose of Phase 2 was to study the relationships between the use of particular policies for computing and the outcomes of computing use in those cities for planning, management, and service delivery. A total of six policies were investigated: degree of automation, degree of sophistication of computing, degree of decentralization of computing resources, degree of integration of systems and data, degree of user involvement in system design, and use of charging policies for computing. Cities were classified along a continuum ranging from low to high for each policy. A low position meant the city was not using the policy; a high position meant the policy was in place. Cities at the extreme ends of the continuum were selected for each of the six policies, which provided maximum differentiation in use of the policies among the cities studied. For statistical reasons, a total of twenty cities at the high end and twenty cities at the low end of each policy continuum was needed. Thus, a total of forty cities was selected; among these were twenty high and twenty low on the policy continua for the six policies.

Each of the forty cities that made up the sample for Phase 2 was visited by a team of one to three principal investigators for periods ranging from one to three weeks. During these visits data were collected in four ways. First, interviews were conducted with twenty to fifty city employees who used computing in a set of information processing tasks selected for study (budget monitoring, budget reporting, planning/management tasks, patrol manpower allocation in police, detective investigation support in police, and traffic ticket processing). Second, a very detailed profile of the city's computing ac-

Figure 1.2 CITIES SURVEYED IN THE URBIS AND OECD STUDIES

URBIS Cities

Albany, N.Y.	Milwaukee, Wis.
Atlanta, Ga.	Montgomery, Ala.
Baltimore, Md.	New Orleans, La.
Brockton, Mass.	New Rochelle, N.Y.
Burbank, Calif.	Oshkosh, Wis.
Chesapeake, Va.	Paterson, N.J.
Cleveland, Ohio	Philadelphia, Pa.
Evansville, Ind.	Portsmouth, Va.
Florissant, Mo.	Quincy, Mass.
Fort Lauderdale, Fla.	Riverside, Calif.
Grand Rapids, Mich.	Sacramento, Calif.[a]
Hampton, Va.	San Francisco, Calif.
Lancaster, Pa.	San Jose, Calif.[a]
Las Vegas, Nev.	St. Louis, Mo.
Lincoln, Neb.	Seattle, Wash.
Little Rock, Ark.	Spokane, Wash.
Long Beach, Calif.	Stockton, Calif.
Louisville, Ky.	Tampa, Fla.
Miami Beach, Fla.	Tulsa, Okla.
Kansas City, Mo.	Warren, Mich.

OECD Cities

Vienna, Austria	Duisburg, W. Germany
Vaerloese, Denmark	Nurtingen, W. Germany
Aarhus, Denmark	Jonkoping, Sweden
Helsinki, Finland	Leeds, United Kingdom
Gagny, France	Torbay, United Kingdom
Montpellier, France	Calgary, Canada
Toulouse, France	Maebashi, Japan
Backnang, W. Germany	Nishinomiya, Japan

[a] These cities were also surveyed, although not originally selected, as part of the 40-city URBIS Phase 2 population. The data from these cities were included in the analysis, while data from two other cities on the list (Quincy, Mass. and New Rochelle, N.Y.) were excluded from analysis because they did not have a level of computer use sufficient for some studies.

tivities was assembled through completion of a self-administered questionnaire by the staff of each computing center in the city. Third, a sample of fifty to seventy computer-using employees was selected to complete a self-administered questionnaire on the impact of computing on employees' jobs and performance. Finally, a detailed case-study report was written by the investigators who visited the cities to provide background on the history of computing and its role in the larger political and administrative context of the city.

The two phases of the URBIS project yielded a wealth of data. In all, over two million data elements were collected (a data element is one answer to one question from one respondent). These data have been analyzed by a number of the URBIS researchers, and the results of the analyses reported in a large number of publications, including two previous books (Kraemer, Dutton, and Northrop 1981; Danziger, Dutton, Kling, and Kraemer 1982). This book continues that analytical tradition. The data used for this book are taken primarily from the forty-city Phase 2 User Core Questionnaire, administered to approximately 2,300 respondents in the study cities. Detailed discussion of the specific data used can be found in the appendix to this book.

THE OECD PROJECT

At approximately the same time the URBIS Phase 2 study was conducted, the Panel on Information Technology and Urban Management of the Organization for Economic Cooperation and Development (OECD) undertook a detailed study of computing use and impacts in sixteen cities in nine OECD member nations (figure 1.3). This study grew out of a tradition of studies by OECD's Computer Utilization Group, which between 1969 and 1978 produced twelve major publications on computer use in government known as the OECD Informatics Series. This research had established the OECD Computer Utilization Group as one of the foremost authorities in the use of computers in government.

The methodology of the OECD study was a combination of survey research and case study. Five major mechanisms were used for data collection: existing studies, secondary data, prestructured surveys, existing documents from study sites, and contextual materials gathered from site visits. Sites were selected by the panel's representatives from the individual member nations, according to a set of guiding criteria (which parallel those in the URBIS study). Research and data collection took place in late 1975 and early 1976 and culminated in preparation of a set of general reports from the nine participating nations' delegations, as well as several summary papers dealing with topical issues such as management of data processing in the cities studied. Although all the data collected during the study were empirical, and some preliminary analyses were done, it was not possible for the panel to conduct the extensive empirical analyses that they had planned due to constraints of time and analytic resources (Gaits 1978). The OECD data existed in a raw but complete state, and these raw data provided the OECD input to the research reported in this book.

THE OPPORTUNITY PROVIDED IN THIS RESEARCH

This research study was undertaken because it represented a unique opportunity to perform an international analysis of computing in cities. This analysis could extend knowledge about the policy alternatives available to national governments and to cities beyond what could be provided by analysis of only one data base. The OECD cities represented policy positions not found in the URBIS cities, but which had been considered periodically and which were expected to be found in U.S. cities in the future. For example, OECD cities differed from URBIS cities in that they automate social service functions more intensively, use cooperative and other centralized computing arrangements more frequently, and share data across agency and jurisdiction lines more extensively. Conversely, URBIS cities were expected to be more technologically advanced in computing use than many of the OECD cities. This provided an opportunity to determine whether use of sophisticated technology produces the expected benefits or brings unanticipated problems. The URBIS cities, therefore, represented an opportunity to investigate computing benefits and problems in technology-intensive environments.

Another research opportunity was provided by the fact that the URBIS and OECD cities vary significantly in their national policy contexts. These policy contexts were expected to relate both to the extent of development of computing and to service requirements that create demands for computing services. They also were expected to differentially affect the policies that local governments adopt to manage computing. U.S. national policy toward local government computing can be described as laissez innover: an extremely decentralized conglomeration of small policies and incentives for particular projects, with individual institutions and sectors left to develop their own arrangements (Kraemer and King 1978b). In contrast, many European countries and Japan have followed very specific national policies of centralized computing development or direction, particularly with intergovernmental systems in the areas of population registry, land registry, and social services.

These contextual differences were considered interesting in their own right, but their importance for national policymaking is illustrated by the changes that are occurring in the United States and in the OECD countries that participated in the study. In the United States several developments took place in the 1970s and early 1980s that suggested a possible evolution toward greater centralization of information control and, in some cases, of computing arrangements. Among these developments were the growth of national information systems such as the National Crime Information Center linking together local, state, and federal governments; the advent of electronic funds transfer systems that might lead to changes in the ways intergovernmental funds transfers are made; the growing demand by the federal government for locally gathered information; and the prospect of a major shift in the management of certain social services from the states to the federal government and vice-versa through the New Federalism. In the OECD countries an analogous trend has been seen in the decentralization of computing activities as a result of the growing availability of less expensive computers and the increasing technical expertise among local governments that makes decentralization possible. The comparative study of the URBIS and OECD cities would contribute to our understanding of the ramifications of such changes in the United States and the OECD contexts.

The fundamental purpose of this research, then, was to combine, synthesize, and analyze the URBIS and OECD study data related to policies, uses, and outcomes of computing in city governance. These objectives were accomplished in the research. Beyond these objectives a number of significant opportunities emerged that were exploited in the creation of this book. Most important was the opportunity to evaluate the efficacy of various policies for the management of computing as recommended by the research literature. Another was the opportunity to explore the differences in context between the URBIS and OECD cities to stimulate our thinking about the role of context in the growth of evolving patterns of computing use. Finally, we were able to investigate the similarities in experience with the use of computing that prevail even across these major contextual differences. In all, the methodological advantage of this research arose from the opportunity to examine two data bases that were independent and different in important respects, but concentrated on the same issues. By working back and forth across the two data sets we developed new ideas that could be further explored in our analyses. In this way the study took on a dynamic character of its own, and allowed us to move beyond the original goals of the research.

The Research Model

The basic model of this research is shown in figure 1.3. This model incorporates our three areas of concern noted earlier: control, technology, and people. Controls are embodied in the formulation and execution of policies by which choices about when, where, and how computing will be used are made and carried out. Technology is contained in the computing environment within organizations that results from computing policy. People, of course, play many different roles in the model: constituents of the local government, elected and appointed policymakers, technical professionals, users, and those outside the organization and the local community (e.g., officials in other governmental jurisdictions, people within the computing field, vendors).

The model shown in figure 1.3 is derived from the earlier models presented in Kraemer, Dutton, and Northrop (1981) and Danziger, Dutton, Kling, and Kraemer (1982) and is a basic product of the URBIS

Figure 1.3 THE BASIC RESEARCH MODEL

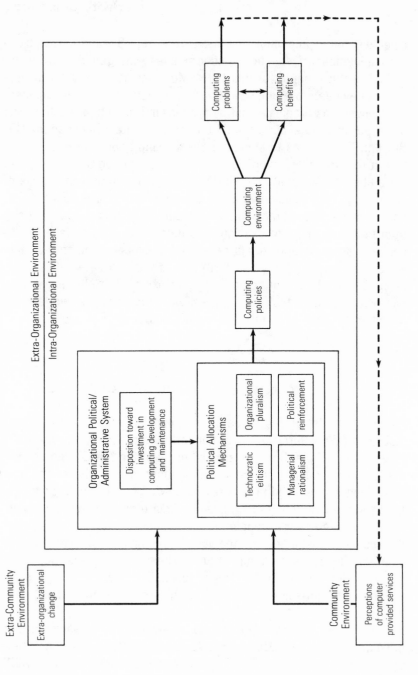

Research Project. The model represents the mechanisms influencing the changes in computing activities and effects over time. In this model the organization exists within a larger, extra-organizational environment. This extra-organizational environment influences the organizational environment through changing local leadership, altering support for the city government through controls on taxation, and providing funding to support special projects. Within the organization most policymaking takes place within a system of protocols and rules we call the organizational political/administrative system. The details of the operation of this system are discussed below. The organizational political/administrative system is influenced by the extra-organizational environment as well as the intra-organizational environment, and serves as the "control point" in the changes in computing. This system's most important outputs are policy decisions affecting the operations of the organization, in this case computing. The result of these decisions is the creation of a computing environment that consists of the basic hardware, software, and organizational knowledge to implement computer-based systems. The use of this environment by the organization results in outcomes that can be broadly classified as either benefits or problems. Depending upon the nature of computing outcomes, a feedback occurs from the outcomes of computing to the organizational political/administrative system. This feedback influences the control system as do the influences from the extra-organizational environment.

Thus, this model is a cybernetic model containing a set of independent variables (the extra-organizational environment and the organizational political/administrative system), a set of control variables (computing policies and the computing environment) and a set of dependent variables (outcomes of computing use). The fundamental rationale behind the model from the standpoint of our interest in policy for the management of computing is that policies are promulgated by a control mechanism that takes input from the extra-organizational environment and the intra-organizational environment, and executes control through a set of control variables: policies that establish a given computing environment. This set of policies and the environment they nurture provide the context within which formal plans are made and are enforced and resources are controlled in the use of computing. By monitoring the results of computing use within this context, it is possible for the actors in the organizational political/administrative system to make changes in policy, given these internal cues and input from the extra-organizational environment. The dependent variables influence the independent variables in this model, making the model cybernetic.

The overall cybernetic model was first developed in the URBIS project proposal to the National Science Foundation (PPRO 1974), and elaborated in the first URBIS book (Kraemer, Dutton, and Northrop 1981). The detailed exploration of the mechanisms by which policies are made within the organizational political/administrative system was explained in the second URBIS book (Danziger, Dutton, Kling, and Kraemer 1982). This analysis produced the four basic modes of policymaking behavior noted in figure 1.3: managerial rationalism, technocratic elitism, organizational pluralism, and political reinforcement.

These four modes should not be taken as mutually exclusive, but as representative of different behaviors that can be found under different circumstances in different organizations. Managerial rationalism is the mode in which critical decisions about computing adoption and use are made by the organization's elected and appointed leaders with the intent of serving the broader interests of the organization in carrying out its basic mandates. In the case of city governments, these basic mandates are to provide public services in efficient and effective ways. This mode is often characterized as the "ideal" mode of decision-making behavior in the management of computing (Fuller 1970; Kanter 1977; Ahituv and Neumann 1982; Nolan 1973a; Simon 1973).

Technocratic elitism is the mode in which a technical elite comprised of technical specialists (programmers, analysts, data-processing managers) and key technical users (budget analysts, planners) dominate computing decisions through their monopoly on technical expertise and control computing growth in use in ways that suit their elite interests. This mode of behavior has not been as widely discussed as managerial rationalism, but some commentators have focused attention on it (Boguslaw 1965; Downs 1967; Kraemer and King 1976; Danziger 1979).

Organizational pluralism is a mode in which no single group

dominates computing decision making, but decisions are made through pluralistic establishment of compromises and coalitions among the varied interests competing for computing resources. This mode is believed to result in allocation policies that meet the minimal needs of dominant interests, and that decision-making patterns change as the coalitions change (Price 1965; Laudon 1974; Lambright 1976).

Political reinforcement is a mode in which computing decisions are made to serve different organizational interests in different situations (e.g., in rationalistic, technocratic, or pluralistic ways), but only within the boundaries permitted by the dominant policymakers of the organization who ensure that the results of decisions reinforce their own political positions. This mode of decisionmaking behavior has been elaborated by URBIS researchers (Dutton and Kraemer 1977; Danziger, Dutton, Kling, and Kraemer 1982).

We adopt the general conclusions of the Danziger et al. (1982) work, including the claim that in most cases computing policies are made in a manner that serves to reinforce the existing political elites within the local government. However, the concern of this book is less with the mechanisms by which policies are formed than with the relationships among policies, computing environments, and computing outcomes. Our focus is therefore on the area in figure 1.3 to the right of the organizational political/administrative system. Through our analyses we attempt to develop a more complete understanding of the pathways by which computing in organizations change within the general model. The cybernetic model assumes that the results of computing use somehow feed back to affect subsequent decisions about computing policy. Our goal is to better explain how this takes place. In particular, we want to determine whether the process of use/outcome/feedback is as rational as the prevailing literature on the management of computing suggests.

A Brief Overview of the Book

This chapter has introduced the three major themes of the book: to examine computing use and outcomes at one point in time, to examine the relationships among various aspects of the computing phenomenon in light of literature predictions, and to use the results of these analyses to sharpen our theories about changes in computing in organizations over time.

Chapter 2 serves as a foundation for the other chapters in this book. It provides an overview of the nature of the comparison sites and the condition of computing in our study cities as of the time of the URBIS and OECD studies, as well as some insight into the comparative nature of computing growth in cities in the United States and the nine OECD countries. The analysis in this chapter reveals that, as of 1976, URBIS cities were more automated than OECD cities, with more computing capacity, a larger number of municipal functions, and greater expenditures on computing. The OECD cities, on the other hand, differ in important respects from URBIS cities. They tend to share computing resources with other cities in their own countries; and in many cases, the OECD cities appear to have made remarkable advancement in computing use in a short period of time. More generally, our analyses show a relationship between size of government and extent and character of computing activity. Size serves as a demarcation factor for the time at which cities enter into computing activity and the speed with which they develop their capabilities. Larger cities have more computing capacity, usually adopt the technology sooner, and have been quicker to adopt new developments. Smaller cities tend to follow the lead of larger cities and utilize the facilities of larger cities or a service bureau while learning about computing and preparing for developing their own capabilities.

The data also suggest that computing development in cities is influenced strongly by the national and local political and administrative contexts in which it occurs. The city organizations appear to shape technologies at least as much as the technologies shape them. Computing is usually adapted to fit the existing organizational context and is put to work in the service of existing organizational interests.

From chapter 2 we carry forward two observations: that computing is used extensively in both the URBIS and OECD cities, and the extent of computing use correlates with organizational size; and that national and local contexts play an important role in the patterns of computing adoption and application.

Chapter 3 presents our findings on the realization of benefits from computing in the cities. Computing apparently has lived up to its promotion as a useful tool for improving the efficiency of operations by increasing the speed of operations, improving data accuracy, and providing an opportunity to avoid future costs. It does not, however, seem to result in much cost saving. Computing's benefit for management and planning activities is somewhat less than that for efficiency and service delivery, possibly because computing has been less extensively applied to these activities. Nevertheless, where computing has been applied to management and planning tasks, it has been generally beneficial. There is evidence of benefits for community planning, especially in the URBIS cities, which are somewhat more advanced in such uses of computing than the OECD cities. In all, computing's benefits are greatest for routine efficiency and service delivery applications in most of the cities. These applications are the most "rational" (e.g., accounting), and are often the first to be built. There is less widespread evidence of extensive management and community planning benefits from computing, but this might be simply because there are relatively fewer applications for such activities in the cities.

Chapter 4 presents our findings on computing problems in the cities. Problems appear to be pervasive. Every city has some problems, and many of the problems listed are shared by over half of the cities in each population. Problems related to computing staff, obtaining computing support, managing technical aspects of computing, and unresponsiveness of computing people to user needs appear very frequently. The somewhat less-developed OECD cities have their greatest problems in getting resources and support for computing. The more developed URBIS cities have greater difficulties with interactions between computing staff and users, but seldom report support problems. These data suggest that in the earlier stages of computing development, the problems of mobilizing support and effort for development are most serious, while after computing has been established, more difficult problems of socio-technical interface (e.g., computing staff/user problems) become more pronounced.

In chapter 5 we explore the relationship among policies for the management of computing, city environment variables, and the computing environment. Policies for the management of computing are shown to be somewhat independent of the city environment: they are manipulable variables that are not necessarily bound by factors such as the size of the city or its budget. On close examination, the relationships we do find between computing policies and city environment appear to be a function of the year computing began to be used in the city. Larger cities tended to be among the first to adopt computing, have more experience with computing, and have more developed computing environments. Thus, the overall relationship between size and the variables of policy, computing environment, and outcomes appears to be complex. Further analysis of size as an independent variable is required and provided in chapter 6. Computing policies do appear to be related to the computing environment and its level of development. This suggests that computing policies are importantly connected to computing environment and might influence the development of the computing environment, as indicated in figure 1.3.

In chapter 6 we bring together policy, environment, benefit, and problem variables to assess their associations with one another. We begin with a detailed analysis of size and its relationship to the other variables and conclude that size *per se* is not the dominant independent variable on which all other variables depend. Superficial analyses are shown to mask the more basic relationships between need for and resources for computing, on one hand, and the policies, technical features, and outcomes related to computing, on the other. This conclusion leaves us free to conduct our assessment of the possible contingencies in the management of computing; that is, those circumstances in which computing policies succeed or fail in association with benefits or problems as predicted by the prescriptive literature on the management of computing. Our results are surprising. They show that the cities vary considerably in the benefits and problems they experience, and that this variance is not attributable simply to the presence of the policies predicted to be most "appropriate" in the literature. Benefits tend to accrue in line with the level of computing development: less developed cities show greater benefits for routine applications, while more developed cities show greater benefit from more advanced applications. Benefits appear to be more closely related to computing environment than computing policy. Most importantly, many of the problems that are supposed to be alleviated by certain "appropriate" management policies are shown to be strongly associated with those policies. This counter-intuitive finding raises the question of whether policies, in fact, do provide the leverage managers seek in attempting to control and exploit computing.

In the final chapter we resume our discussion of computing change over time in an effort to make sense out of our findings. What accounts for the relative ineffectiveness of policies for alleviating computing problems in the cities? We adopt a more longitudinal perspective than that allowed by our cross-sectional data base to construct a possible answer. Using existing theories on the "stages" of computing growth over time, we develop an account of the patterns of growth in our cities. The resulting theory suggests that the factors contributing to the growth and use of computing are very powerful and in many cases not likely to be fully controllable by policy actions of management. Rather, once a threshold of computing investment in the organization is reached, beyond which there is no internal political support for greater expenditure, the competitive actions of various organizational actors take over to influence the allocation of the restricted resource base. Because the changes in the supply-push and demand-pull factors driving computing growth continue to occur rapidly, it is nearly impossible for managers to develop a set of truly "appropriate" policies that will survive and be successful. Management of computing in this scenario is a task of coping with a somewhat unmanageable situation.

We incorporate this stage theory into a refined version of the model presented in figure 1.3 to account for the findings of our research, and this new model provides the mechanistic explanation for how changes in computing take place within the larger context of our stages. This integrated theory, which we call the dynamics of computing, suggests possible fruitful lines for further research, with which we conclude both the stories in this book.

Notes

1. When new technologies are fully adopted by organizations and become routine, the technologies and procedures they replace are usually allowed to atrophy. As a result, organizations give up some options for action in the process of adopting new technologies. For ex-

ample, the sprawling development of modern urban areas encouraged by the transportation technology of automobiles and highways has greatly constrained the option of retrofitting those areas with fixed-guideway rapid transit systems. The purpose of decision making is to eliminate alternatives, so it is not surprising that the decision to adopt and incorporate a technology often has the effect of locking that technology into use for a considerable period of time. This phenomenon can be expressed succinctly by the observation of an engineer working on a large water system project carrying water from Northern to Southern California: "If we don't build this canal, we won't need it."

2. For example, the remarkable characteristics of computers as symbol manipulators first became apparent in the work of Alvin Turing, who proved that it was possible to construct a machine that could follow a formal procedure to imitate the behavior of any other formal procedure, and then actually supervised construction of the first "Turing machine" (Turing 1936; Minsky 1967). The application of this remarkable discovery and its potential analogy to human thought has been extensively explored since (von Neumann 1958; Feigenbaum and Feldman 1963; Newell and Simon 1972; Schank and Colby 1973; Weizenbaum 1976). Whether or not computers can ever be developed to the point that they can "think," they can and are now being applied to a remarkable array of complex tasks, especially in the operations and management of organizations.

3. The costs of computer processing as a function of processing power, have been declining at a remarkable rate in the past two decades (Boehm 1981). This remarkable achievement in production technology, which certainly surpasses most other such achievements in history, has helped to move computing power into small organizations and even into people's homes and onto their wrists in the form of calculator wristwatches.

4. The marketing of computing technology has been actively pursued ever since the first mechanical calculators appeared on the market in the late nineteenth century. Modern companies such as Burroughs, Sperry-Rand, IBM, and others trace their origins from those early days. An interesting account of the sales practices of computer vendors of today can be found in Kling and Crabtree (1978).

5. Many characterizations of the impetus behind adoption of computing technology rely on highly rationalistic explanations of the technology's usefulness in doing productive work. However, a glance at the phenomenal growth in popularity of computer-based video games suggests that the entertainment potential of computing technology is also an important factor in its rapid and widespread acceptance. Beyond the immediate entertainment value of the technology, whether in the form of video games or computer-aided design systems, computing is a politically powerful technology that has important effects on the behavior of individuals in organizations (Laudon 1974; Kraemer and Dutton 1979; Kraemer and King 1976; Danziger, Dutton, Kling, and Kraemer 1982).

6. A central tenet of welfare economics noted here is the independence of the household in economic decision making, sometimes called the principle of consumer sovereignty. This tenet maintains that only the people directly affected by the decision are in a position to know how their welfare is affected by their decision (Hicks 1939; Nash 1950; McGuire 1982). This assumption is weakened, however, by the forces of monopoly, and the fact that in some cases individuals do not have sufficient information on which to make reasonable decisions affecting their welfare (Rothenburg 1968; Arrow 1970).

7. The IBM OS/360 project incurred great cost overruns in development within IBM, and the story of its development was the subject of a very interesting book by Brooks (1975). The conversion to IBM OS/360 was traumatic for many user organizations as well. As an executive for Shell Oil, who was at the time in charge of Shell computing activities worldwide, explained

to us in 1979, the organizational disruptions resulting from conversion to OS/360 required five years of effort to overcome within the company.

8. The articles in these three volumes were considered to be related to the management of computing and information systems if they were primarily concerned with top-management decisions for making more effective use of computers or for dealing with problems in computing use (e.g., controlling costs, organization of computing activity, computer systems planning, insuring compliance with privacy and security needs), instead of applying computer technology to the needs of managers (e.g., computerized decision systems, inventory systems, investment analysis systems). The articles noted here, and in many other places in this book, focus primarily on business uses of computing. Until relatively recently there has been considerably less work in the area of computing in the federal, state, and local government sectors. The General Accounting Office has written a large number of reports dealing with problems related to specific federal government computing issues, and typically issues one or more reports per month. The growing concerns about the burden of paperwork in the federal government culminated in the Commission on Federal Paperwork's recent adoption of the concept of "information resource management," arising from the work of McDonough (1963), as a means of dealing with computing and information problems in the federal government (Commission on Federal Paperwork 1977), and this has sparked considerable interest as reflected in subsequent work (Horton and Marchand's 1982 reader provides a good overview of this). At the state level, the National Association of State Information Systems has conducted annual surveys of computer use. The Urban and Regional Information Systems Association holds annual professional conferences on applications of computing in local government, and in some cases the proceedings produce important contributions to understanding of computing in those areas. Some instructional materials on government information systems have been written (e.g., Bassler and Enger 1976), and at the government level, practical guides have been published (Kraemer and King 1981b, c, d). In addition to the work conducted at the Public Policy Research Organization, there have been a limited number of detailed research efforts examining computing in government (Colton 1978; Laudon 1976; Chartrand 1972, 1976; Library of Congress 1977; Council of State Government 1974). Other than *Computers, Environment and Urban Systems,* there are no research journals that deal directly with public sector information systems. There are no formal programs in information systems in U.S. schools of public administration, and most computing professionals in the public sector receive their training in other professional schools (e.g., computer science, engineering, business). As a result, most of the policy guidance for dealing with computing in local governments, and in the public sector generally, comes from private sector experiences.

9. We hasten to point out here that we are not criticizing the management literature based on consulting, analytical, or experimental methods. Indeed, much of the most insightful and useful advice to be found in the management of computing comes from such sources. For example, the work of John Dearden, which is based primarily on his experience and understanding of the tasks of high-level management, is classic in its applicability and practicality (Dearden 1965, 1966, 1972). The work on stage theories of computing by Nolan and others has provided an important new slant on conceptions of how computing evolves in organizations (Gibson and Nolan 1974; Nolan 1973a, 1977a, 1979). And the empirical work of Lucas and others has shed new light on the problems of building successful computing systems in complex organizations (Lucas 1974a; Alter 1980). Rather, our concern is that such research has only scratched the surface of the important issues that still lie unresolved in the management of computing in organizations generally.

10. The difficulties of implementing chargeback systems were revealed to us on a con-

sulting assignment to a large midwestern city in the late 1970s. The organization had declared the computing center an "enterprise" organization, responsible for collecting all of its budgetary support from user departments through chargeback mechanisms. The accounting system on the computer was inadequate, so users soon lost confidence in the fairness of the charges they were incurring. The billing procedures were cumbersome, requiring a formal bill-back even for very small consultative jobs, with the result that users forwent requests for small maintenance jobs that were essential to keeping their systems useful. Perhaps most importantly, the users took the problems with the chargeback system to be indicative of more widespread problems in the computing center and began to seek the system development services of outside firms, thereby eroding internal support for the organization's computing center.

11. The two projects, which are described later in this section and in the appendix, were the Urban Information Systems (URBIS) Project conducted by the Public Policy Research Organization between 1974 and 1980 and the OECD Panel on Information Technology and Urban Management Study conducted by the Organization for Economic Cooperation and Development between 1974 and 1978. Both studies, while carefully developed and executed in keeping with principles of social science research, have limitations of generalizability and validity that accompany most such research efforts. These limitations are described in this book where they are important.

12. The "package" metaphor has become an important concept for focusing the research carried on at the Public Policy Research Organization. It is derived from several sources. Ivan Illich (1971) describes the transfer of educational programs in the context of a package of components, including educational philosophy, technology, and administrative mechanisms. Stewart (1977) expanded on this concept in his analysis of the transfer of physical technologies to developing countries. In our studies of information technology we have adopted the concept in a variety of analyses: King and Kraemer (1978), Kling and Scacchi (1979, 1982), Scacchi (1981), and Danziger, Dutton, Kling, and Kraemer (1982).

CHAPTER TWO
AN OVERVIEW
OF COMPUTING
IN THE STUDY CITIES

THE USE of computer technology to assist in the management, planning, and operations in city governments has been growing steadily over the past three decades, in a manner that parallels its growth in other organizational sectors (Glaser et al. 1983). This technology's potential for improving productivity and expanding the capabilities of local government management is widely recognized. And knowledge, which is useful in furthering the technology's exploitation, continues to be gained in many countries.[1]

The use of computers in city governments was the focus of the studies that provided the data used in this book. This chapter presents the state of computing practice in cities at the time the data were collected. It is organized in four parts: an overview of the cities studied; a comparison of diffusion patterns of computing adoption among the cities; the financial and technical aspects of computing use in the cities; and the breadth of computing applications in the cities.

The data presented here are not current at the time of this book's publication, having been collected in 1976. We assume that there have been significant changes—especially in the areas of computing characteristics and use—since the URBIS and OECD studies. These data, then, are not intended to provide a current "state of the art" profile; their utility in this chapter is to provide a "state of practice" baseline about computing development, as well as environmental information about the cities, that will form a background for the data presented in later chapters and set the stage for our further assessment of computing dynamics in cities.

A Profile of the Cities

As shown in table 2.1, the population ranges of URBIS cities and OECD cities are similar, with the average populaton at 309,000 in URBIS cities and 365,000 in OECD cities (see Penitzka 1978). The political character of the two groups differs somewhat, with URBIS cities governed most often by either the council-manager or the strong mayor/council form of city government, and OECD cities favoring the commission form of government.

As shown in table 2.2, the average population of the smaller cities (those under 200,000) is substantially larger in the URBIS sample than in the OECD sample. This is because the bottom-line cutoff for cities studied in URBIS was 50,000 population. As a result, the sampling was more restricted than that for the OECD study. Yet the OECD cities differ consistently from URBIS cities in certain respects: in spite of the substantial difference in population averages among the smaller cities, the number of city employees and the average city operating budgets are comparable between OECD and URBIS; and among larger cities (above 200,000), the OECD cities have proportionately larger government organizations and spend more than do the URBIS cities. This comparatively greater size and spending level among OECD city governments may be due to a propensity of Western European cities, in particular, to provide certain major services such as education, public health, and social service that in the United States are commonly provided by special districts, counties, the states, or the federal government.

These size and expenditure differentials between the two groups

Table 2.1 PROFILE OF THE STUDY CITIES

City	Population (1,000s)	Land Area (sq. mi.)	Form of Gov't[a]	No. of City Employees[b]
		URBIS Cities		
Albany, N.Y.	111	20.9	SM/C	3,481
Atlanta, Ga.	451	131.6	SM/C	7,412
Baltimore, Md.	878	78.3	SM/C	38,413
Brockton, Mass.	93	21.2	SM/C	2,624
Burbank, Calif.	86	17.1	CM	1,207
Chesapeake, Va.	97	346.8	CM	3,203
Cleveland, Ohio	679	75.9	SM/C	12,596
Costa Mesa, Calif.	75	15.6	CM	192
Evansville, Ind.	136	36.0	SM/C	1,275
Florissant, Mo.	67	9.0	SM/C	192
Ft. Lauderdale, Fla.	156	31.0	CM	2,231
Grand Rapids, Mich.	191	44.9	CM	2,001
Hampton, Va.	128	54.7	CM	3,688
Kansas City, Mo.	488	316.3	CM	6,461
Lancaster, Pa.	57	6.1	SM/C	706
Las Vegas, Nev.	144	53.2	CM	1,447
Lincoln, Neb.	163	51.5	SM/C	2,269
Little Rock, Ark.	142	55.8	CM	1,531
Long Beach, Calif.	347	50.1	CM	4,559
Louisville, Ky.	336	60.0	SM/C	4,714
Miami Beach, Fla.	95	6.4	CM	1,621
Milwaukee, Wis.	691	95.0	SM/C	9,388
Montgomery, Ala.	153	50.3	Comm.	1,940
New Orleans, La.	573	197.1	SM/C	10,958
Newton, Mass.	91	10.4	CM	940
Oshkosh, Wis.	52	10.8	CM	1,342
Paterson, N.J.	143	8.5	SM/C	3,445
Philadelphia, Pa.	1862	128.5	SM/C	36,952
Portsmouth, Va.	109	29.0	CM	3,975
Riverside, Calif.	155	71.7	CM	1,549
Sacramento, Calif.	267	93.9	CM	3,041
San Francisco, Calif.	687	45.4	SM/C	20,943
San Jose, Calif.	523	146.3	CM	3,210
St. Louis, Mo.	588	61.2	SM/C	14,094
Seattle, Wash.	503	83.6	SM/C	10,475
Spokane, Wash.	174	50.8	CM	1,740
Stockton, Calif.	114	33.8	CM	1,094
Tampa, Fla.	276	84.5	SM/C	4,259
Tulsa, Okla.	335	175.7	Comm.	3,251
Warren, Mich.	176	34.2	SM/C	1,108

Table 2.1 cont.

Country City	Population (1,000s)	Land Area (sq. mi.)	Form of Gov't[a]	No. of City Employees[b]
OECD Cities				
Austria				
Vienna	1614	159.9	SM/C	57,000
Canada				
Calgary	454	158.4	Comm.	8,000
Denmark				
Aarhus	246	180.0	Comm.	11,268
Vaerloese	17	13.3	Comm.	1,050
Finland				
Helsinki	510	71.4	Comm.	30,000
France				
Gagny[c]	116	12.5	Comm.	1,332
Montpellier	190	21.9	Comm.	1,260
Toulouse	450	NA	Comm.	7,200
Germany				
Backnang	31	15.2	SM/C	343
Duisberg	600	89.9	CM	NA
Nurtigen	30	18.1	SM/C	NA
Japan				
Maebashi	250	56.8	Comm.	2,291
Nishinomy	402	37.7	Comm.	4,500
Sweden				
Jonkoping[d]	108	573.0	Comm.	3,345
United Kingdom				
Leeds	739	217.0	WM/C	27,540
Torbay	110	24.2	WM/C	1,509

[a] Designations refer to: WM/C = Weak Mayor/Council; Comm = Commission; SM/C = Strong Mayor/Council; CM = Council/Manager.

[b] These figures indicate only the relative size of individual municipal government organizations—some cities have larger numbers of employees than cities comparable in size because they provide services such as education and utilities.

[c] Gagny actually represents a collective of five small local authorities known as SAECOMMA (Syndicat d'Arenagement et d'Equipement du Cours Moyen de la Marne-Development and Equipment Board for the Middle Reaches of the River Marne).

[d] Jonkoping is a local authority that encompasses three cities (Jonkoping, Husqvarna, and Granna), the borough of Norrahammar, and several small villages including the land between them. Hence the large land area encompassed by the city.

of cities, while not significant for overall comparisons, do have significance for certain measures of computing extensiveness and use that will be pointed out later in this chapter. In general, it is agreed among national experts on the OECD Advisory Committee that the mix

Table 2.2 COMPARISON CONTEXTUAL DATA ON OECD AND URBIS CITIES BY POPULATION

Cities less than 200,000 Population	Average Population (1000s)	Distribution of Forms Government[a]	Average Land Area (sq. mi.)	Average No. of City Employees	Average Operating Budget ($ million)
OECD cities (N = 7)	86	Comm = 4 SM/C = 2 C/Comm = 1	18[b]	1,473	$38
URBIS cities (N = 24)	121	Comm = 1 C/M = 14 SM/C = 9	31[c]	1,867	$36
Cities between 200,000 and 450,000					
OECD cities (N = 4)	337	Comm = 4	114	6,305	$116
URBIS cities (N = 5)	312	Comm = 1 C/M = 2 SM/C = 2	93	3,965	$106
Cities greater than 450,000					
OECD cities (N = 5)	783	WM/C = 1 Comm = 2 C/M = 1 SM/C = 1	135	30,635	$486
URBIS cities (N = 11)	718	SM/C = 9 CM = 2	124	15,537	$397

[a] Designations refer to: WM/C = Weak Mayor/Council; Comm = Commission; SM/C = Strong Mayor/Council; CM = Council/Manager.
[b] Excludes the city of Jonkoping, which is disproportionately large in land area.
[c] Excludes the city of Chesapeake, which is disproportionately large in land area.

of OECD cities is sufficient to form a "rough" indicator of the local government computing environment in western developed nations outside the United States. Comparisons among individual countries are used only for highlighting the broader comparison between the UR-BIS and OECD cities.

Diffusion of Computing Use

The most direct measure of the diffusion of computer technology across cities is the number of cities in each country that have adopted computing, expressed as a percentage of all cities (Kraemer and King 1977a; Perry and Kraemer 1979).[2] By "adoption" of computing is meant active application of computing to at least one municipal function. It is not necessary that the city have its own computing installation, or even that it be part of a group of local governments using computing; computing can be procured from any source to qualify a city for classification as a user.

Table 2.3 provides data on the use of computing by cities in five of the ten countries for which reliable data are available. It is interesting to note that although United States cities are often regarded as the most advanced users of computing, the United States lags behind the other four countries listed in the table in tems of the proportion of cities using computing. The leader of the group (and probably the leader among all nine OECD countries) is Denmark, which provides computing through a central organization to nearly all cities. Copenhagen and a few other cities have their own systems, but all other cities must use the shared facilities of Kommunedata, AB, a national service organization for local goverment computing. Sweden is second with 72 percent of the cities using computing under an arrangement similar to that in Denmark; the United Kingdom is third with 67 percent; and Japan is fourth with 64 percent. The U.S. figure of 51 percent may be slightly inflated compared to the other countries, since the percentage calculation is based upon only U.S. cities over 10,000 in population rather than all U.S. cities. The data from Denmark, Sweden, United Kingdom, and Japan reflect the status of computing in *all* municipalities in those countries.

Table 2.3 PERCENTAGE OF CITIES USING COMPUTING IN FOUR STUDY COUNTRIES IN THE MID-1970S

Country	No. of Cities	Percentage Using Computers	Date of Survey
Denmark	276	90%	1975
Sweden	464	72%	1973
United Kingdom	521	67%	1978
Japan	3,274	64%	1975
United States	2,294	51%	1975

SOURCES: Denmark and Sweden: OECD, 1974b; United Kingdom: Local Authorities Management and Systems Analysis Center, London; Japan: Local Authorities Systems Development Center, Tokyo; United States: Kraemer and King 1977a.

The rate of adoption of computing indicates the relative speed with which computing has been adopted by cities over time. Ideally, it would be best to compare the rates of adoption in each country to one another, but that is impossible without detailed data on computing in all cities in each country. Instead, we compare the rate of adoption among the URBIS cities and U.S. cities generally (organized according to various population groups) with the sixteen OECD cities (figure 2.1).

The adoption pattern for all cities follows the traditional "S" shape for diffusion of innovations (Perry and Kraemer 1979). Because the OECD cities tend to represent the more advanced sites in individual countries, and the URBIS cities include primarily advanced but also some non-advanced sites, the adoption curves on all U.S. cities of over 10,000 population have been included. The most striking feature of the comparison is that the OECD cities typically started later as a group than did the URBIS cities, but reached full adoption sooner.

Figure 2.1 CUMULATIVE PERCENTAGES THROUGH 1975 OF CITIES USING COMPUTING IN OECD AND URBIS, BY YEAR OF ADOPTION, SHOWN GRAPHICALLY

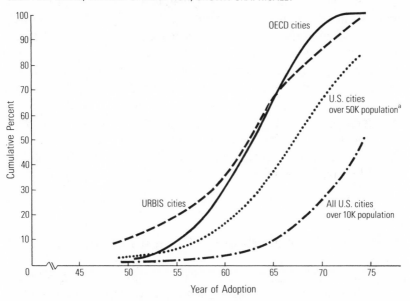

[a]Data on cities below 10,000 population are from the International City Management Association as reported in Kraemer, Dutton, and Matthews 1975.

Application of computing in cities started first in the United States (around 1950) and began later in other countries (e.g., 1955 in the United Kingdom). Yet, at least four of the OECD countries show broader diffusion of the technology than does the United States. The OECD cities as a group appear to have adopted computing technology much more rapidly than have U.S. cities as a group. Of course, these data indicate only the average rates of adoption, and in the case of the OECD cities, the rate is certainly not representative of individual countries. Nevertheless, the difference between the U.S. rate of adoption and that of the OECD cities is unxpected.

A possible explanation for this phenomenon is the difference in the nature of national support for local government computing development between the United States and the OECD countries. In general, the development of local government information systems in the United States has been a local affair. The U.S. federal government's main contribution has been to pave the way for computing development by experiments with new applications and techniques. The local government associations (e.g., the International City Management Association, the National League of Cities, the National Association of Counties) and the state governments have played only a minor role in computing development in cities (King 1982). In contrast, many of the countries represented by the OECD cities exhibit much greater national and regional support for such computing development through coordination efforts of the central government and nation-wide local government associations. This support ranges from establishment of large national/regional centers for providing computer service, to operation of national/regional centers for software development and advice to local governments. This concentrated support, we feel, has stimulated movement of the technology out to the OECD cities more quickly than has been the case in URBIS cities.

Organization for Computing Activities

The provision of computing services for city government can be organized in several ways. These range from ownership and operation of the equipment by the city in a centralized installation serving all departments, to more decentralized arrangements whereby departments buy time or even run their own computing operations, to cooperative arrangements where cities band together and organize a shared computing installation to service their collective needs. Figure 2.2 indicates these options.

According to the widely accepted scenario of computing de-

Figure 2.2 ALTERNATIVE ARRANGEMENTS FOR OWNERSHIP AND MANAGEMENT OF COMPUTING

Ownership of Equipment

	Local Government	Outside Organization
Local Government	Owned and managed by the local government Advantages: Full government control of the equipment and its use, as well as potential for economies of scale. Disadvantages: High investment and maintenance costs, even if the system is underused.	Rental or lease arrangements Advantages: Low investment costs, and relative ease in changing the system. Disadvantages: Less government control over system, and usually much higher overall equipment cost in long run.
Outside Organization	Facility Management Facility is owned by the local government, but is operated on a contract basis by a private firm. Advantages: Government control over the system, frequently lower operating costs, removal of need for government management. Disadvantages: Less government control over management activities, absolute need for a good contract, and problems of changeover if converting from a government-managed situation.	Service Bureaus and Shared Facilities Facilities are owned and managed by a private firm or by a consortium of public agencies that sells computer service to municipalities. Advantages: Flexible utility, easy to adapt to needs, less management for participating governments, and often lower costs. Disadvantages: Little control for individual governments; cost-sharing difficult to make equitable, may be unreliable, requires much cooperation.

Management of the Facilities

SOURCE: Adapted from Kraemer and King (1977b)

velopment in U.S. cities, in the earlier days computing was most often located in the finance or city controller department.[3] Other departments wishing to make use of computing found it necessary to bargain with the finance department or to develop their own departmental computing capability in order to be able to get prompt, reliable service. When the computer's use expanded outside finance to include many other functions, local governments tended to move computing out of the finance department and into a new, separate department of data processing under the chief executive, and to centralize all computing in this department (i.e., do away with each department's having its own equipment). Very recently, with the advent of mini- and microcomputers, there again has been a tendency for individual departments to acquire their own systems (King 1982).

These trends are seldom viewed as satisfactory by all parties at interest (King 1978, 1983). The computer was originally located in finance because that department was perceived as the biggest potential user. But finance tended to dominate use and this spurred the proliferation of separate computing facilities among other departments. Centralization of computing activity emerged to eliminate this proliferation and bring economies of scale to computing and to locate control under the chief executive in order to make the technology available to all municipal operations with no single department dominating.[4] But large, centralized installations often become unmanageable and, in the minds of users, insufficiently responsive to the wide range of departments that now need computing service. Recent decentralization efforts have attempted to take advantage of lower hardware costs, which reduce the need to achieve economies from scale, and to move computing closer to users. But now there are problems in maintaining overall control (King and Kraemer 1980; King 1980, 1983).

As a group, the URBIS cities reflect all of these trends. As shown in figure 2.3, out of the 40 URBIS cities, 21 cities were using single, centralized installations at the time of the study. Eight cities show two installations, two cities show three installations, and three cities show four, five, and six installations respectively. Those cities with two installations typically maintain a large single installation handling most computing for the city, with a smaller dedicated com-

Figure 2.3 ORGANIZATION AND DISTRIBUTION OF COMPUTING ARRANGEMENTS IN OECD AND URBIS CITIES, 1976

OECD Cities: 16 cities total
   12 with single, centralized installations, all under control of the local chief executive
   4 receiving computing service from public regional installations
URBIS Cities: 40 cities total
Distribution by number of installations
   21 cities with single, centralized installations
   8 cities with 2 installations
   2 cities with 3 installations
   1 city with 4 installations
   1 city with 5 installations
   1 city with 6 installations
   2 cities using facilities management
   3 cities using public regional installations
Distribution by location of installations
   18 installations under the chief executive
   17 installations under the finance department
   9 installations under the police department
   7 installations under the public works/utilities departments
   3 installations under the courts
   1 installation under the health department
   1 installation under the assessment department
   1 installation under the fire department
   1 installation under the personnel department
   1 installation under the transportation department
   1 installation under the library department

---

puting operation serving a highly specialized function, usually the police department. Two cities in the study used facilities management (where a private firm comes in and takes over the city-owned installation and runs it fo the city), and three cities obtained computing services from shared computing installations. Of these many computing installations, 18 were located under the city chief executive, 17 under the finance department, nine under police control, seven in public works/utilities, three in courts, and one each in health, assessment, fire, personnel, transportation, and library departments.

    This contrasts markedly with the situation in OECD cities at the time of the studies. Of the 16 cities, twelve showed centralized single installations under control of the city chief executive, and four were receiving computing service from a shared computing installation. In addition, of the twelve that show in-house installations, four were providing services to other local governments in excess of 15 percent of their total operations. Thus, out of 16 cities, one-half were involved in sharing computing resources with other governments. In the Scandinavian countries, moreover, sharing is extremely common, with a large majority of cities receiving computing from large nation-wide centers set up to serve local governments. This is a remarkably high level of sharing compared to the URBIS cities; less than 8 percent were involved in shared computing arrangements. Similarly, those OECD cities with in-house computing invariably created centralized installations under control of the city chief executive. This contrasts with the URBIS cities, where over one-third of the cities owning their own computing facilities also maintained more than one installation, and where less than one-half of the cities had computing located under the chief executive.

Financial and Technical Characteristics

The character of computing in the OECD and URBIS cities in 1976 is illustrated by (a) the level of resources devoted to computing, measured as the level of expenditures for computing; and (b) the level of technical capability available to the city, measured by the number of computer mainframes used in the cities, computing core capacity available to the cities, and the number of on-line computer terminals used in the cities.

FINANCIAL CHARACTERISTICS
Expenditure patterns for computing have varied considerably across U.S. cities, which were found to spend an average of about one percent of their operating budgets on computing (Kraemer and King 1977a), and between $1.00 and $5.00 per capita on computing each year. The range of expenditures on computing varies slightly with population, with the smallest cities spending somewhat less than larger cities. The URBIS cities, being somewhat more sophisticated than the average U.S. city, were expected to spend more, and they do. As shown in table 2.4, the average URBIS city expenditure for computing in 1976

Table 2.4 EXPENDITURES FOR COMPUTING IN URBIS AND OECD CITIES, 1976

	URBIS Cities	OECD Cities
Mean percent of city operating budget spent on computing[a]	1.30%	.82%
Range of percentages	.11–4.00%	.24–2.10%
Mean expenditure on computing per capita (U.S. $)[b]	$3.98	$2.96
Range of per capita expenditures (U.S. $)	$.63–11.77	$1.20–6.53

[a] Data unavailable for one OECD city and four URBIS cities.
[b] Data unavailable for three URBIS cities.

as a percentage of operating budget is 1.30 percent, and the average per capita expenditure was $3.98. The list of expenditures shows considerable variance across the cities, with a high of 4.0 percent of operating budget spent on computing and $11.77 per capita on computing, and lows of .11 percent and $.63 per capita.

In comparison, the OECD cities in 1976 spent much less on computing. Their range of expenditures shows highs of 2.10 percent and $6.53, and lows of .24 percent and $1.20. Their average expenditures were only .82 percent and $2.96 per capita. These figures represent only about two-thirds to three-quarters as much computing expenditure as found in the URBIS cities. Since level of expenditure on computing, particularly as a percentage of operating budget, correlates closely with both the quantity and sophistication of computing activity, we infer in a tentative way that the U.S. cities were substantially more developed in use of computing than the OECD cities in 1976. We do not infer, however, that higher levels of expenditures for computing in the U.S. cities results in qualitatively superior computing use compared to that in the OECD cities. Rather, it simply means that the extent of use in U.S. cities in 1976, as measured by investment, was greater.

TECHNICAL CHARACTERISTICS

Three indicators serve as guides to the technical level of computing in a city: the number of computer mainframes; the total amount of computer core capacity available as a sum of the capacities of the computers; and the number of on-line computer terminals

Table 2.5 COMPARISON OF MAKES, NUMBERS, AND CORE SIZE OF COMPUTERS, PLUS NUMBER OF ON-LINE TERMINALS IN URBIS AND OECD CITIES

OECD City	Machines in Each City	No. CPUS	City Core[b]	No. of Term'ls
1	IBM 370/145; IBM 370/158	na	na	3
2	(2) IBM 370/145	na	na	0
3	(2) IBM 370/145	na	na	0
4	(2) Univac 1106	na	na	7
5	IBM 370/125	1	85K	0
6	Honeywell/Bull 58	1	10K	16
7	IBM 370/135	1	192K	4
8	IBM 370/145	1	748K	12
9	HITAC 8.250	1	132K	2
10	FACOM U-200	1	32K	6
11	IBM 370/145	1	512K	30
12	C II IRIS-50	1	256K	14
13	DATASAAB D22; IBM 370/145	2	848K	20
14	IBM 370/158	1	806K	13
15	ICL 1904A; ICL 19045	2	1320K	40
16	(2) IBM 370/158	2	2000K	55
Average[a]		1.25	621K	16.5

URBIS City				
1	IBM Syst. 3; Xerox 530	2	192K	19
2	(2) IBM 370/145; Varian V74	3	1108K	75
3	(3) IBM 370/145; (2) IBM Syst. 7; IBM 360/40; IBM 1401; IBM 370/125	8	1704K	80
4	Univac 9840	1	98K	0
5	IBM 370/125	1	256K	20
6	IBM 370/115; DEC PDP 11/45	2	288K	8
7	(2) IBM 370/158; IBM Syst. 7; DEC PDP 11/45	3	3074K	157
8	NCR Century 200	1	33K	1
9	Zytron; IBM System 3/10	2	32K	2
10	NCR 399	2	8K	0
11	RCA 45; Wang 2200; DATA GENERAL NOVA 3	3	344K	5
12	Burroughs B3500; (2) Burroughs TCS1020; PDP 8; PDP 11/30	5	538K	49
13	IBM 370/135	1	256K	17
14	(2) IBM 370/158; DEC PDP 11; IBM Syst. 7; NCR Century	5	2564K	174
15	IBM Syst. 3/15	1	192K	4
16	IBM 2020; IBM 1130; IBM 370/145; DEC PDP 11/45	4	660K	3
17	IBM 370/145	1	512K	29
18	(2) Varian V73	2	256K	20
19	IBM 370/145; IBM 370/158	2	2500K	85
20	IBM 370/155; Mohawk 2400	2	1040K	21
21	Burroughs B2700	1	150K	3

OECD City	Machines in Each City	No. CPUS	City Core[b]	No. of Term'ls
22	IBM 370/145; IBM 370/135; (2) DEC PDP 11; (2) Interdata 74	6	608K	116
23	NCR Century 200; DEC PDP 8	2	48K	5
24	IBM 370/155; IBM 370/158; Burroughs 1726	3	2179K	147
25	Honeywell 600; Basic Four 600	2	600K	4
26	Univac 9300	1	32K	0
27	IBM 370/115	1	128K	4
28	(2) IBM 370/145; IBM 370/135; (2) IBM Syst. 3; HP 3000	6	1970K	178
29	Honeywell 2050A	1	256K	40
30	Burroughs 3500	1	256K	24
31	NA	na	na	na
32	(2) IBM 370/158; DEC PDP 12; COMTEN 476	4	4324K	269
33	IBM 360/20; Burroughs 3741	2	316K	2
34	IBM 370/158; IBM 370/155; IBM 360/140; IBM 360/20; (3) Four Phase; DEC PDP 8; Univac 9010	9	3550K	269
35	NCR 251; (2) DEC PDP 11/45	3	372K	18
36	NCR Century 200	1	64K	4
37	Univac 9314	1	32K	0
38	RCA 70/45; RCA 70/2; Interdata 70; Raytheon 704	4	470K	10
39	Honeywell 6040; (2) DataGeneral NOVA 840	3	256K	44
40	Univac 9300	1	16K	0
Average		2.64	790K	46.8

[a] Excludes those sites marked na.
[b] Adjusted to reflect amounts of time sold to other local authorities.

being used. Table 2.5 provides data on the makes, numbers, and core sizes of computers in the URBIS and OECD cities, as well as the number of computer terminals in each site. Excluding the four OECD cities that were receiving computing from shared installations (excluded because it is impossible to assign a portion of a machine to a single user when the breakdowns of use by all users are unavailable, as they were in this case), the average for the OECD cities was 1.25 computers per city, with an average of 621 K bytes of core memory capacity, and an average number of 16 computer terminals.

In contrast, the URBIS cities in 1976 (excluding, again, those using public regional installations) showed an average of 2.64 computers per city, with average core capacity of 790 K bytes, and an average of 47 terminals. The level of computer capacity in the URBIS cities substantially exceeds that of the OECD cities for this period. Moreover, the URBIS cities show a large number of minicomputer systems in use (computers such as the Digital Equipment PDP 11, Data General Nova, Interdata 74, Four Phase, and IBM System 7). Mini-computers were not used in the OECD cities at the time of the studies. These cities in 1976 had installations similar to those found in many U.S. cities during the early 1970s—one or two large, powerful computer mainframes, and no smaller, special-purpose machines.

It is important to note that these measures are only rough indicators, and exhibit some peculiar problems. First, simply having a larger number of computers does not mean that a city has greater computing capacity than a city with fewer computers; capacity depends on the size of the machines. Second, computer core memory sizes are not really additive in the strictest sense. A single machine with one megabyte of core storage is more powerful for some jobs than four machines with 256 K bytes of storage, since the larger single machine can work flexibly with all or portions of its capacity, while the small machines are limited to their maximum individual capacities. However, these measures do, on average, provide a useful indication of the relative level of computing capability of cities.

Although our subsequent analyses do not concern the distribution of various vendors' equipment among the cities, as a matter of interest we do provide that distribution in table 2.6. We note three characteristics of this distribution: IBM clearly dominates in both the United States and the OECD countries; the dominance of IBM in OECD cities is substantially stronger than in the URBIS cities; and five brands of computers used in the OECD cities are not being used in URBIS cities, while 15 brands of computers used in URBIS cities are not used in the OECD cities. This suggests that the international marketing capabilities of smaller companies are considerably less than the capabilities of the large, established computer firms.

Breadth of Computing Use

The major indicators of breadth of computing use are the number of operational applications each city has and the spread of those applications over various functions performed by the city. An application

Table 2.6 DISTRIBUTION AND PROPORTIONS OF COMPUTERS BY MANUFACTURER IN OECD AND URBIS CITIES, 1976

Manufacturer	Number	Percent of Total
OECD cities		
IBM	13	65%
ICL	2	10
Honeywell	1	5
Datasaab	1	5
HITAC	1	5
FACOM	1	5
C II	1	5
Totals	20	100
URBIS cities		
IBM	45	47%
Digital equipment	12	13
Burroughs	7	8
NCR	5	5
Univac	5	5
Data General	3	3
Honeywell	3	3
RCA	3	3
Varian	3	3
Interdata	2	2
Basic Four	1	1
Hewlett Packard	1	1
Mohawk	1	1
Raytheon	1	1
Wang	1	1
Xerox	1	1
Zytron	1	1
Totals	95	100

is a program or set of programs that matches the capabilities of the computer to a clearly definable organizational task. Examples of applications are general ledger accounting, payroll calculation and check printing, engineering calculations, criminal records for police, and traffic ticket processing. Table 2.7 shows a substantial difference between OECD and URBIS cities in the average number of operational computer applications in 1976. The OECD cities range from four applications to a high of 85, with an average of 24. The URBIS cities range from four applications to 152, with an average of 63—an average over twice as high as that of OECD cities. Moreover, as shown in table

Table 2.7 NUMBERS OF OPERATIONAL APPLICATIONS IN URBIS AND OECD CITIES, 1976

	OECD Cities	URBIS Cities
Number of cities	16	40
Total applications	384	2,520
Mean number of applications	24	63
Range of number of applications	4 to 85	4 to 152

2.8, the URBIS cities in 1976 showed much broader uses of computing; that is, computers were applied to a larger number of functional
areas in the government. The OECD cities as a group show ten functional areas with at least 2 percent of all applications, while the UR-
BIS cities as a group show fifteen such functional areas.

These similarities and differences in applications are noteworthy. Both OECD and URBIS cities in 1976 were devoting roughly
half of their computing applications to the area of governmental administration, particularly financial and budgetary aspects. The OECD
cities show a stronger concentration on applications for accounting,
treasury, and collection than do the URBIS cities, but the URBIS cities show a stronger concentration on budgetary and general fiscal
management applications. The URBIS cities also devote significantly
more applications to data-processing activity itself, and to the comparatively sophisticated tasks of geographic data processing. Thus,
within government administration, the URBIS cities engage in a more
diversified application of the technology and include generally more
sophisticated applications.

In the area of community development the OECD cities in 1976
were devoting substantially more applications to the task of plan-
ning/zoning/renewal. These tasks tend to be more important in the
municipal governmental activities of the countries making up the OECD
survey than in the United States, and we feel this accounts for much
of this difference. Also, many planning departments in the United States
contract-out services for planning-related data processing, so the
URBIS figure may be slightly deflated. In other aspects of community
development, both the URBIS and OECD cities seem to be rather close
in application of computing.

Table 2.8 COMPARISON OF APPLICATIONS BY FUNCTIONAL AREAS IN THE CITIES, 1976

Functional Areas	OECD Cities (N = 15) % of applications in this area	URBIS Cities (N = 40) % of applications in this area
Public safety		
police protection	1.6%	11.2%
fire protection	0	4.0
courts	0	4.2
	1.6	19.4
Government administration		
accounting/treasury/collection	20.0	13.6
assessment	6.4	5.7
budgeting/general fiscal management	9.7	17.5
data processing	0.6	6.3
geoprocessing	1.6	3.0
public services/general government	6.9	5.0
	44.7	51.1
Community development		
planning/zoning/renewal	11.4	5.5
licensing	1.4	2.6
engineering	1.9	1.0
transportation/roads	4.4	3.1
sanitation	1.7	1.7
water supply/utilities	7.2	6.3
	28.0	20.2
Human resources		
public health	8.9	2.5
welfare	10.0	2.0
parks/recreation	1.7	0.8
vital statistics	0.6	0.6
libraries	1.7	1.6
voter registration	2.8	1.8
	25.7	9.3
Number of functional areas having at least 2.0% of all applications	10	15

Striking differences between URBIS and OECD cities appear in the areas of public safety and human resources. In public safety the OECD cities show virtually no application, while the URBIS cities show a very substantial amount—nearly one-fifth of all applications. Two factors probably account for this. First, police and fire activities are usually the responsibility of city governments in the United States, while in many of the OECD countries these are performed by other levels of government. Second, police automation has been a focus of very large federally-sponsored development programs in the United States in recent years. One program alone, the U.S. Department of Justice's Law Enforcement Assistance Administration, spent as much as $50 million dollars per year for police automation in cities in the middle to late 1970s, which spurred development of police applications (Kraemer and King 1978b).

The human resources category, on the other hand, showed considerably less development in the URBIS cities than in OECD cities in 1976, particularly in the areas of public health and welfare. Two factors might contribute to this situation. First, most public health and welfare services in the United States are administered through local programs at county or regional levels rather than the city level, or through direct federal government-to-recipient programs, such as social security. It was noticed in the URBIS study that the few city-level health and welfare computing applications took place in large cities, which have taken on these tasks at the behest of state governments, or in consolidated city-county governments. The second factor is the considerably higher level of publicly-provided health and welfare services in many of the OECD countries, particularly those in Western Europe. Because these tasks are well suited to computing assistance (a fact that was made evident by the large number of health and welfare applications operational in U.S. counties surveyed in the first phase of the URBIS Project), it is not surprising to see active development in these areas among the OECD cities, where city governments often act as delivery agents for national health and welfare programs.

Taken together, these measures of computing development—number of applications operational and functional areas of application—indicate that the URBIS cities in 1976 displayed intensive and broader development of computing applications than did the OECD cities. However, as noted earlier, considering the later start of the OECD cities and their consistently lower relative expenditures on computing, it is fair to say that even as early as 1976 the OECD cities had become fairly well developed in use of the technology. The major differences appear to be in two areas: the URBIS cities had much more computing overall, and they tended to show computing in a wider variety of applications.

Summary

These data serve as a foundation for the other chapters in this book, and as an overview of the nature of the comparison sites and the condition of computing in these local governments at the time of the URBIS and OECD studies. To a lesser extent, these data also provide some insight into the comparative nature of computing growth in cities in the United States and the nine OECD countries.

As of 1976 URBIS cities were more automated than OECD cities. They had more computing capacity, a larger number of municipal functions, and spent considerably more on computing than most of the OECD cities. The OECD cities tended to share computing resources with other cities in their own countries to a much greater extent than did the URBIS cities. In countries represented by the study cities, the proportion of cities using computers was substantial. A vast majority of the cities in Denmark, Sweden, Japan, and the United Kingdom were using computers, and over half of the U.S. cities were as well. Even though cities in the OECD countries adopted computing somewhat later than did those in the United States, the OECD cities made remarkable advances in a short period of time in application of the technology, possibly due to the emphasis the central governments and local government associations in the OECD countries place on nationwide or regional sharing of computer facilities. The U.S. approach to development of computing in urban management was more decentralized and individualistic than the approach of most OECD countries, although some of the OECD countries (United Kingdom, Canada) are similar to the United States in this regard.

There appears to be a relationship between size of government and extent and character of computing activity. Larger organizations tend to require larger support services such as computing to meet their needs, but size is significant in more interesting ways. For one thing, size serves as a demarcation factor for the time at which cities enter into computing activity and the speed with which they develop their capabilities. Larger cities not only have more computing capacity as a rule, but they have usually adopted the technology sooner and have been quicker to adopt new developments. It is interesting to note in the URBIS cities, for example, that the adoption of minicomputers has been greater among the larger cities (which adopted minicomputers as supplements to their larger mainframes) than among smaller cities, which were expected to be quick to take advantage of the smaller computers. Typically, smaller cities tend to follow the lead of larger cities and utilize the facilities of larger cities or a service bureau while learning about computing and preparing to develop their own capabilities. Large cities very seldom are involved in procuring computing from other cities.

Size plays an important role in the adoption of computing in cities. Larger size affords opportunity to capitalize on the computer's capacity for rapidly and cheaply processing large-volume, routine transactions. Larger size also allows economies of scale not available to smaller cities, as with procurement of larger machines with higher computing power-to-cost ratios. Size also provides greater organizational slack, or the "reserve capacity," that most organizations maintain to deal with unexpected needs or fluctuations in workflow, and this slack can often be utilized in development of new computer applications. Finally, larger organizations can employ larger workforces, with greater job specialization and more exotic skills (e.g., in telecommunications or data base management).

The data further suggest that computing development in local government is influenced strongly by the national and local political and administrative contexts in which it occurs. Although technologies can help transform the organizations in which they are used, our findings suggest that organizations shape technologies at least as much as the technologies shape them. Our findings suggest that computing is usually adapted to fit the existing organizational context and is put to work in the service of existing organizational interests. For example, the highly decentralized nature of local government units in the United States is mirrored by the highly decentralized in-house computing arrangements within U.S. local governments. The comparatively centralized governmental organization found in many of the countries represented in the OECD study is mirrored by highly centralized arrangements for computing. Further, the political demands made on governmental organizations for particular services appear to influence the kinds of computing applications developed. URBIS cities emphasize the application of computing for law enforcement, whereas the OECD cities tend to emphasize applications for welfare and health. Both sets of cities give greatest emphasis, however, to applications aimed at revenue generation and expenditure control. This emphasis on fiscal efficiency has traditionally been part of the political/administration culture of local governments in Western developed nations. In all three cases, these patterns of the technology's use reflect the political demands and organizational contexts of their application environment.

From this chapter we carry forward two basic observations. First, computing is used extensively in local governments in both the URBIS and OECD cities, and, in both populations, extent of computing use correlates with organizational size. Larger cities tend to make more extensive use of computing, suggesting that the net benefits of computing use are related to the size of the demands facing cities and the amount of resources that can be brought to bear in adopting and implementing computerized systems. The second observation is that national and local contexts play an important role in the patterns of computing adoption and application. National policies and practices can encourage computing use in different ways, and the mandates under which cities function naturally dictate the tasks to which computing systems are put. In both URBIS and OECD cities, however, there are similarities in the core applications to financial management and administration.

Notes

1. The various publications by the OECD (listed under the author "OECD" in the references) provide a good overview of use of computing in cities internationally.

2. Diffusion of a technology means the movement of a technology for a particular task from its place of initial use to another, similar place of use—in this case, the spread of computing among cities. Diffusion of innovations is a subject of considerable discussion in the literature: see Downs and Mohr (1976); Rogers and Shoemaker (1971); Rogers (1975); Roessner (1979); Tornatzky et al. (1983); and Perry and Kraemer (1979).

3. The computer was initially brought into the organization through the efforts of the department with the greatest perceived need for, and fit with, computer assistance—usually the finance department.

4. The general centralization/decentralization debate in computing focuses on two arguments: proponents of centralization claim that centralization costs less (economies of scale),

provides a higher quality and quantity of computing capability, and ensures better managerial control; proponents of decentralization claim that there is little or no difference in costs, that decentralization yields a quality and quantity of service more consistent with user needs, and puts greater control in the hands of users without loss of managerial prerogatives. See King (1978, 1980, 1983).

CHAPTER THREE
THE
BENEFITS
OF COMPUTING

I N CHAPTER 1 the question was asked "why has there been such spectacular growth in the use of computing?" All of the supply-push and demand-pull factors that were presented reduce, in at least some respects, to the proposition that computing use has grown because it provides benefits to those that use it. The range of possible benefits from computing is large, from direct and demonstrable cost savings of replacing human labor with machine labor, to the entertainment benefits of a new and exciting technology. This chapter addresses two major classes of benefits that are believed to result from computing use in city governments. The first we call *benefits for operational efficiency and service delivery;* the second we call *benefits for organizational management and planning.* Both were considered in the URBIS and OECD studies, and the data collected from the studies provide a solid base for assessing the benefits of computing for city governments.[1]

Operational Efficiency and Service Delivery

The promotional literature, and indeed much of the common belief about computing, holds that computers improve efficiency and productivity by taking over repetitive data-processing tasks and by providing better ways of managing and using data.[2] Beyond these efficiency improvements there is the computer's ability to do certain things that could not be done at all with manual data-processing methods. As these improvements are realized, the organization can become better at what it does. In the case of a service-providing organization such as a local government, the expected result of improvements in efficiency is an improvement in service delivery.

The efficiency benefits that can come from computing are:

1. *Increased speed of operations;*
2. *Improved accuracy of data;*
3. *Staff savings;*
4. *Cost savings or avoidance.*

As major service providers, local governments also become repositories for many required records on citizens and organizations, and their extensive information management activities consume considerable staff time and other resources. Increased speed of operations, if achieved without simultaneous increase in the net resources expended, results in an efficiency improvement. Such results occur most often in applications requiring large amounts of calculating and printing (utility or tax billing), and in record searching (customer inquiry, selective updating).

The major data-handling duties of local governments require considerable concern about data accuracy. It is essential that the government ensure the accuracy of important public records and government accounts, and baseline data must be accurate so that errors do not propagate and cause costly mistakes. Thus improved accuracy of data is an important goal in the use of computing in local governments. The computer seldom makes "errors," and its storage media are very reliable. If sufficient care is taken to see that accurate data are entered into the machine, computing can allow virtually error-free data management capability.

Many of the services provided by local governments are dependent on large-scale information flows, and these operations are necessarily labor-intensive. If computing reduces the time required to manage information and at the same time improves accuracy, the number of person-hours devoted to these activities can be reduced greatly. These potential staff savings can yield major benefits for the local government, in the form of cost savings or cost avoidance.

Cost savings can be achieved as a result of staff savings when the staff members freed from information-processing tasks are eliminated from the payroll or are put to tasks that generate direct new revenue. If there are no layoffs or increases in revenue due to labor reallocation, there are no cost savings. Cost avoidance is a benefit that occurs when the use of computing makes it possible to accommodate an unavoidable increase in workload without a proportional increase in staff.

Sometimes it happens that computing brings improvements in speed, accuracy, and staff savings, but no real or proportional reductions in costs of government operations. In such cases the benefit of the computer must be found in a qualitative improvement in the effectiveness of government service delivery. Such a benefit occurs when, for example, staff hours previously devoted to processing water bills and correcting clerical errors are released to provide additional labor for improving the water department's conservation campaign or its counter service to the public. Another kind of service delivery improvement can come in the form of new services provided because of the computer's unique capabilities. For example, the low per-unit cost for printing, addressing, and mailing notices to the public can result in improved public notification of important issues, meetings, and elections.

The indicators of efficiency and service delivery used in this analysis are shown in figure 3.1. The findings on efficiency and service delivery benefits are based on data presented in tables 3.1 and 3.2.

SPEED OF OPERATIONS

Both URBIS and OECD cities have experienced benefits in the speed of operations. Two measures related to the effects of speed of

Figure 3.1 INDIVIDUAL INDICATORS USED FOR MEASUREMENTS OF EFFICIENCY AND SERVICE DELIVERY BENEFITS FOR URBIS AND OECD CITIES

URBIS Cities

Speed
Computers save me time in looking for information.

It takes too long to get the information I need from the computer.

Accuracy
Computerized data are less accurate than data stored on manual files.

Staffing
Where they have been applied, computers have reduced the number of people necessary to perform tasks in my department.

Cost
Where they have been applied, computers have reduced the cost of department operations.

Service Delivery
Computers have failed to increase the effectiveness of my department in serving the public.

OECD Cities

Speed
Has the introduction of the application, as compared to previous system, if any, led to more efficient transaction of business?

. . . led to increased capacity to handle workload?

Accuracy
Has the introduction of the application, as compared to previous system, if any, led to reduced error rate?

Staffing
Has the introduction of the applications, as compared to previous system, if any, led to staff savings?

Cost
What are the annual savings/cost when compared to (previous, manual) alternatives?

Service Delivery
Has the introduction of the application, as compared to previous system, (if any):

. . . led to greater ability to cope with nonstandard situations?

. . . led to provision of better analysis?

. . . led to provisions for more integrated presentation of data?

operations were used for the analysis of the URBIS cities: whether computers save time in looking for information, and whether the amount of time required to get needed information from the computer is acceptable. URBIS respondents in about half of the cities feel computing has increased the speed of information searches, but whether this is an "adequate" payoff is unclear. Respondents in one-third of the cities believe that computing does not impede the timely flow of information, and may improve it.

In OECD cities, speed of operations was measured by the

Table 3.1 EFFICIENCY AND SERVICE DELIVERY BENEFITS FROM COMPUTING IN URBIS
CITIES (N = 39)

Type of Benefit	Little or none	Moderate	High
	Percent of Cities Indicating Extent of Benefit is:		
Speed of operations			
Computers save me time in looking for information.	51%	39%	10%
It takes too long to get the information I need from the computer. (Item reversed: high score means it does not take too long)	33	49	18
Average speed benefit	46	41	13
Accuracy of data			
Computerized data are less accurate than data stored on manual files. (item reversed: high score means greater accuracy)	8	51	41
Staff savings			
Where they have been applied, computers have reduced the number of people necessary to perform tasks in my department.	69	26	5
Cost savings			
Where they have been applied, computers have reduced the cost of department operations.	80	15	5
Service delivery effectiveness			
Computers have failed to increase the effectiveness of my department in serving the public. (item reversed: high score means effectiveness has been improved)	15	54	31

section heads' assessments of applications as leading to more efficient transaction of business and as increasing capacity to handle the workload. Overall, more than 90 percent of the cities have experienced these efficiency benefits. Indeed, for a majority of these cities speed-related benefits are high. It appears that computing has generally improved the speed of operations in OECD cities.

Table 3.2 EFFICIENCY AND SERVICE DELIVERY BENEFITS OF COMPUTING IN OECD CITIES (N = 15)

Type of Benefit	Percent of Cities Indicating Extent of Benefit is:		
	Little or none	Moderate	High
Speed of operations			
Has the introduction of the application, as compared to previous system, if any, led to more efficient transaction of business?	20%	13%	67%
. . . led to increased capacity to handle workload?	20	20	60
Average speed benefit	7	33	60
Accuracy of data			
Has the introduction of the application, as compared to previous system, if any, led to reduced error rate?	27	47	27
Staff savings			
Has the introduction of the application, as compared to previous system, if any, led to staff savings?	20	33	47
Cost savings			
What are the annual savings/cost when compared to (previous, manual) alternatives? (high score indicates cost savings)	46	31	23
Service delivery effectiveness			
Has the introduction of the application, as compared to previous system, if any, led to greater ability to cope with non-standard situations?	47	33	20
. . . led to provision of better analysis?	33	27	40
. . . led to provisions for more integrated presentation of data?	20	40	40
Average service delivery benefit	20	53	27

ACCURACY OF DATA

Both URBIS and OECD cities have experienced benefits in the accuracy of data. Computer-based data are held by most URBIS cities to be at least as accurate as data in manual files, and the strength of the response indicates that computing may have improved accuracy over manual information systems. Among OECD cities responding, nearly three-fourths feel computing has resulted in greater accuracy. However, for most of the OECD cities an increase in speed of operations has been realized more than a reduction in the error rate.

STAFF SAVINGS

There seems to be a difference between the perceptions of URBIS and OECD cities regarding staff savings from computing. Surprisingly, respondents in most of the URBIS cities feel that computing does not reduce the staff necessary to perform tasks. On the other hand, OECD respondents in nearly one-half of the cities claim to have experienced staff savings from computing.

COST SAVINGS

For URBIS cities cost savings are even more weakly realized than staff savings. In only one-fifth of the cities do respondents indicate at least some savings in department operations. OECD cities also are less likely to attribute cost savings to computing. This is particularly striking since respondents were asked to compare the cost of the use of applications with the manual alternative. For 46 percent of the cities no cost savings appear to have been realized.

SERVICE DELIVERY EFFECTIVENESS

It is unfortunate that important as this issue is, neither the URBIS nor the OECD questions satisfactorily tapped the service delivery effectiveness benefits from computing. The best question on the subject comes from URBIS, asking whether computing has increased the department's effectiveness in serving the public. For OECD respondents, three questions address service delivery benefits: "Has computing led to an improvement in ability . . . to cope with non-standard situations, . . . better analysis, and . . . more integrated presentation of data?" Because these three OECD question are quite weak as indicators of service delivery impact, we suggest a caveat in interpreting these findings. Generally, URBIS cities report substantial benefit for service delivery effectiveness: 85 percent claim at least moderate benefits. Of the OECD cities, about 80 percent on average feel that computing has improved their ability to conduct service-delivery-related tasks. This is an average measure, and the actual scores for the three questions vary considerable. For example, only about half of the cities claim computing has improved their ability to deal with nonstandard situations. The strongest benefit is in provisions for integrated presentation of data to be used in organizing service delivery.

SOME OBSERVATIONS ON OPERATIONAL EFFICIENCY AND SERVICE DELIVERY BENEFITS

The URBIS and OECD cities both have experienced efficiency and service delivery benefits from computing in four areas: speed of operations, accuracy of data, cost savings, and service delivery effectiveness. Generally, computing does appear to contribute to speed of operations and to accuracy of data in local government operations, although it does not result in many direct cost savings for local government operations. Expectations that naive users of computing hold about the possibilities of cost savings are probably too simplistic and exaggerated. Some cities do claim cost savings, but we reserve our investigations of the characteristics of those cities and the uses they make of the technology until chapter 6.

There is one contrary finding on efficiency impacts between the URBIS and OECD cities: the URBIS respondents generally report that computing does not result in staff savings, but OECD respondents generally report that it does. As described earlier, two kinds of staff savings might be effected by the use of computing: (a) those from job elimination—elimination of the need for staff in given operations, allowing those positions to be eliminated from the payroll; and (b) those from job transfer—elimination of the need for some of the tasks performed by staff in given operations, freeing them for other tasks but not resulting in their dismissal. It seemed that we might be measuring both of these factors, and that the URBIS respondents were viewing their staffing questions with respect to the latter.

We tested this possibility two ways. First, we utilized a question from the URBIS User Core Questionnaire, which asks whether computers allow departments to handle a greater volume of service without corresponding increases in cost. It is reasonable to view this question in light of personnel requirements, as personnel costs tend to be the greatest costs of most local government departments, and greater volumes of service without increases in productivity of labor tend to mean greater operating costs. As shown in table 3.3, the scores for this question are more positive than those for the two other questions about cost and staffing. Thus for the URBIS cities we modify our general conclusion: computing can reduce the number of staff hours required to do certain tasks, which allows a reduction in the size of the work force, a reallocation of staff hours to tasks that have been short on labor, or the creation of new services. Given the strong responses to the direct questions on staff and cost benefits, we conclude that most cities do not lay off staff whose labor is no longer needed in computerized tasks. Rather, those employees are given other tasks and are retained on the payroll. This would coincide with the general finding that computing improves departmental effectiveness, but without reducing costs.

The other way of testing the possibility of two kinds of staff benefits used OECD study data. We do not have equivalent measures for URBIS and OECD cities with which to test our hypothesis, but we did utilize the OECD case study reports that were prepared on each of the sites by the expert interviewing teams. In carefully perusing these reports, we found that in nearly every city there was a distinction made between staff reduction and staff reassignment related to

Table 3.3 COMPARISON OF THREE KINDS OF STAFF AND COST BENEFITS FROM COMPUTING IN THE URBIS CITIES

	Extent of Benefit		
Question	No Benefit	Moderate	High
Computers allow departments to handle a greater volume of service without corresponding increases in costs.	42%	46%	12%
Where they have been applied, computers have reduced the number of staff necessary to perform tasks in my department.	62	33	5
Where they have been applied, computers have reduced the cost of department operations.	68	30	2

computing. No cities had actually eliminated staff as a result of computing, but all claimed to have experienced reductions in staff hours needed to perform tasks to which computing has been applied. These staff hours appear to have been reallocated to other needs, in keeping with the generally consistent claim that local government staff resources were in short supply.

We conclude that in OECD cities as well as in URBIS cities computing does not reduce staff in local governments, but can allow more effective and productive use of the existing staff and, possibly, reduce the need for new hires. This ability to do more with the same staff appears to be a major benefit from computing, although it has meant that computers seldom have *decreased* the cost of operations. Instead, they have contributed to "cost avoidance"—the ability to incur greater work demands, achieve better service delivery, or develop new services without a proportional increase in costs.

In general, computing has produced efficiency and service delivery benefits in URBIS and OECD cities. Computing has increased the speed of certain local government operations by increasing the rate of routine processing and by improving the ability of local staff to get timely access to the information they need. This has assisted the staff in keeping up with the normal workflow, and in some cases has provided a "buffer" against unexpected surges in workflow that formerly might have led to major operating problems. Computers also have brought about improvements in data accuracy for local government records management.

Organizational Management and Planning

Computers have been held to offer considerable potential for assisting local government managers and planners in running the affairs of government. These basic advantages of computerization lie in the ability to gather together information from many sources and analyze it to provide profiles on issues of concern. We classify three kinds of management and planning benefits that can result from computing:

1. *Management control:* the computer's benefits for the day-to-day and week-to-week running of a government.
2. *Management planning:* the computer's benefits for the making of policy for the conduct of government affairs.
3. *Community planning:* the computer's benefits for physical and economic planning for the city as a whole.

Each of these kinds of benefits has its unique characteristics, and each results from particular kinds of applications.

MANAGEMENT CONTROL

Management control—directing daily organizational or departmental activities—generally means overseeing and supervising the work of subordinates within the resource-and-constraint environment of their unit. The manager must see to it that the resources at his or her disposal (e.g., personnel, equipment, funds) are applied efficiently and effectively to completion of the unit's assigned tasks. This requires the setting of goals and objectives, allocation of resources, organization of subordinates' tasks and time, supervision of the work for both adherence to schedule and maintenance of quality, integration of subtasks, and continued monitoring of operations to ensure completion of tasks within budget. Moreover, managers must be concerned about the survival and integrity of their units to keep productivity and morale high. Finally, managers must work with other managers and with top-level policymakers so that the work of the various units merges in a manner consonant with the organization's mandates and objectives.

The contributions of computing to management control are said to come in three ways. First, computing can bring improvement in control over staff. The computer allows collection, management, and aggregation of data from many sources, and permits these data to be organized in a manner useful to management. Data that are routinely collected on subordinates' work, such as hours spent on different jobs, amount of work done, and productivity evaluation, allow the manager to create both ongoing and summary reports on the performance of given employees and employee groups. This provision of information, in theory, allows the manager greater control over subordinates.

A second potential contribution of computing is improvement in daily decision making. Many decisions are made on an almost daily basis, such as expenditure decisions, hiring decisions, reallocation of staff, promotion decisions, and short-term planning. The computer's ability to collect and store operating information that is used as a basis for such daily decisions makes it a potentially powerful tool for the decision maker. Examples of computer outputs useful in daily decisions are daily account updates, available case reports, employee attendance records, and trial balances.

The third area of potential contribution is improvement in major decisions. Computing can allow for aggregation of data and for manipulation of data for salary negotiations, budget projections, revenue projections, and other major issues.

CONTROL OVER STAFF

Computing seems to have had little benefit for control over lower-level staff. Two measures were used to evaluate these effects in URBIS cities: the contribution of computing to control of lower-level staff and units; and the utility of computing for identifying abuses or inefficiencies in subordinate units. As shown in table 3.4, computing has yielded moderate benefits for each of these areas in about two-thirds of the cities.

Two questions asked of the OECD cities relate to management control over staff. One asks section heads about computing's benefit for management control generally, but given the context of the question in the interview, we feel it relates primarily to management control issues. The other asks department heads whether computing is used to increase management control. As shown in table 3.5, department heads in only about one-third of the cities claim such benefits from computing. Section heads in about half of the cities make the more general claim that computing has led to better management control.

DAILY DECISION MAKING

URBIS and OECD cities differ in their assessment of computing's benefits for daily decision making by managers. However, in neither case can it be said that the computer's impact is strong. For

Table 3.4 URBIS CITY COMPUTING BENEFITS FOR MANAGEMENT CONTROL

Category	Questionnaire Item	Percent of Cities Where Benefits for Management Control Perceived as:		
		Little or none	Moderate	High
Management control over staff	How much does computing increase your ability to control staff or units under your responsibility? (N = 40)	33%	67%	0%
	How useful to you has computer-based information been in identifying abuses or inefficiencies in units you supervise? (N = 40)	38	60	2
Daily decision making	How useful to you has computer-based information been for day-to-day expenditure decisions? (N = 40)	8	75	17
	How useful has computer-based information been in allocating manpower? (N = 40)	50	45	5
Major decision making	How useful has computer-based information been during annual budget cycle? (N = 40)	5	55	40
	How useful has computer-based information been for (decision on) salary questions and negotiations? (N = 40)	40	50	10

URBIS, the two questions related to day-to-day management decisions asked: whether computing has been useful for considering day-to-day expenditure decisions; and whether computing has been useful in allocating department manpower. The responses to these questions, shown in table 3.5, differ a good deal. A large majority of cit-

Table 3.5 OECD CITY COMPUTING BENEFITS FOR MANAGEMENT CONTROL

		Percent of Cities Where Benefits for Management Control:	
Category	*Department Head Perceptions* *Questionnaire Item*	*Not mentioned*	*Mentioned*
Management control over staff	Computing is used to increase management control (N = 15)	66.7%	33.3%
Daily decision making	Computing is used for making day-to-day decisions (N = 15)	93.3	6.7
Major decision making	Computing is used to make major decisions (N = 15)	60	40

	Percent of Cities Where Benefits for Management Control Perceived as:		
Section Head Perceptions	*Little or none*	*Moderate*	*High*
Has introduction of computing applications, as compared to the previous system, led to better management control? (N = 15)	43%	25%	25%

ies—about nine-tenths—responded positively to the first question, but only one-half responded positively to the second. These results are not surprising. The majority of management-oriented applications of computing in URBIS cities relates to financial matters (finance applications are the most common in the cities), and relatively few are directed to manpower allocation matters.

OECD city department heads were asked how they use computer technology in performing their daily official duties, and they indicated a very low level of use (table 3.5). In fact, only one site mentions this type of use of computer technology. We conclude that computing in the OECD cities has had little benefit for daily decision-making by managers.

MAJOR DECISION MAKING.

There are greater computing benefits for major management decisions than for day-to-day decision making in both URBIS and OECD cities. The URBIS study provided two questions related to major management decisions, one inquiring whether computing has been helpful in making decisions about the annual budget cycle and another inquiring whether computing has proved useful for decisions about salary negotiations. Table 3.4 shows over 95 percent of the cities indicating benefits for management decision making during the annual budget cycle, and 40 percent claim major benefits, although relatively fewer claim managerial benefit for salary-negotiation decisions. URBIS cities have many financial applications related to departmental accounting and budgeting that would be most useful during the budget cycle, but there are fewer applications that would be useful in salary negotiation; such applications, being much more analytical (using, for example, simulation and modeling), are less common.

For OECD cities, the department heads responding to the questions concerning the uses of the technology indicate much greater benefits from use of computing for major decision making than for daily decision making (table 3.5). We hypothesize that the OECD cities lag behind URBIS cities in development of more sophisticated applications, so management impacts realized in URBIS have not yet been obtained in OECD cities. Since among both URBIS and OECD cities a significant portion indicate benefits for major management decisions, this application of computing appears to be growing and showing promise.

MANAGERIAL PLANNING

Computing has long been heralded as a major boon to managerial planning because it offers planners two critical forms of assistance: the ability to assemble large, randomly accessible and dynamic data bases containing data that are needed for planning decisions; and the calculating power to rapidly perform mathematical calculation and sorting tasks necessary for more advanced tasks of analysis simulation.

Rudimentary uses of computing for planning include creation of statistical summaries of key data items (e.g., population) to either assess given conditions or project future ones. The monitoring of government conditions can be done from a variety of perspectives, such as city expenditures by program and revenue sources by type. This kind of application allows for on-the-spot checking and special analyses to serve the needs of policy makers. Faster and more precise identification of management-related city problems can be accomplished through the computer's ability to link together separate data elements that feed into a particular problem's analysis. In its more advanced uses, computing can improve problem solving by providing such capabilities as geographically-based analyses and simulations based on many variables, enabling the modeling of proposed solutions. For example, computerized models can be used to predict the man-loading required for given tasks under different conditions.

The URBIS study provides several questionnaire items specifically concerning uses of computing for managerial planning. In order to develop an overall index of benefits for managerial planning, every URBIS city's Management Oriented Computing Interview questionnaire and site report was studied and a synthesized score developed (see appendix). Responses in the URBIS data have been taken from department heads, chief executives, top management staff, and planners. Some data provided by department heads in the URBIS User Core Questionnaire have been used to provide greater detail. The OECD study provides less data on the subject of computing and planning than does URBIS, but it does contain two general questions regarding planning benefits. These OECD study data are supplemented by the discussions of planning uses of computing in the site reports, and by use of the OECD original questionnaires to determine what kinds of planning the respondents were talking about in each case. This search strategy allowed us to create an overall summary for uses of computing in both internal operations planning and physical development planning in the OECD cities based on responses from chief executives, department heads, section heads, and data-processing managers.

Overall, we find computing is used for managerial planning purposes in the cities studied, and that this use is considered beneficial. However, this use is much less extensive and sophisticated than one might expect from reading promotional literature. Further, while there is general belief that computing will affect managerial planning more in the future than it has so far, there is considerable skepticism about whether computing really can be very helpful in managerial planning.

The indices of use and benefits of computing for managerial planning for both URBIS and OECD are shown in table 3.6. Generally, the table shows that computing is successfully used for managerial planning on a substantial or extensive basis in only half of the sites in both studies. The use and benefit scores for the URBIS cities are somewhat higher than those for the OECD cities. We expect that this use of computing is strongly associated with factors such as size of government, sophistication of computing, and professional management orientation; factors that are investigated in associative analyses discussed in chapter 6.

The responses from URBIS and OECD cities to specific questions about management planning impacts are shown in tables 3.7 and 3.8, respectively. Table 3.7 shows responses from URBIS department heads about benefits for identification of city problems and determination of solutions to them. Over three-quarters of the respondents feel computing has been useful in identifying city problems, although a large majority of these feel the technology has been only "somewhat useful." In contrast only half of the cities report that computing has been helpful in determining solutions to city problems and, in nearly all of these cities, computing is said to have been only somewhat useful.

OECD cities indicate that computing has had benefits for provision of information about service delivery performance and about

Table 3.6 USE AND BENEFIT OF COMPUTING FOR MANAGEMENT PLANNING

		Cities in Each Rating Category (%)	
Questionnaire Item	Rating Category	URBIS Cities (N = 37)	OECD Cities (N = 16)
The extent to which computing is used for and has benefited internal operations planning	Low use and benefit	40%	56%
	Substantial use and benefit	57	38
	Extensive use and benefit	3	6
		100	100

Table 3.7 SPECIFIC INDICATORS OF COMPUTING'S BENEFIT FOR MANAGEMENT PLANNING
IN URBIS CITIES (N = 40)

	Cities Indicating Benefit for Management Planning Has Been:		
Questionnaire Item	Not at all Useful	Somewhat Useful	Useful
How useful to you has computer-based information been in *identifying* city problems?	22%	63%	15%
How useful to you has computer-based information been in *determining solutions* to city problems?	50	48	2

demand for services (table 3.8). Such provision is an aspect of monitoring conditions and identifying problems. Somewhat less than half indicate that computing has improved the information about service delivery, while somewhat more than half indicate that computing has improved the information about demand. About one-fifth of the cities in each case indicate that this impact has been major. Not surprisingly, over one-half of the cities indicate that computing provides a better basis for planning services delivery; and fully one-fourth report that this benefit has been strong.

Table 3.8 SPECIFIC INDICATORS OF COMPUTING'S BENEFIT FOR MANAGEMENT PLANNING
IN OECD CITIES (N = 15)

	Percent of Cities Indicating Benefit for Management Planning Has Been:		
Questionnaire Item	Not at all useful	Somewhat useful	Useful
Has the introduction of the application, as compared to previous system, if any, led to:			
Better bases for planning future delivery of services?	46%	27%	27%
Better management information on delivery performance?	60	20	20
Better management information on the demand for services (type and level)?	47	33	20

COMMUNITY PLANNING

Community planning refers to land-use planning, transportation planning, facilities location planning, and other kinds of planning involving design and siting of physical development. This kind of planning usually involves creation of data bases on specific questions (e.g., housing preferences, use of park facilities), including statistical descriptives (e.g., population and demographic data) from which subsets of data relevant to particular physical development questions can be drawn. It also involves creation of software to allow various kinds of data analyses necessary for addressing community planning concerns. Such planning is usually conducted in departments specifically concerned with the function in question. For example, transportation planning would usually be done by the road or transportation department, land-use planning by the city planning department, and educational planning by the school department. Often, the plans of specialized departments such as education and transportation are developed in conjunction with the city planning department, and, with greater use of computing in community planning, the data-processing department is becoming increasingly involved with such planning projects.

Computing can assist in community planning in the same two ways it can assist managerial planning: in condition monitoring and problem finding, and in problem solving. As with the assessment of impact on managerial planning, we constructed summary indices of impact on community planning for both URBIS and OECD cities (see appendix). These indices are based on URBIS questionnaire responses from chief executives, top management staff, department heads and planners, and on OECD questionnaire responses from chief executives, department heads, and data-processing managers. Several questions unique to the URBIS user core and management-oriented computing questionnaires provide more detail and are included separately.

ANALYSIS OF BENEFITS OF COMPUTING FOR COMMUNITY PLANNING

Table 3.9 shows the summary scores for use and benefits of computing for community planning. The table indicates for both UR-

Table 3.9 USE AND BENEFITS OF COMPUTING FOR COMMUNITY PLANNING

		Percent of Cities in Each Rating Category	
Questionnaire Item	Rating Category	URBIS Cities (N = 38)	OECD Cities (N = 16)
The extent to which computing is used for and has benefited physical development planning:	Low use and benefit	34%	50%
	Substantial use and benefit	40	44
	Extensive use and benefit	26	6
		100	100

BIS and OECD cities that computing's use and benefits have been greater for community planning than for management planning. Again, these scores are higher for URBIS cities than for OECD cities. Nearly two-thirds of the URBIS cities made substantial or extensive use of computing applied to physical development planning, with beneficial results. Among OECD cities, only half had such experience.

We used data from URBIS alone to investigate benefits for the two subareas of community planning activity mentioned above: condition monitoring and problem identification; and determining solutions to community problems. In the first area, two questionnaire items were used. The data for these, shown in table 3.10, are collected from the point of view of chief executives and planners. The data show considerable differences in perception depending on point of view. Planners in three-quarters of the cities felt computing had been useful for performing needs assessment of communities, while the chief executives in less than half of the cities claimed computing had been useful for this purpose. Planners in about two-thirds of the cities felt computing had been helpful in identifying community problems, but chief executives in less than one-third of the cities felt this was so.

Apparently, those actors most closely associated with planning activity, the planners, rate computing's benefit for planning most positively; those farther from the role of community planning in their

Table 3.10 COMPUTING BENEFITS FOR MONITORING OF COMMUNITY CONDITIONS IN URBIS CITIES ONLY

Questionnaire Item	Chief Executives	Planners
Have you used computers for needs assessments of communities?		
Not mentioned	58% (21)	23% (9)
Mentioned	42% (15)	77% (30)
	100% (36)	100% (39)
Do data reports and analyses you use lead to any new or clearer perceptions of community problems?		
No	72% (28)	36% (14)
Yes	28% (11)	64% (25)
	100% (39)	100% (39)
Have you used computing for planning— social services, transportation, land use, housing, etc.?		
Not mentioned	62% (24)	22% (9)
Mentioned	38% (15)	78% (31)
	100% (39)	100% (40)
Have these reports and analyses ever led to programmatic recommendations?		
No	36% (13)	24% (9)
Yes	64% (23)	76% (28)
	100% (36)	100% (37)

jobs, the chief executives, have a lower estimate of the utility of computing for planning purposes. The comparatively negative response of chief executives may also be due to their less frequent use of data banks, the subject of these questions.

Based on the data, we feel that the benefits of computing for community planning has been limited overall. Benefits that do occur have been most beneficial in the areas of monitoring community conditions and identifying problems. These benefits generally manifest themselves in an improved ability to evaluate particular community conditions by running sample statistical summaries or indicators for which data are collected on an as-needed basis. Also, computers appear to be useful in conducting reviews of conditions in the community to help locate and evaluate problem situations. While these are certainly helpful to the planning task, they are not the sort of exotic and sophisticated planning uses of urban data banks that have been predicted.

Benefits for determining solutions to city problems also were assessed using only URBIS data, presented in table 3.10. Planners in over three-fourths of the cities felt computing had contributed to the planning of service delivery, while chief executives in two-thirds of cities felt it had not, showing the same discrepancy of perception shown in the other areas of impact. However, there is greater agreement over the benefits of computing for developing programmatic recommendations, where planning department heads in three-quarters of the cities and chief executives in two-thirds of the cities claimed beneficial impact.

We feel two factors are being measured here. One is computing's contribution to the formulation of programs and plans for service delivery; the other is computing's contribution to the actual determination of policy for solving specific problems. The former use of computing lies somewhere between "problem identification," where it is fairly widespread, and "problem solution," where there is comparatively little evidence of a major computing contribution. Thus computing assists in providing data on alternatives for problem solution, but does not contribute substantially to the choice of a solution to a problem.

Although there were no questions from OECD specifically related to the kinds of planning applications mentioned above, we were able to utilize the responses from the two OECD questionnaire items that relate to planning. One seeks a response (i.e., "improved planning") to the general question about ways computing has improved efficiency; the other is a more direct question about whether the computer has been useful in planning local futures. As shown in table 3.11, only 25 percent of the cities reported with conviction that computers had been helpful in these areas. These questions are vague, and cannot be easily interpreted in light of the specific kind of planning use intended, but the data generally indicate slightly less conviction about the positive planning impacts of computing than do the data for URBIS cities. This could be accounted for by the fact that computing seems to be more frequently and extensively applied to planning in URBIS cities.

Table 3.11 BENEFITS OF COMPUTING FOR PLANNING IN OECD CITIES ONLY (N = 16)

Questionnaire Item	Percent of Cities Where Benefits for Community Planning Were:	
	Not mentioned	Mentioned
Computers have improved efficiency by improving planning.	75%	25%

	Percent of Cities Indicating:		
	No	Yes, but uncertain	Yes, with evidence presented
Have computers been useful in planning local futures?	37.5%	37.5%	25%

To summarize our findings, computing's benefits for community planning in local governments have been beneficial but thus far limited. Computing has had greater benefit for planning activities related to community development than for managerial planning activities, and these benefits have been more pronounced in the URBIS cities than in the OECD cities. Using data only from the URBIS cities, we find that within the area of community planning, computing has had its greatest benefit in helping identify city problems, less benefit in determining solutions to city problems, and the least impact on monitoring community conditions.

DISCUSSION OF FINDINGS ON ORGANIZATIONAL MANAGEMENT AND PLANNING BENEFITS

The foregoing findings on organizational management and planning benefits from computing suggest that the impact of computing in these areas has been limited but generally beneficial.

Two notable findings emerge from our analysis of *management benefits* from computing. First, there is a clear difference between URBIS and OECD cities in the level of these benefits. We believe the discrepancy to be due to several factors. Management-oriented applications tend to be much more pronounced in sites with more developed computing capability, and by and large URBIS sites are more developed than are the OECD sites. Assuming that benefits will usually accrue where attempts are made to use the technology,

the greater extent and level of development of management applications in the URBIS cities would indicate that the level of benefits for
management in those cities would be greater.

Although it is difficult to test with the data we had, we have
a strong impression that key decision makers in the URBIS cities are
more supportive than those in the OECD cities of computing's application to management. Several things lead us to this conclusion. Other
research from the URBIS study has shown that propensity to use
computing is positively associated with level of professional or "reformed" government structures that encourage use of appointed, highly
qualified professional executives to manage city affairs (Kraemer,
Dutton, and Northrop 1981). These professionals typically have training in modern management techniques, including use of management
technologies such as computing. On average, such individuals will be
more disposed to adoption and use of computing, both generally in
the government and in their own jobs, than will elected executives.
Such "reformed" governments are more common in the United States
than in the OECD cities. In addition, there tends to be a stronger element of "faith in technology" operating in U.S. local governments than
in the OECD cities. This faith in technology predisposes a government
to use computing, and this predisposition leads to greater experimen-
tation and, in many cases, to higher levels of successful application.
Finally, in European countries especially, local government employees are often members of trade unions. Trade unions in Europe have
much more substantial influence on policy than those in the United
States, and one thing they have been concerned about is the potential employment impacts of computing on local government workers.
The faith in technology in U.S. cities and the concern of trade unions
in European cities seems to have given computing an ideological "head
start" in URBIS cities as compared to OECD cities.

The second notable finding from the analysis is that there is
a relationship between the benefits of computing for management and
the "time-dependent workflow" of managerial activity. Time-dependent workflow refers to the character and frequency of various management tasks. Some tasks are highly discrete and come only periodically; for example, preparation of the departmental budget for the
coming fiscal year. Many record-keeping and decision processes that

go on throughout the year lead up to this task, but the actual task itself is performed only once per year and in a relatively short time (say several months). By contrast, daily decision making and control over subordinates are activities that, while discrete on the level of individual decisions or control problems, tend to be more of a continuous workflow when viewed over time. Such decision and control tasks are usually quite small in themselves, but there are many of them and they follow one another in a fairly consistent stream.

The data from the OECD cities indicate strongly that computing has had a much more substantial impact on the making of major decisions than on the making of daily decisions. The URBIS cities provide another, somewhat subtler picture. Computing seems to have been about equally useful in day-to-day expenditure decisions and in major budgetary decisions (relatively useful in both cases), and also about equally *not* useful in allocating manpower and in salary negotiations. Earlier research demonstrated from URBIS data that computing has been utilized most extensively by management in the making of small incremental decisions, and relatively less in the making of major decisions (Kraemer, Dutton, and Northrop 1981). Factoring out these different indicators of impact requires an understanding of the nature and frequency of different kinds of managerial decision making tha. might be assisted by computing, and an understanding of the differences in state of development between URBIS and OECD cities.

Managerial decisions about daily allocation of funds and about yearly budget construction require precise data on the quantifiable commodity of money. Manpower allocation and salary negotiation decisions are different, requiring specification of softer commodities (e.g., man-hours required for a task) that are more difficult to specify with precision. Minor mistakes in allocation of man-hours to tasks can be handled more flexibly than mistakes with the precise commodity of money. Also, in the case of salary questions and negotiations, the overall questions are as political as they are financial. Computing use is beneficial when it helps make clear the consequences of granting a certain pay raise, or if it can better pinpoint the existing state of fiscal health. But the decisions of whether and how much to grant in a raise are based on many considerations beyond the information the computer can provide. Thus, computing can more directly assist decisions related to allocation and control of money than decisions involving less precise commodities or decisions heavily influenced by political factors, such as manpower allocation or salary negotiation. Since daily decisions are made much more frequently than are major decisions, the net benefit of computing may eventually be greater for daily decision-making.

We believe that the more clearly shown difference in impact on daily decision making and on major decision making in OECD cities might be due to these cities' levels of computing development compared to URBIS cities. The OECD cities at this time were somewhat less advanced in development of computing. Since applications capable of affecting major decisions (e.g., batch-oriented financial accounting systems that can do year-end aggregations) are usually among the earliest to be implemented, they show greater benefit. Computing tends to be exploited first in those areas that offer the greatest relative payoff, and at the time the data were collected these were operationally-based systems from which managerial data could be spun-off. The URBIS cities may have been at a stage of development, on average, where more of such managerially useful data could be made available.

The benefits of computing use for *managerial planning* have been predicted to be substantial, since ongoing internal operations are always a focus of managerial effort and systems can be designed to provide data to support such planning. However, the URBIS and OECD data show that such systems are not very commonly used. We feel this is largely because there has not been a concerted push to develop systems for this purpose in the local governments. Promotion of planning-oriented management information systems has been hyperbolic, but their actual development has been slow for two reasons. One is that creating and maintaining the operational systems of government takes precedence over the development of applications for management planning. Second, managers and policymakers appear to have reservations about the use of computerized aids for finding solutions to problems of managerial planning. A policymaker's response to highly political and judgmental demands usually cannot be informed simply by getting more data.

Where computers are applied to internal planning, they do seem to have beneficial impacts. Most such application is in the area of financial planning, where operational systems such as budget monitoring or payroll-personnel processing can provide historical data that are useful for extrapolating future expenditure patterns. This indeed shows up as an area of computer benefit for managerial planning. We expect that future development of systems to assist in management of internal operations will gradually result in greater use of computing for management planning as well.

At first glance, a comparison of the findings on benefits for managerial planning shows such benefits to be much stronger in OECD cities than in URBIS cities. In fact, we feel that the responses are quite close in intent, and that variance is due primarily to the differential specificity of the questions. Among both URBIS and OECD cities, approximately one-half indicate benefits from computing for condition monitoring and problem identification. The URBIS question on this subject asks about the benefit for identifying city problems. The OECD questions are more precise, and inquire about benefits for monitoring and identifying needs for service delivery. Similarly, the major differences in response between the URBIS question of benefit for determining solutions to problems and the OECD question of benefit for planning service delivery are probably the result of the nature of the questions more than anything else. However, in this case it may be that managers in OECD cities have had somewhat more beneficial experience using computing in determining solutions to city problems than have managers in URBIS cities. Given our data, it is not possible to tell precisely if this is so.

Community planning seems to have benefited from computing more than has managerial planning in both OECD and URBIS cities. This, we believe, is because over the past fifteen years considerable amounts of money have been poured into developing systems to aid community planning. Much effort has been concentrated on the development of urban data banks that collect large amounts of information on particular community and regional conditions (e.g., housing, transportation, demography, employment) and store it for potential use in the planning process. It must be said, however, that the overall experience with such data bank efforts has been disappointing. The costs of maintaining these data banks have proved to be very high, and the subsequent use of them rather low (Kraemer 1969; Kraemer and King 1979a; King 1982). However, as our data assess only the perceived benefits rather than measures of the net value of such applications, the data illustrate only the immediate contribution of computing to the process of community planning, independent of the overall payoff of such application.

Computing's greatest benefit for community planning has been in identification of city problems. There has been less benefit for determination of solutions to problems, and even less for monitoring community conditions. These differences seem logical, given the nature of the planning-oriented systems in use, and the characteristics of planning activity in local government. By and large, planning-oriented systems are built around relatively static data bases that are useful for providing information on baseline conditions in the community. The best example of such a data base is the U.S. Census data that are provided by the U.S. federal government to each local government that requests them. These data contain information on population, housing, and other community conditions for the period in which the data were collected. The census data base is not frequently updated by the local government because of the high cost of such updates, so each collection of the census data represents only a single slice in time. However, some cities have developed large data bases against which regular monitoring inquiries can be run. Such data bases might include land-use inventories, housing inventories, business establishment inventories, and traffic and parking inventories. However, these are rare in local governments due to a weak data infrastructure to support such analyses. The lack of comprehensive data often results in a relative lack of computing use for monitoring community conditions and it is likely that the costs of maintaining a sophisticated computer-based monitoring capability would swamp the benefits to be gained from such an endeavor.

Computers are used more frequently for specialized, often ad hoc studies of community conditions in an effort to identify problems in the city. Such studies are not the large, monitoring-type studies that survey conditions on an ongoing basis, but rather are one-shot probes into city conditions to ascertain whether a suspected problem is indeed a problem. For example, the supposition that citizens in a particular area are unfairly short of park and recreational services given their population might result in an ad hoc analysis of census population data by area, coupled with a listing of city parks and recreational resources per capita. This analysis would give insight into the problem of disproportionately allocated benefits. Computers are being applied with success to such tasks.

Computers are not being applied as extensively to the solution of city problems as they are to the identification of city problems. This is to be expected. First, computer applications for providing descriptive statistics and even simulations are more common than applications that directly assist solution development. This is true for organizations in both the public and private sector. Some promotional literature on computing's promise for planning, written during the early 1960s, portrayed computers as actually "making decisions" within the organization (see Greenberger 1962). This has not come about, largely because of the limitations of the technology. Second, even if the computer could deliver such capabilites, it is not clear that managers or policymakers would want to use them for that purpose. Much of the manager's and the policymaker's job forces reliance on personal judgment, political sensitivity, and an overall sense of organizational conditions that cannot easily be programmed into or represented by a computer system. These factors are critical to the development of solutions, for even the best suggestion cannot be a solution unless it is viable politically and organizationally as well as technically. We expect that systems that directly affect decision making at the level of city planning policy will be more highly developed in the future, and to some extent modern computer-assisted fiscal planning/budgeting systems already serve this role (Dutton and Kraemer 1983). However, major decision making will remain one of the last domains of local government activity to be affected by computing, both because the political stakes in decision outcomes are too high and because the utility of the technology is still too limited.

The analysis of computing benefits for organizational management and community planning illustrates the differences in perceptions that actors in different roles hold with respect to the same issues. Generally, we found that planners claimed the greatest benefits from computing, chief executives were less strong in their claims, and department heads were the least enthusiastic. Thus in every case we had to weigh carefully the responses against the kinds of applications we were discussing, then check the site reports and other indicators (e.g., actual answers to some questionnaire items) before deriving a conclusion about computing's benefit. This illustrates the necessity for carefully measuring the attitudes of several respondent groups when seeking to analyze benefits that may span across those groups. For example, had we chosen only planners as a response group, we might have drawn the erroneous conclusion that computing has had great benefit for community planning; conversely, if we had chosen only department heads as respondents, we might have concluded wrongly that computing has had little or no benefit for community planning.

Conclusion

Computing apparently has lived up to its promotion as a useful tool for improving the efficiency of operations. It improves the speed of operations, it results in improved data accuracy, and it results in staff savings. It does not, however, seem to result in much cost saving. The major savings come through cost avoidance.

It is important to note that the benefits of cost avoidance and improved service delivery effectiveness are perhaps the most difficult kinds of benefits to demonstrate. Actual cost savings can be demonstrated by the expenditures of the government, but cost avoidance depends on the claim that the increased level of work done as a result of computing was absolutely necessary, and would certainly have resulted in increased labor or other costs if computing had not been used. Service delivery improvements are very difficult to pin down because they often entail "intangible benefits" such as greater accessibility of staff to citizens or better dissemination of notices to the public. The question of what value there is in more staff accessibility or better dissemination of notices remains unanswered. Thus, while the data indicate that computing has improved efficiency and service delivery, there is no clear evidence of what this kind of improvement is worth, and what it has cost to attain. This kind of cost-benefit assessment of computing use in local governments remains for future research to tackle (King and Schrems 1978).

There is considerable similarity in assessment of the efficiency and service delivery benefits of computing in both URBIS and OECD cities. This suggests that computerization has similar results for such applications across countries and cultures. This was indeed our expectation, since the most common reasons for adopting computing have been to improve efficiency and enable the organization to cope with heavy workloads. This similarity might also be due to the fact that information technology as it is currently used has emanated largely from the United States, and advances in the technology and its use tend to originate either in the United States or in those computer industries and organizations in other countries that are very similar to those of the United States. There are probably endemic similarities among the organizations studied in this research project that result from adoption of a common technology and its application to a rather restricted range of applications. The similarity of perceptions of basic operational functions among the local government respondents demonstrates the universality of problems and promises that can result from computing's application to local government operations worldwide. We speculate that the efficiency and service delivery benefits of computing revealed in the URBIS and OECD study cities obtain in nearly all local government computing environments.

As expected, the benefits of computing for management and planning activities have not been as great as the benefits found for efficiency and service delivery activities. We believe this is primarily because computing has been less extensively applied to these tasks. Nevertheless, where computing has been applied to management and planning tasks it has been generally beneficial. We can offer some general conclusions about benefits for management and planning, based on the data presented above, in the context of the written comments in the site reports and our own experiences in the field.

In the area of managerial control, computing has potential to assist managers in maintaining control over staff, making daily decisions, and making major decisions. Contrary to expectations voiced in the literature, computing's benefits for managerial control over staff have been slight. This is probably because there are as yet few systems capable of providing such assistance. Where there are such systems there is slight indication that computing does improve managerial control over staff, but until there is more experience with these systems there can be no firm conclusion that the help they offer will be worth their cost. Similarly, computing's benefits for daily decision making have been slight and limited to the area of financial control, which is comparatively highly automated, especially in URBIS cities. Computing has had its greatest managerial benefit in the making of major decisions, but again only in the relatively few areas where applications have been developed sufficiently to be useful. It is likely that the greatest short-run benefits of computing for management will be related to major decision-making processes, because these are sufficiently important to warrant development of new systems, and because existing operational and "housekeeping" systems can be modified to provide data for the more analytical managerial systems. However, further development of systems to assist in daily decision making might also eventually result in substantial benefits, given the frequency with which such decisions must be made and the importance of their aggregate effects on organizational performance.

There has been comparatively less benefit from computing for managerial planning than for managerial control. Its application to managerial planning seems to be very weakly developed as of the time of the URBIS and OECD studies, probably due to the great difficulty of designing and building systems that can aggregate data from many sources, perform analytical routines on the data repeatedly while changing assumptions or conditions, and do this all in the short timeframe required by managers. Also, there is the major problem of the "rationality" of computer-assisted systems as compared to the political and organizational uncertainty that surrounds many important managerial decisions. As long as computerized systems can provide only limited and deterministic pictures for managers to consider, even if they are built around implicit biases, they will at best offer alternatives to or supporting evidence for the political and administrative plans top managers must make. We believe that computing will have relatively little benefit for managerial planning in the near future, although the long-run potential for the technology may be much greater. In the area of community planning, computing has shown somewhat greater benefit, although nothing approaching the benefits found for efficiency and service delivery. Community planning benefits tend to be more pronounced in URBIS cities than in OECD cities, probably because the URBIS cities on average are somewhat more advanced in such uses of computing. Within the area of community planning, computing has affected specific functions differently. It has not shown much benefit for monitoring community conditions, nor for finding solutions to city problems. It has, however, contributed to the task of identifying community problems. The greatest management and planning benefits thus far appear to be in providing data for evaluating conditions over fairly long periods, and for identifying problems and opportunities. The closer an application moves to providing real-time information and conditions, the more difficult it will be to build and maintain the system. Thus fewer such systems will be built in the near future, lessening the chance that computing will produce major benefits for this area of local government activity.

Notes

1. The URBIS study data used in this chapter come primarily from the responses by section heads to the User Core Questionnaire, although some data were taken from the interviews conducted with management and service staff in the URBIS Phase 2 cities. The OECD data are taken primarily from the OECD Section Heads Interview Schedules, although additional data were taken from the Department Head Schedules and the Site Visit Reports. Generally, the URBIS data are responses to specific questions about different kinds of benefits from computing. The OECD data, on the other hand, were collected in the context of specific applications that have provided benefits for the city. All data reported in this chapter are reported at the city level, as were the data in chapter 1. URBIS city-level scores were created by initially tabulating the responses of individual respondents, then calculating aggregated mean responses for all respondents in the city. THE OECD city-level scores were similarly aggregated to provide means for the city. The aggregated mean scores for both the URBIS and OECD respondents for each city were then trichotomized to produce three general categories of response: below .33 meaning "no benefit," between .33 and .66 meaning "moderate benefit," and above .67 meaning "high benefit." (See the appendix for additional details.)

2. In several places in this chapter we refer to "promotional" rhetoric on the potential benefits of computing. We do not mean by this simplistic and uncritical assumptions about the

kinds of benefits computing might provide, but rather a prevailing bias evident in much of the literature on computing and its application to organizations. This bias has been evident for many years. Early examples can be found in Chapin (1955), Canning (1956), Kozmetzky and Kircher (1956), Leavitt and Whisler (1958), Shultz and Whisler (1960), Simon (1960), Hoos (1960), and Gregory and Van Horn (1960). A thoroughly engrossing set of predictions about the possible benefits of computers can be found in the talks by Jay Forrester, Herbert Simon, Alan Newell, John Kemeny, Alan Perlis, and John Pierce in Greenberger (1962). This tradition has been carried on to the present in a wide array of books and articles on computing and organizations, including (as a brief sample) Simon (1965), Dearden (1966), Meyers (1967), Boutell (1968), Heany (1968), Orlicky (1969), Humphrey and Yearsley (1970), Pendleton (1971), Lucas (1973b), Davis (1973), McFarlan, Nolan, and Norton (1973), Murdick and Ross (1975), Alter (1977), Smith (1979), and Glaser, Torrance, and Schwartz (1983).

CHAPTER FOUR
PROBLEMS
OF
COMPUTING

THE INITIAL use of most new technology is accompanied by problems, and the full range of these problems often is not apparent until after the development and implementation of the new technology. While some of the problems can be rendered harmless, others are more intractable and might actually be inherent in the technology. Even when the effects of problems are mitigated, new ones may arise out of the solutions or may appear in entirely different areas. As the use of computers has increased, a growing awareness has arisen that along with the technology's potential benefits come problems that confound its application.

Applying computer technology can be more costly and more difficult than anticipated. Lack of knowledge about the technology and what it can do is widespread, and addressing this problem is made difficult by continuous change in the technology. Support for the technology is difficult to maintain over the extended periods required for its development and implementation. Resistance to the technology's implementation arises because of uncertainty about its potential benefits and its potential disruptive effects on current operations, the work environment, and interdepartmental relationships. Even after the technology is in place and operating for a time, over-inflated expectations and the difficulty of developing criteria to evaluate the technology's performance may lead to a sense that it has failed to perform.

A Typology of Computing Management Problems

This chapter on the problems of computing addresses their relation to its successful implementation.[1] It investigates seven types of problems found in the URBIS and OECD cities. These problems are listed in figure 4.1, in terms of their importance and incidence in the cities, and they are each discussed next.

Staff problems occur in the computing staff-user interface. These difficulties mainly focus on inadequacies of the computing staff rather than of users, and involve poor communication, insensitivity to users, and "professional" rather than "client service" values. Staff problems are viewed as a failure of computing managers and staff in dealing with their interpersonal and professional relationships. In the URBIS cities, staff problems are indicated by user responses that "data-processing staff are more interested in working on new computer uses than in making improvements in the ones we now use," "data-processing staff are more intrigued with what the computer can do than with solving the problems of my department," and "data-processing staff confuse our conversations with their technical language." In the OECD cities, these problems are indicated by responses that "EDP staff are not sensitive to the problems they create for users," "EDP staff do not involve users sufficiently in the design of systems," and "communication problems exist between EDP staff and users."

Technical problems are related to the reliability of the existing computer hardware, software, and services in the day-to-day, routine operational performance of computing. Reliability is particularly important to managers and users who depend upon the consistent and timely performance of the technology in their daily work. Technical problems are viewed as a failure of computing managers and staff in the management and operation of their own internal operations. In

Figure 4.1 TYPOLOGY OF COMPUTING MANAGEMENT PROBLEMS

Problems	Illustrations
Staff	
Difficulties in the computing staff-user interface.	Poor communication, insensitivity to users, "professional" vs. "client service" values.
Technical	
Doubtful reliability of existing computer hardware, software, and services in day-to-day routine computing.	Foul-ups, frequent technical change, development projects late, routine processing not timely.
Responsiveness	
Inflexibility of data-processing services and systems.	Slowness in handling special requests for information, difficulty in modifying current computerized systems.
Resource	
Insufficient staff, budget, hardware, software, or data.	Limited financial resources, limited machine capacity, too few staff, too few applications.
Support	
Lack of acceptance of data processing by politicians, managers, and users.	Department resistance to computerization, lack of political support/pressure for computerization.
Knowledge	
Lack of understanding of the potentials and limitations of computing on the part of politicians, managers, and users.	Uncertainty about whether computerization will pay off, lack of knowledge about how to use the computer.
Institutional	
Constraints in the organizational environment.	Government operations not standardized, data bases very poor.

the URBIS cities, technical problems are indicated by user responses that "foul-ups occur in day-to-day computer operations," "frequent technical and organizational changes occur in data-processing services," and "the quality of data-processing services is poor." In the OECD cities, technical problems are indicated by user responses that "computer processing is not timely," "development projects are not completed on time," "inputting data is difficult," and "documentation of systems is poor."

Responsiveness problems are related to the flexibility of computing services and systems. Here the concern of managers and users is with the readiness of computing staff to handle requests for special information, service, or modifications to existing computerized systems. Responsiveness problems are viewed as a failure of computing staff to deal adequately with the needs of managers and users.

In the URBIS cities, responsiveness problems are indicated by user responses that "data processing is slow to respond to special requests for information," "computer-based data is not available," and "getting priority in using the computer is difficult." In the OECD cities, responsiveness problems are indicated by user responses that "current (local) computerized systems are inadequate and inflexible," and "current national or regional computerized systems are inadequate and inflexible."

Resource problems are related to the lack of sufficient staff, budget, hardware, software, data, or other resources needed to satisfy the demand for computing services. These problems are viewed as a constraint on computing, and frequently as beyond the immediate control of computing managers. In the URBIS cities, resource problems are indicated by user responses that "the cost of computer use is high," and "accessing computer-based data gathered or held by other departments is difficult." In the OECD cities, resource problems are indicated by user responses that "financial resources are limited," "machine capacity is limited," "there are too few EDP staff," and "there are too few computer applications available."

Support problems concern the level of acceptance of computing within the government, whether that acceptance is based on an understanding of computing or not. The extent of interest and optimism on the part of local government politicians, managers, and users is believed to be a major factor affecting the successful development of computing. Lack of support is viewed as a failure of computing management to build good relationships with government officials and staff, which has a negative effect on computing development. In the URBIS cities, support problems are measured by responses which indicate that "computers and data processing have not lived up to expectations" and that "computers will not greatly improve the operations of the government over the next five years." In the OECD cities, support is indicated by responses to a query about constraints on the further development and use of computing. "Department resistance to computerization," "lack of political support/pressure for computerization," and "loss of confidence in EDP because of previous problems with systems" are the specific indicators used.

Knowledge problems refer to managers' and users' lack of

understanding about the potentials and limitations of computing. Specifically, they refer to users' uncertainty about whether and how to use computing and how to adapt to its job impacts. Knowledge problems are viewed as a failure of computing management to orient managers and users to computers and data processing and to train them adequately for adaptation to computing in their jobs. These problems are believed to be related to support problems in that lack of adequate knowledge may lead to unrealistic expectations about what the computer can do and to manager and user resistance to computerization. Knowledge problems were measured only in the OECD cities and are indicated by responses regarding "lack of knowledge about how to use the computer, or how to use it beyond current routine applications," "uncertainty about whether computerization will really pay off," and "lack of knowledge about how department staff should adapt to computerization in their jobs."

Institutional problems refer to constraints in the organizational environment which affect the applicability of computing. These problems are initially largely beyond the control of computing managers but might be brought under their control. Institutional problems were measured only in the OECD cities and are indicated by user responses that "government operations are not sufficiently standardized for computerization," and "existing data bases are poor."

Problems of Computing in URBIS Cities

The URBIS data were collected from forty cities, yielding a sufficiently large data base to allow us to factor analyze data on the entire range of problems about which URBIS respondents were queried. Thus we were able to cluster the data statistically to determine whether and to what extent the typology of problems we developed was parallel to how problems are perceived by local government personnel. The data from these factor analyses are shown in table 4.1.

The URBIS data clustered around five problem categories: computing staff and user interface problems, technical problems, computing service responsiveness problems, resource problems, and

Table 4.1 FACTOR LOADINGS FOR DIMENSIONS OF COMPUTING PROBLEMS IN THE URBIS CITIES (N = 40)

Questionnaire Items	Type of Computing Problem				
	Staff	Technical	Resource	Respon-siveness	Support
Data-processing staff are more interested in working on new computer uses rather than making improvements in ones we now use.	.94	.28	.06	.02	−.19
Data-processing staff are more intrigued with what the computer can do than with solving the problems of my department.	.81	−.04	.00	.19	.14
Data-processing staff confuse our conversation with their technical language.	.59	.21	.27	.24	.15
Frequent technical and organizational changes in data-processing services.	.01	.82	.17	.06	−.04
Foul-ups in day-to-day computer operation.	.24	.76	.04	.32	.05
Quality of data-processing services provided.	.26	.43	−.06	.36	−.01
Difficulties in accessing computer-based data gathered or held by other departments/agencies.	.20	−.06	.92	.36	.05
High cost of computer use.	−.03	.24	.54	.10	−.18
Slow response of data processing to requests for information.	.08	.11	.20	.35	−.03
Difficulty in getting priority in using the computer.	.14	.30	.04	.67	−.10
Computer-based data not available for the analysis of specific questions or problems.	.28	.13	.29	.52	.23
In general, computers and data processing having failed to live up to my expectations.	.21	−.01	−.13	.33	.71
Within the next five years, computers will not greatly improve the operations of this government.	−.07	−.01	−.09	−.21	.56
Percent Variance Explained	33%	14%	11%	10%	8%

Note: The items underlined within each column represent a single factor.

user support problems. Our analytical framework was substantiated by this close fit of the responses, so we constructed our further problems analysis around this typology.

Problems with computing appear to be pervasive in the URBIS

cities, but they are not overwhelming. Approximately one-fifth to two-thirds of the URBIS cities experience problems with computing staff, technology, responsiveness, resources, or support (table 4.2).

The most pervasive and most serious problems are with computing staff. Approximately 60 percent of the cities report problems with the computing staff due to their interest in working on new computer uses rather than making improvements in current applications, their interest in what the computer can do rather than in solving departmental computing problems, and their tendency to confuse con-

Table 4.2 PERCENT OF URBIS CITIES EXPERIENCING COMPUTING PROBLEMS (N = 40)

Type of Computing Problem	Percent URBIS Cities with Problem	
	Moderate	Major
Staff		
Data-processing staff are more interested in working on new computer uses rather than making improvements in ones we now use.	50%	12%
Data-processing staff are more intrigued with what the computer can do than with solving the problems of my department.	45	10
Data-processing staff confuse our conversations with their technical language.	53	12
Technical		
Foul-ups in day-to-day computer operations.	20	2
Frequent technical and organizational changes in data-processing services.	15	—
Quality of the data-processing services provided.	53	8
Responsiveness		
Slow response of data-processing to requests for information.	30	—
Computer-based data not available for the analysis of specific questions or problems.	50	8
Difficulty in getting priority in using the computer.	38	—
Resource		
High cost of computer use.	45	12
Difficulties in accessing computer-based data gathered or held by other departments and agencies.	28	2
Support		
In general, computers and data-processing have failed to live up to my expectations.	2	—
Within the next five years, computers will not greatly improve the operations of this government.	20	—

versations with technical computing language. Ten percent of the cities report "major" problems with the computing staff in these areas. Technology problems in the URBIS cities are somewhat less pervasive. In 53 percent of the cities, users report moderate problems with quality of computing services and in another 8 percent these are major problems. About one-fifth of the cities also report foul-ups in day-to-day computer operations and problems arising from frequent technical and organizational changes in services. The kinds of change most frequently experienced by the URBIS cities include changes in computer mainframe, computer vendor, development priorities, and computing manager. While such changes might be routine to the computing staff, apparently they create problems for users who are less familiar with the technology and whose work can be easily disrupted by change. For example, the change to a new computer mainframe or computer vendor inevitably produces operational problems with the technology, such as downtime, bugs in the operating system, and conversion of application programs. It also produces change in user interface procedures which are unfamiliar and disruptive to users. The less familiar users are with the technology, the more unnecessary these changes appear and the more they frustrate users. At the same time, these changes may be inconsequential to computing staff who therefore may be insensitive to their impact on users. The pervasiveness of staff problems in the URBIS cities supports this interpretation.

The responsiveness of the computing service also is a problem in at least one-third of the URBIS cities. Users indicate that computing service is slow in responding to requests for information, that computer-based data are not available for analysis, and that they have difficulty in getting priority in using the computer. The URBIS fieldwork suggests that most of these problems center around the handling of special requests for information. These requests might range from fact retrievals to reports to complex analyses, but they usually share the common feature of requiring special programming and/or special data to handle them; hence the frequently slow response from data processing. Because many unsophisticated users believe the promotional literature, which depicts the computer as a massive data bank and an instant producer of information, few understand why the computing service should not be able to respond more quickly. Sophisticated users, on the other hand, tend to complain because they hold the computing service responsible for data management, they know that responsiveness is a matter of priorities, and they disagree with the low priority given to special requests.

Resource problems, particularly cost, are "moderate" in nearly half the cities and "major" in another 12 percent of the cities. Although most user departments do not directly pay for routine computing, users feel that the cost of computer use is high. They probably are aware of costs because many municipal computing departments report the costs of services to them, and because the departments often do pay directly for new development and for special requests.

Despite the problems with computing, users in the URBIS cities are basically supportive of computers and data processing. Only 2 percent of the cities indicate that computing has not lived up to expectations, and only 20 percent doubt that computing will greatly improve the operations of the government over the next five years. This suggests that while users have problems with computing and with EDP staff, they have not become soured by their experiences and probably will support expanded use of the technology within the government.

Problems of Computing in OECD Cities

The OECD cities also indicate that computing problems are pervasive. Approximately 20 to 40 percent exhibit at least moderate problems with computing staff, technology, responsiveness, resources, support, and knowledge. The most pervasive and most serious problems are with computing resources (particularly costs) and responsiveness (table 4.3).

Users in 69 percent of the cities report that the costs of computing are too high or financial resources are too limited; and in 31 percent this is a "major" problem. As might be expected with cost/financial problems, the OECD cities also experience other resource problems. These include limited machine capacity (in 25 per-

Table 4.3 PERCENT OF OECD CITIES EXPERIENCING COMPUTING PROBLEMS (N = 16)

Type of Computer Problem	Percent OECD Cities with Problem	
	Moderate	Major
Staff		
EDP staff are not sensitive to problems they create for users.	19%	6%
EDP staff do not involve users sufficiently in design of systems.	25	0
Communication problems between EDP staff and users.	25	12
Technology		
Difficulty in inputting data	0	12
Timeliness of computer processing	25	25
Timeliness of development projects	12	0
Poor documentation of systems	6	—
Responsiveness		
Inflexibility or inadequacy of systems	38	12
Inflexibility or inadequacy of national or regional systems	6	25
Resource		
Financial resources are too limited/costs are too high	38	31
Limited machine capacity	25	—
Too few EDP staff	31	6
Too few applications	44	6
Support		
Department resistance to computerization	19	12
Lack of political (elected officials, chief executives) pressure/support for computerization	25	6
Loss of confidence in EDP because of previous problems with systems	12	—
Knowledge		
Lack of knowledge about how to use computer or how to use it beyond current routine applications	19	12
Uncertainty about whether computerization will really pay off	19	6
Lack of knowledge about how department staff should adapt to computerization in their jobs	6	12
Institutional		
Lack of standard operations	0	12
Lack of good data bases	—	6

cent of the cities), too few computing staff (in 37 percent), and too few applications (in 50 percent). Financial resources probably are a major constraint on machine and staff capacity; in turn, these factors undoubtedly combine to limit the number of applications that can be developed and probably help to account for the large percentage of cities with too few applications. These relationships are suggested by the comments of users:

Personnel availability is a problem. For example, four or five programs are on hold until an accounting-oriented systems analyst and several programmers can be hired.

The systems need further enhancement in that there is not sufficient detail held on the master files. The data-processing department is unable to give time to work on enhancements due to the large number of new systems and other tasks that are on their list of work to be done.

The responsiveness of computerized systems is a problem at two different levels in the OECD cities. Approximately one-half of the cities have problems with inflexibility or inadequacy of local EDP systems, and approximately one-third have such problems with national or regional systems. Most of the cities experiencing problems with national systems have "major" problems. The major complaints of users are that systems were not adequately designed to provide the information they need in the first place or they cannot get the systems modified to provide what they need. National and regional systems are described by users as having the inherent problem that, being generalized, they are not designed to meet "local" conditions and cannot be modified to meet them. Thus while such systems might be well-designed on their own terms, they still are inadequate from the standpoint of the users. The following comments illustrate the responsiveness problem:

We are dependent on what is offered by the (computer) center and have no influence on developments there. We cannot take the initiative because the applications are to be developed uniformly on the (national, regional) level. Now if we wanted a modification or a completely new program which would better fit our purposes, we would hardly have a chance of getting it done. The programs are not built to handle cases the way we need them to be handled.

The way of work of the DP center implies a low degree of flexibility both as regards the general turn-around time and technical changes. There are certain adjustment cases that cannot be handled by the system, but have to be done manually. It is difficult to get applications modified exactly as we would like.

We are exploiting all of the possibilities which have been offered, but the national systems imply some limitations.

Problems with computing staff occur in one-fourth to one-third of the OECD cities. One problem mentioned by managers and users is that computing staff are not sensitive to the problems they create for users when they change hardware, software, and procedures or when they introduce new systems:

There are more errors made than before. The applications are developed to be uniform and there is a lot of pressure to implement them as quickly as possible. Testing times at the (national, regional) center are too short, and as administrative deadlines draw nearer the programs are run before they are thoroughly tested. The results are abortive runs on the computer, loss of time, and additional costs. Also, the center staff sometimes cause serious trouble by errors in running currently operational programs.

We are overloaded with work because there was an unrealistic reduction of our department personnel due to a wrong assessment of savings achievable with the computer.

Computing staff also do not involve users sufficiently in the design of systems and fail to communicate adequately (e.g., fail to inform users of changes, confuse conversations with technical language). Communication problems were "moderate" in 25 percent of the OECD cities and "major" in another 12 percent. Most of the users' concern over staff problems seemed to be related to national and regional systems rather than to purely local systems.

Most technical problems with computing are not very pervasive in the OECD cities. Generally, only about 10 percent of the cities experience problems with timeliness of development projects, poor documentation of systems, or difficulties in inputting data. But one-half of the cities experience problems with the timeliness of computer processing and half of these experience "major" problems. This problem of timeliness again appears to be related to user experience with national and regional systems, but it also occurs with purely local systems. For example:

Relations with the center are somewhat tense. You see, we have to keep deadlines, legally fixed terms, at which to deliver (bills, assessments, reports, etc.) on time, and the center has not always been able to meet the deadline. That added to our workload because we just had to keep the deadline.

A problem arises when the DP center informs us that a technical error encountered will not be corrected in time (to meet our deadlines); it is left up to the municipality to remedy the consequences.

CRT is on a telephone line, has been down for two weeks, and has slow response time. Only weekly update, therefore information is always one week old. Information from the CRT is limited. Time delay in receiving hard copy reports (seven working days).

      Problems with support of data processing occur in about one-third of the OECD cities. Chief among these problems are department resistence to computerization and lack of political pressure or support for computerization (which would presumably overcome department resistance). Department resistance to computerization is variously attributed to lack of department staff knowledge about computers and what they can do, fear on the part of department managers that the poor quality of their operations will be discovered, and uncertainty about the benefits and costs of computerization. Chief executives commented that:

A major constraint relates to the psychological receptivity of the departments. In effect, there exists some opposition, all the more dangerous when it is underhanded. There exists a fear of computers, especially among the department directors who, not having always correctly managed their departments, are afraid of certain discoveries and who, on the other hand, because they are not up to the job of management, are afraid of not knowing how to adapt. One also runs up against the mediocrity of certain members of the department staff.

Department resistance is a problem. The problems associated with earlier changes of hardware and the load and strain these imposed on the department resulted in a loss of confidence which set back the thinking of department users for several years.

The second comment (above) is especially interesting because it introduces a factor that might be related to department resistance in some cases. It is important to note that 12 percent of the cities reported moderate problems with the loss of confidence in computing because of previous problems with systems.

As these comments suggest, the OECD cities also have problems with regard to managers' and users' knowledge about the technology and its use. Chief among these are lack of knowledge about how to use the computer (including how to use it beyond current routine applications), lack of knowledge about the benefits of computerization, and lack of knowledge about how department staff should adapt to computerization in their jobs.

A few OECD cities reported major problems with the degree to which their institutional setting lends itself to computerization. These problems centered around the lack of standardized operations in the government which would warrant computerization. It is unclear whether the users' responses in this area really constitute a unique set of problems or merely a sophisiticated form of resistance to computerization. Some people might argue that these problems indicate a major reason why computerization should be undertaken: to rationalize and systematize government operations and data bases. Thus they are not problems in computing; they are problems meant to be addressed by computing.

Summary

The data indicate that computing problems occur frequently in both URBIS and OECD cities. Several comparative observations can be made about the nature of computing problems in both populations.

First, we notice that the problem lists of the two populations are different in length, with the OECD list a bit longer. This might be due to a difference in problems experienced in the OECD cities as compared to URBIS cities, but we believe this difference is essentially an artifact of the difference in research design between the URBIS and OECD studies. The URBIS questionnaires listed a set of problems to which users and computing personnel could respond. This increased the likelihood that problems that exist but were not on the list might have been overlooked. The OECD questionnaire, on the other hand, was open-ended, making it more likely that the full range of possible problems would appear even though the exact distribution of problems across the OECD cities might be difficult to assess given variance in respondents' abilities to recall all of their problems when being interviewed. Thus the mix of problems reported in the two studies can be taken as a whole.

Second, we see that computing problems are quite pervasive in both URBIS and OECD cities. Every city has some problems, and many of the problems listed are shared by over half of the cities in each population. In few cases did a problem exist in less than 20 percent of the cities. Thus, assuming that at least some of the cities in each population must be well-organized and managed with respect to computing, we see that computing problems appear to be somewhat endemic to computing activity regardless of management. And certain kinds of problems, especially staff, support, technical, and responsiveness problems, appear very frequently in both URBIS and OECD cities.

Third, the two populations of cities exhibited different "top" problems (i.e., class of problem experienced by the largest proportion of the cities). In URBIS the top problem class was the computing staff and user interface; in OECD the top problem class was resource limitations on computing. The actual breakdowns of problem reporting for URBIS and OECD cities is shown in table 4.4. Over half of the URBIS and OECD cities have experienced high levels of technological, resource, and responsiveness problems.

Finally, it appears that the OECD cities have somewhat more problematic computing environments than do the URBIS cities. The data indicate that the OECD cities have a larger number of "major" problems with computing. Taking into account the open-ended nature of the OECD interviews, the OECD cities would have tended to underreport problems as compared to the URBIS cities if the differences in responses between the two were simply differences in data collection methodology. But as the OECD cities indicate more problems with computing, it is likely that they do in fact experience higher levels of problems.

Several of these comparative findings indicate a general trend. The OECD cities, which tend to be somewhat behind the URBIS cities

Table 4.4 SUMMARY COMPARISON OF COMPUTING PROBLEMS IN URBIS AND OECD CITIES

	Percent or Percent-Range of Cities with Problem[a]	
Category	URBIS Cities	OECD Cities
Top problem category		
Staff	55–65%	25–37%
Cost	57	69
Problem categories shared by 50% or more of the cities in both groups		
Technology	15–61	6–50
Responsiveness	30–58	31–50
Resource	30–57	25–69
Lowest categories of problems shared by both groups		
Support	2–20	12–31
Knowledge	—	18–31
Institutional	—	6–12
Top individual problems shared by 50% or more of one group		
Communication difficulties	65	37
DP staff interests	62	—
Quality of service provided	61	—
Computer data not available	58	—
Cost	57	69
DP staff intrigued by computer	55	—
Difficulty in getting priority	38	—
Too few applications	—	50
Timeliness of computer processing	—	50
Inflexibility of systems	—	50
Individual problems classified as "major" by more than 10% of the cities from either group		
Communication difficulties	12	12
DP staff interests	12	—
High cost of computer use	12	31
Department resistance	—	12
Lack of standard operations	—	12
How to use the computer	—	12
Staff adaptation	—	12
Difficulty in inputting data	—	12
Timeliness of computer processing	—	25
Inflexibility or inadequacy of systems	—	12
Inflexibility or inadequacy of national or regional systems	—	25

[a] Percent-range means the upper and lower percentage boundaries having the problem.

overall in the level of computing development, also show a slightly different problem mix. The OECD cities have trouble getting resources and support for computing; URBIS cities have difficulties with interactions between computing staff and users, but relatively few support problems. Perhaps in the earlier stages of computing development the problems of mobilizing support and effort for development are most serious, while after computing has been established more difficult problems of socio-technical interface (e.g., computing staff/user problems) become more pronounced. This possible difference cannot easily be tested using the data available because they were not designed specifically to answer such a question. However, these data do provide an indication of a link between level of development and kind of problem that will be investigated more thoroughly in chapters 6 and 7, and that must subsequently be addressed with further research.

Note

1. The data used in this chapter are taken from the responses of chief executives, department heads, and section heads in the URBIS and OECD cities to questions about problems, constraints, and satisfaction with computers and data processing. Data from the URBIS cities are responses of users to pre-structured Likert-type questions. Four-point items were dichotomized such that "0" was equal to "no problem" and "1" equaled agreement that "a problem existed." To obtain a city-level score for analysis, these dichotomized responses were then averaged across all respondents for the city. Each questionnaire item's score could vary from 0 to 1.00. The items were then categorized such that if the average score for a city on the item was greater than .66, that city was classified as experiencing a "major problem." Data from the OECD cities are responses of city officials to questions about the constraints they face in using and further exploiting computing and about the quality of computing services they receive. Categories of problems were constructed based on the common themes found within responses to these questions, and city-level scores were derived on the basis of whether problems had been mentioned. If respondents failed to mention a problem, the city was classified as having "no problem" on that item. If at least one respondent mentioned a problem, the city was classified as having a "moderate problem." If several respondents mentioned a problem with some intensity, the city was classified as having a "major problem" with the item. Details about the analyses of problems can be found in the appendix.

CHAPTER FIVE
ENVIRONMENT AND POLICIES IN THE MANAGEMENT OF COMPUTING

THE ANALYSES in chapters 2, 3, and 4 yielded three interesting results. First, computing use is widespread and increasing in city governments, but the extent of use and kinds of use made of the technology vary from place to place. Second, computing appears to produce a variety of benefits, but these benefits do not accrue in an across-the-board pattern; many of the basic economic benefits of computing seem to accrue in the most routine and simple applications of the technology, while applications to more demanding managerial and planning tasks show less promising payoffs. Third, problems with computing seem to be ubiquitous among the cities studied, but these too vary in kind and intensity from place to place. The unifying characteristic of these findings is that the use and impact of computing varies significantly across cities. What accounts for these variances?

Here we must refer to our framework presented in chapter 1, figure 1.3. The framework posits that the outcomes of computing (benefits and problems) as well as the state of computing in the organization (computing environment) are dependent on computing policies. Policies are widely believed to be critical factors in the outcomes of computing use because they modify the computing environment to reduce problems and increase benefits (Lucas 1974a; Zani 1970; Nolan 1973a, 1979; Gibson and Nolan 1974; Ein-Dor and Segev 1978; Kraemer, Dutton, and Northrop 1981; Allen 1981). This may indeed be the case, and a major purpose of this research is to determine the connections between policies and outcomes of computing use in the cities studied. But as figure 1.3 also shows, policies are believed to be dependent on environmental factors. We are immediately faced with the question of whether the policies are truly influential in determining the outcomes of computing use, or whether the real independent variables are the environmental factors that affect computing policies.

This chapter focuses on the relationship between computing policies and computing environment variables, after determining whether those variables are sufficiently independent of city environment factors to be meaningful as independent variables in their own right.

The Influence of City Environment

The influence of city environment on the variables of computing policies and computing environment can be ascertained indirectly by correlating these variables to see whether they co-vary. The specific variables of interest are shown in figure 1.3, and are explained in greater detail here. Specific descriptions of how the variables were constructed and measured can be found in the appendix.

CITY ENVIRONMENT VARIABLES

We used two city environment variables in this research. City size is measured by the city's population. As a general rule, the scale of city operations varies directly with the population and size of the city. The major factor that might account for differences in operations among cities of the same size is the other environmental variable, city wealth as measured by the size of the government's budget. As a general rule, wealthier cities are able to provide greater service than are poorer cities of the same size. These variables are considered "environment" variables because neither is under direct policy control of the government itself.

MANAGEMENT POLICY VARIABLES

We classify management policies for computing in three categories: technological development policies, structural arrangement policies, and socio-technical interface policies. (This construction for the computing policies variables is adapted from Kraemer, Dutton, and Northrop 1981.) Management policy variables, as noted in chapter 1, correspond to the area of concern we call "control." Yet it also directly embodies the other two areas of concern, "technology" and "people." Policies are made by people, and it is through policy action that the technology of computing is adopted and deployed into a particular computing environment. Policy variables are therefore best considered intermediary variables, between the relatively uncontrollable variables of city environment and the (presumably) controllable variables of computing environment and computing outcomes.

TECHNOLOGICAL DEVELOPMENT

Outcomes of computing use are sometimes viewed as highly dependent upon the state of technological development in organizations (Gibson and Nolan 1974; Pendleton 1971). It is assumed that up to a hypothetical saturation point, the relationship between extent of computing and benefits from computing is linear: the more automated a site is, the more it benefits from automation. This belief, which seems to be widespread among both technical and user communities, results in what has been termed a "faith in technology" attitude toward computing. Most users and technical specialists appear to believe that once a computer technology is developed to its full capacity, the benefits of the technology will be realized to their greatest extent; thus local governments must keep up with the state of the art.

We divide policies for technology development into two classes: software development and hardware development. Under software development we include policies related to adoption of relatively new software advancements such as integration of data files (measured by degree of data linkage), changes in priority of development, number of applications planned, number of applications undergoing major modification, level of sophistication of reports generated by the systems, and level of sophistication in use of output. These variables collectively measure the extent to which city policymakers advocate adoption and development of advanced software technology.

Under hardware development we include the extent to which the city has adopted on-line computing and multiprogramming, and the city's tendency to upgrade hardware. These variables measure city policymakers' propensity to encourage adoption of new and advanced hardware.

STRUCTURAL ARRANGEMENTS

Another perspective suggests that outcomes from computing use are dependent on the structural arrangements that govern its use. Structural reorganization is a basic strategy for increasing the payoffs of a technology. This perspective assumes that problems with technology largely stem from organizational arrangements affecting the locus of control over computing resources. Reorganization, then, might create better conditions for managing the technology and thus for achieving benefits.

We identify three kinds of structural arrangements. First: arrangements for the technology, which includes centralization and decentralization (i.e., whether there are consolidated or distributed computing facilities), and the extent of ongoing changes in these arrangements. Second: decision making about computing activity, which includes centralized and decentralized control of decision making and computing, the presence and functions of a computing policy board, and the extent of managerial involvement in decision-making. Third: charging policy, which deals with the question of whether users are charged for computing services.

SOCIO-TECHNICAL INTERFACE

Another set of factors that can shape the outcomes of computing use are related to the way in which the technology has been integrated into the organization. It has been suggested that the successful use of computing is contingent on user involvement with the technology (Lucas 1974a; Kling 1979). This perspective suggests that computing benefits might best be achieved by more complete training of users, for example, or by changing the way in which users interface with the technology. Through use of the "right" policies, EDP staff might be sensitized to the problems that computing can create for users and to the potential conflicts between their commitments to professionalism and to client service. One approach is to have analysts and programmers employed by the user departments, or at least assigned by the computing installation to specific user departments. Such policies, it is suggested, can help integrate computing into the organization by changing the attitudes, behaviors, and interactions of the providers and the users of data-processing services.

COMPUTING ENVIRONMENT VARIABLES

Computing environment variables are basically dependent on computing policies. We include three kinds of variables in this class. Resource dedication includes measures such as the level of budgeted funds for computing and the number of computing staff. Technology development includes measures such as the degree of automation throughout the city, the computing power available (total core capacity), and the utilization level of the equipment (hours per week operational). Experience with computing is measured by the year computing began in the city. Generally, one would expect that the greater the level of resource dedication and technology development and the longer the period of experience, the greater would be the success of computing in terms of positive impacts and few problems.

THE INTERACTIONS AMONG THE VARIABLES

The question we face here is whether city environment variables closely relate to computing policies and the computing environment. We can hypothesize that they exert a powerful effect on both, in the sense that these variables are responsible for the broader context of opportunities and constraints within which policymakers must work. If the conditions imposed by city environment factors are very strong and very restrictive, management policies can be expected to have little more independent effect than making outcomes a little better or a little worse.

Let us examine this hypothesis with a specific example. Assume that computing success correlates strongly with extensiveness of computing (i.e., the more successful computing sites will be the more extensively developed sites). From this proposition we can further postulate that the more extensively developed sites are those that have a stronger need and the resources to develop computing. Both need and abundance of resources are related to wealth and size. The model in figure 5.1 illustrates the causal chain in this hypothesis. Larger organizations have both a greater need for automation and greater wherewithal to support it, and they therefore use more of it. More automation leads to more substantial computing impacts, so by way of the intermediary variable of computing environment, the environment variables "control" computing outcomes. Thus positive outcomes could be expected to correlate strongly with both population size and level of government budget.

In order to determine the relationship among city environment, computing environment, and computing policy, we correlated computing environment and policy variables with the indicators of city environment: city population and government budget.

Our correlation analysis indicates four broad relationships in the URBIS cities (table 5.1). First, size is related to policies for hardware development and to nearly all measures of the computing environment. Larger cities clearly have more advanced computing equipment and a more developed computing environment. With respect to computing equipment, larger cities tend to have on-line capability, many terminals deployed, multiprogramming capability, and upgraded central processing units. With respect to the computing environment, larger cities tend to have large computing budgets and staffs, many computer applications, many departments with at least some automation, large total core capacity on the computer mainframe, and high mainframe utilization. Second, size is generally unrelated to management policies for software development, structural arrangements, and socio-technical interface. Thus, most management policies do not appear to be a function of the size of the city. Third, experience with computing (a variable in the computing environment) is associated with the size of city: larger cities clearly have had computing for a longer period of time.

Fourth, with the sole exception of number of terminals avail-

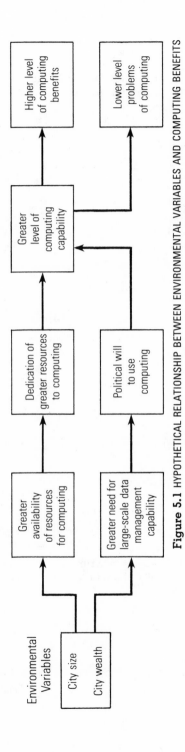

Figure 5.1 HYPOTHETICAL RELATIONSHIP BETWEEN ENVIRONMENTAL VARIABLES AND COMPUTING BENEFITS

Table 5.1 PEARSON CORRELATIONS BETWEEN THE CITY ENVIRONMENT AND MANAGEMENT POLICIES AND COMPUTING ENVIRONMENT IN URBIS CITIES (N = 40)

	City Environment	
	Size of city	Government budget
MANAGEMENT POLICIES		
Technological Development		
Software		
Degree of data linkage	.01	.00
Degree of report sophistication	.23	.25
Total applications in development	.33*	.19
Total applications planned	−.06	.06
Change in development priorities	−.05	−.06
Hardware		
On-line capability	.28*	.20
Number of terminals[a]	.35*	.48*
Multiprogramming	.30*	.23
Hardware upgrading	.27*	.24
Structural arrangements		
Technology management		
Centralization	−.25	−.22
Recent reorganization	.19	.07
Decisionmaking		
Control of priorities	.15	.09
Policy board	.05	.02
Board influence in applications[b]	−.18	−.05
Board influence in management[b]	.07	−.13
Chief executive involvement	−.13	−.07
Department head involvement	.11	.14
Charging policy		
Charge for use	−.07	.01
Socio-technical interface		
User-centered involvement		
User involvement in design	.15	.05
EDP staffing assignments		
Programmers assigned by departments to EDP	.34*	.21
Programmers assigned by EDP to departments	.12	.23
Training		
User training	.32*	.27
Department head training	.05	−.02
COMPUTING ENVIRONMENT		
Resource dedication		
EDP budget per capita	.28*	.36*
Percent EDP budget of total budget	−.06	−.21
Total EDP staff	.73*	.78*

	City Environment	
Technology	Size of city	Government budget
Degree of automation	.40*	.44*
Degree of functional automation	.54*	.50*
Total core capacity	.29*	.36*
Total clock hours per week	.47*	.35*
Experience with computing		
Year EDP began in city	−.49*	−.50*

[a] Includes only those cities with on-line capability; n = 28
[b] Includes only those cities with a policy board; n = 15
*p < .05

able, government budget does not correlate with computing policies but strongly correlates with computing environment. Moreover, the association between government budget and computing environment is identical to that between city size and computing environment.

The OECD cities show similar patterns of association, but there are some significant exceptions (table 5.2). Larger OECD cities are more likely to have their own local computing installations (shown by the centralization variable) and to use local policy boards to control these installations. These relationships could be predicted given the special characteristics of many of the OECD cities. In particular, smaller ones tend to utilize regional computing installations, and local policy boards usually do not exist in the cities using regional installations. Another noteworthy difference in OECD cities is the fact that larger and wealthier cities tend to have fewer applications planned than do smaller and less wealthy cities. This relationship was not expected, but as the analyses in chapters 6 and 7 will show, there is a theoretical means of explaining it. In general, however, the results in the OECD cities are similar to those from the URBIS cities: city environment variables seem to relate more strongly to computing environment variables than to computing policy variables.

What do these relationships suggest for our hypothesis that city environment variables strongly affect policies and computing environment? With few exceptions, city environment does not relate to policies. The exceptions are found in situations where special arrangements (e.g., regional installations) take precedence over local

Table 5.2 PEARSON CORRELATIONS BETWEEN THE CITY ENVIRONMENT AND MANAGEMENT POLICIES AND COMPUTING ENVIRONMENT IN OECD CITIES (N = 16)

	City Environment	
	Size of city	Government budget
MANAGEMENT POLICIES		
Technological development		
Software		
Degree of data linkage	.30	.07
Degree of report sophistication	.29	.19
Degree of sophistication of applications	.19	.14
Total applications planned	−.41	−.57*
Total applications to be modified	−.04	−.06
Hardware		
On-line capability	.33	.33
Number of terminals[a]	.75*	.48
Multiprogramming	.30	.31
Structural arrangements		
Technology management		
Centralization	−.55*	−.41
Decisionmaking		
Control of priorities	.08	−.15
Local policy board	.60*	.75*
Chief executive involvement	.43	.36
Department head involvement	.12	.05
Charging policy		
Charged for development	.17	.13
Charged for operations	.07	−.07
Socio-technical interface		
User-centered involvement		
User involvement	.46*	.41
Training/orientation		
Section head training	.29	.21
Department head training	.27	.40
COMPUTING ENVIRONMENT		
Resource dedication		
EDP budget per capita	.23	.40
Percent EDP budget of total government budget	.12	−.26
Total EDP staff	.84*	.71*
Percent increase in resources needed in 1976	.03	.36
Technology		
Degree of automation	.40	.10
Degree of functional automation	.45*	.15
Total core capacity	.85*	.73*
Percent computer use	.48*	.31
Experience with computing		
Year EDP began in city	−.42*	−.27

[a] Includes only those cities with on-line capability; n = 10.
*$p < .05$

policy and are themselves directly related to city size. City environment, and especially city size, does appear to be strongly related to
computing environment. Since we posit that policies do have an in-
termediate effect on environment and, as we shall see, on outcomes
of computing use, what might account for this strong relationship?
We believe the key is in the variable "experience with computing,"
which measures the length of time organizations have been using
computing. Cities that have been using computing longer would be
expected to be more highly developed in their use. And generally, it
is the larger cities that have been using computing the longest. As
suggested by our hypothesis, larger cities have more demand for the
special contributions computing can make to administrative performance, and they generally have more resources to devote to computing; thus they are early adopters of the technology. The relationship between city environment and computing environment, therefore,
might be explained by the simple fact that larger and wealthier cities
adopted computing earlier and thus have more fully developed computing environments.

The key finding from our analysis here is that city environment
variables do not appear to relate directly to the policies followed in
the management of computing. This allows us to proceed with the
assumption that our analysis of the relationship between policies and
computing environment will reveal whether policies themselves exert
direct influence on computing environment. This provides a key in ascertaining the link between computing policies and outcomes, discussed in chapter 6.

Management Policies and Computing Environment

The relationships between management policies for computing and
computing environment variables are presented in tables 5.3 and 5.4.
These analyses lend credence to our assumption that city environment variables associate with computing environment variables mainly
as a function of how long the city has been using computing.

In the URBIS cities, technological development policies relate

Table 5.3 PEARSON CORRELATIONS BETWEEN COMPUTING ENVIRONMENT AND MANAGEMENT POLICIES IN URBIS CITIES (N = 40)

Management Policies	Computing Environment							
	EDP budget per capita	% EDP budget of total	Total EDP staff	Degree of automation	Degree of functional automation	Total core capacity	Total clock hours per week	Year EDP began
Technological development								
Software								
Degree of data linkage	.31*	.17	.27*	.56*	.49*	.38*	.19	-.16
Degree of report sophistication	.42*	.06	.32*	.45*	.41*	.21	.18	-.28*
Total applications in development	.20	.13	.27*	.29*	.25	.26	.23	-.08
Total applications planned	.02	-.13	-.08	.02	-.01	-.03	-.09	.23
Change in development priorities	-.17	.00	-.11	-.11	-.13	-.04	.01	.01
Hardware								
On-line capability	.38*	.30*	.35*	.43*	.36*	.33*	.47*	-.34*
Number of terminals [a]	.61*	-.07	.74*	.62*	.38*	.71*	.39*	-.32*
Multiprogramming	.28*	.22	.35*	.42*	.36*	.31*	.39*	-.25
Hardware upgrading	.21	.10	.28*	.15	.15	.29*	.23	.01
Structural arrangements								
Technology management								
Centralization	-.06	.02	-.06	.21	-.09	.17	.10	-.08
Recent reorganization	-.03	.12	.03	-.05	-.12	.09	.08	-.20

Decisionmaking								
Control of priorities	.33*	.06	.16	.16	.12	.19	.22	−.19
Policy board influence	.14	.01	.16	.11	.03	.31*	.37*	−.13
Applications[b]	−.10	−.54*	−.01	.21	.01	−.10	−.33	.13
Management[b]	−.37	.22	−.07	.30	.09	−.04	.42	−.11
Chief executive involvement	.00	−.06	−.02	.18	.09	.02	.16	−.09
Department head involvement	.39*	.15	.22	.33*	.18	.31*	.32*	−.20
Charging policy								
Charged for use	.06	.18	.04	.08	−.04	.01	.06	−.15
Socio-technical interface								
User-centered involvement								
User involvement in design	.03	−.11	.19	.31*	.35*	.15	.20	−.24
EDP staffing assignments								
Programmers assigned by departments to EDP	.10	.21	.30*	.13	.18	.18	.32*	−.36*
Programmers assigned by EDP to departments	.25	.07	.25	.30*	.16	.34*	.11	−.10
Training								
User training	.34*	.24	.42*	.60*	.55*	.40*	.38*	−.19
Department head training	.43*	.49*	.34*	.58*	.44*	.47*	.52*	−.20

[a] Includes only those cities with on-line capability; n = 28.
[b] Includes only those cities with a policy board; n = 16.
* p < .05

Table 5.4 PEARSON CORRELATIONS BETWEEN COMPUTING ENVIRONMENT AND MANAGEMENT POLICIES IN OECD CITIES (N = 16)

Computing Policies	Computing Environment								
	EDP budget per capita	Percent EDP budget of total	Total EDP staff	Percent increase needed in 1976	Degree of automation	Degree of functional automation	Total core capacity	Percent computer use	Year EDP began
Technological development									
Software									
Degree of data linkage	.44*	.52*	.47*	−.17	.58*	.62*	.27	.53*	−.35
Degree of report sophistication	.36	.10	.37	−.30	.46*	.32	.19	.46*	−.39
Degree of sophistication of applications	.63*	.35	.52*	−.26	.35	.22	.29	.31	−.48*
Total applications planned	−.49*	.06	−.54*	−.55*	−.06	−.10	−.52*	.06	−.13
Total applications to be modified	.20	.06	.05	−.22	.02	.02	−.10	.29	−.31
Hardware									
On-line capability	.39	.09	.57*	.08	.09	.17	.43*	.80*	−.19
Number of terminals[a]	−.09	.34	.92*	−.07	.31	.45	.90*	.19	−.10
Multiprogramming	.12	.30	.43	.10	.26	.47*	.32	.37	.06

Structural arrangements

	(1)	(2)	(3)	(4)	(5)	(6)	(7)	(8)	(9)
Technology management									
Centralization	−.28	−.51*	−.49*	.04	−.40	−.40	−.40	−.40	.22
Decisionmaking									
Control of priorities	−.41	−.15	−.28	.09	.19	.24	−.18	.19	.01
Local policy board	.86*	.02	.69*	.26	.51*	.41	.49*	.45*	−.21
Chief executive involvement	.14	−.10	.04	.06	.26	.20	.41	−.01	−.24
Department head involvement	−.26	.23	−.08	.14	.10	.12	−.09	−.15	.34
Charging policy									
Charged for development	−.05	.01	.16	−.06	−.22	−.04	.30	.22	−.07
Charged for operations	−.05	.16	.08	.09	.11	.24	.03	.49*	.21
Socio-technical interface									
User-centered involvement									
User involvement	.12	−.03	.32	−.18	.17	.27	.46*	.59*	−.41
Training/orientation									
Section head training	.58*	.56*	.52*	.12	.49*	.30	.11	.27	−.17
Department head training	.16	.01	.49*	.21	.19	.30	.44*	.01	−.05

[a] Includes only those cities with on-line capability; n = 10.

* $p < .05$

to the computing environment more consistently and more strongly than to city environment variables (tables 5.1 and 5.3). This is true with respect to both hardware and software development. Moreover, socio-technical interface policies, which were unrelated to city environment in table 5.1, are strongly related to computing environment in table 5.3. Policies for dealing with socio-technical interface tend to be present in the more developed computing environments. This trend is broken with the structural arrangement policies, which tend not to be associated with computing environment in table 5.3. Overall, computing policies, especially software and hardware development policies, are related to computing environment.

The OECD cities show similar patterns of association between the computing policies and the computing environment. Technological development policies are associated with the computing environment (table 5.4). Both advanced software and development and hardware development are moderately associated with an advanced computing environment. Second, and to a lesser extent, the socio-technical interface policies of user involvement and user training also are associated with an advanced computing environment. As expected, the OECD cities also show some dissimilarities to the URBIS cities in the area of structural arrangements. Local computing installations and local policy boards are associated with more advanced computing environments, whereas regional computing installations tend to be associated with less advanced computing environments.

Summary

The foregoing analyses suggest that policies for the management of computing are somewhat independent of the city environment. Computing policies appear to be manipulable variables that are not bound by the size of the city or its budget. The relationships that we found between computing policies and city size appear to be an artifact of the year EDP began in the city. That is, larger cities tended to be among the first to adopt computing and consequently have more experience with computing and have more highly developed computing environments. While management policies are independent of the city environment, the analyses indicate that policies are related to the computing environment and its level of development. In particular, advanced technological development policies and socio-technical interface policies are more likely to be present in the more highly developed computing environments. However, the structural arrangements for computing are not associated with the level of development in the computing environment.

These findings have implications for our further analysis: first, the relationship we found between computing environment and city environment may bear on benefits and problems from computing; second, the association of centralized structural arrangements with the city environment, found in the OECD cities, will need to be considered in our comparisons of the URBIS and the OECD cities.

The next chapter raises the central question of our analysis: Do the computing environment and management policies explain the variance in levels of benefits and problems from computing found in the URBIS and OECD cities?

CHAPTER SIX
CONTINGENCIES IN THE MANAGEMENT OF COMPUTING

As NOTED in the previous chapter, policies for the management of computing have long been considered necessary to effective implementation of the technology. Specifically, it has been predicted that policies for advanced technological development, controlled decentralization of decision making, explicit charging for services, and increased user involvement would reduce the problems and increase the benefits of computing. Moreover, experienced organizations, those that have been using computing for some time, are expected to have policies that better allow them to cope with its problems and increase its benefits. These advanced policy and computing environments are expected to have evolved toward a state of "maturity" in which problems are mitigated and benefits substantial (Gibson and Nolan 1974; Nolan 1973a, 1977a, 1979).

Findings presented in earlier chapters indicate that the benefits and problems of computing are spread unevenly over the cities studied. This variation is the concern of this chapter. The chapter presents the results of four analyses.[1] First, we analyze statistical associations among policies for computing (technological development, structural arrangements, and socio-technical interface), environments (computing and city environments), and computing benefits. Next, we analyze the relationship among policies, environments, and computing problems. Third, we examine a special case of the influence of the city environment variable, city size, on the associations between policy and computing environment, problems, and benefits. Finally, we analyze the relationship between computing benefits and computing problems in URBIS and OECD cities.[2]

These four analyses are synthesized in a general discussion of the interrelationships among policy, environment, benefits, and problems. The chapter ends with a conclusion drawing these summarized findings together into a profile from which we can build a theory of the dynamics of computing presented in chapter 7.

Policies, Environment, and Computing Benefits

The findings presented in chapter 3 indicate that computing has generally had a positive effect within the cities. It brings improvements in speed of operations and data accuracy. Although it does not usually bring staff or cost reductions, it can bring cost avoidance by reducing the need for new hires. Further, computing generally improves service delivery effectiveness. The benefit of computing for management and planning is weaker, but still evident. Computing brings benefits by increasing managerial control over staff and by providing information for making daily decisions. Its benefits for managerial planning have been limited, but computing has helped in community planning, especially in the identification of problems. Overall, these benefits of computing on efficiency and service delivery, and on management and planning, are the kinds of benefits predicted in the literature. But these benefits are neither overwhelming in their presence nor uniform in their distribution among the cities.

In order to analyze the relationships between benefits and computing policies and environment variables, we developed summary indices for the benefit variables. The indices cover essentially the same broad categories of computing benefits discussed previously in chapter 3, but their specification has been modified somewhat because preliminary analysis indicated that certain variables were intercorrelated.[3] Thus, we classified computing benefits into seven areas as follows:

Speed and accuracy: the most basic efficiency benefits of computers, i.e., speeding up data handling operations and reducing errors once data are properly entered into the automated system.

Cost and staff savings: secondary benefits that result from basic efficiency benefits, through reductions in actual direct costs of processing data, or through reductions in staff time needed to carry out tasks dependent on data processing.

Service delivery effectiveness: benefits from the enabling of government to deliver new services or improved services.

Management control of staff: improved ability of manager to control operations, primarily through increased ability to monitor and evaluate the performance of their staffs and subunits.

Management decision making: improvements resulting from increased availability of decision-relevant data for managers, and from special analytical capability for short-run decisions.

Management planning: improvements from new or better quality data, plus analytical power to simulate possible outcomes of alternative plans, increasing the ability to make short- and long-run organizational plans.

Community planning: improvements from data management and analytical capabilities that facilitate planning for community development or redevelopment.

The relationships of these benefits with computing policies and environment were analyzed using Pearson correlation analysis. The results of this analysis are shown in table 6.1 for URBIS and table 6.2 for OECD. The two will be discussed separately.

URBIS CITIES

At the most general level, our analysis in table 6.1 indicates that computing policy is associated with a broader range of benefits than are the computing environment and the city environment variables in the URBIS cities. Computing policies have some association with six of the seven categories of benefits, whereas computing en-

Table 6.1 PEARSON CORRELATIONS OF COMPUTING BENEFITS WITH POLICY AND ENVIRONMENTAL CHARACTERISTICS OF URBIS CITIES (N = 40)

	Computing Benefits						
	Speed/ accuracy	Cost/ staff savings	Service delivery effec- tiveness	Management control of staff	Management decision- making	Management planning	Community planning
MANAGEMENT POLICY							
Technological development							
Software							
Degree of data linkage	.06	.16	.26	.29*	-.05	.38*	.31*
Degree of report sophistication	-.17	-.13	-.07	.47*	.03	.15	.47*
Total applications in development	-.02	-.10	.26	.26	.04	.18	.34*
Total applications planned	.27*	-.04	.07	-.05	-.25	-.07	.03
Change in development priorities	.22	.05	.14	-.12	.06	-.08	-.22
Hardware							
On-line capability	.11	.03	.23	.11	.21	.30*	.21
Number of terminals[a]	-.20	-.23	-.10	.02	-.34*	.13	.52*
Multiprogramming used	.15	.10	.29*	.08	.12	.35*	.26
Hardware upgrading	.01	-.15	.10	.32*	.01	.04	.16
Structural arrangements							
Technology management							
Centralization	.36*	-.12	.14	-.07	-.09	-.24	-.03
Recent reorganization	.07	-.12	.16	.11	.06	.01	.22

Decisionmaking						
Decentralized control of priorities	−.19	.04	.07	.07	−.26	.08	.25
Policy board	−.21	−.01	.06	−.05	.18	.23	−.20
Board influence in applications[b]	−.19	.03	.09	.00	−.07	−.21	.34
Board influence in management[b]	−.16	−.13	.09	−.53*	.04	−.08	.05
Chief executive involvement	−.04	−.15	−.13	−.29*	−.04	−.21	−.04
Department head involvement	.00	.04	.11	−.01	−.29*	.08	.29*
Charging policy						
Charged for use	−.07	.12	.19	−.19	−.20	−.18	−.02
Socio-technical interface						
User-centered involvement						
User involvement in design	.18	−.04	−.02	.26	.14	.08	.11
EDP staffing assignment						
Programmers assigned by departments to EDP	.00	.06	.12	.20	.32*	.22	.15
Programmers assigned by EDP to departments	.16	−.25	−.15	.18	.01	.05	.26
Training						
User training	.02	−.02	−.02	.28*	−.03	.35*	.43*
Department head training	−.01	−.25	−.05	.01	.00	−.02	.23
COMPUTING ENVIRONMENT						
Resource dedication						
EDP budget per capita	−.23	−.16	−.06	.17	−.08	.40*	.41*
Percent EDP budget of total government budget	−.24	−.11	.02	.06	.16	−.06	−.09

Table 6.1 cont.

	Computing Benefits						
	Speed/ accuracy	Cost/ staff savings	Service delivery effec- tiveness	Management control of staff	Management decision- making	Management planning	Community planning
Total EDP staff	-.21	-.07	.06	.24	.08	.34*	.46*
Technology							
Degree of automation	-.09	-.14	-.01	.22	-.05	.30*	.56*
Degree of functional automation	-.20	-.07	-.04	.39*	.08	.53*	.60*
Total core capacity	-.15	-.19	-.11	-.01	-.10	.28*	.28*
Total clock hours per week	-.30*	-.16	-.01	.05	.24	.24	.22
Experience with computing							
Year EDP began	.32*	.11	.13	-.28*	-.18	-.30*	-.25
CITY ENVIRONMENT							
Size of city	-.27*	-.03	-.10	.27*	.17	.36*	.54*
Size of government budget	-.21	-.05	-.14	.22	.03	.29*	.52*

[a] Includes only those cities with on-line capability; n = 27.
[b] Includes only those cities with a policy board; n = 16.
* p < .05

vironment and city environment are each associated with only four categories of benefits. However, both policies and environments tend to be associated most frequently with benefits resulting from more advanced applications of computing, and not with those resulting from the more basic applications of computing. That is, they tend to be associated with benefits in the areas of management control, management planning, community planning, and, to a lesser extent, management decision making; and they tend to show fewer relationships with speed and accuracy and service delivery effectiveness and none with cost/staff savings. Given that over four-fifths of the cities have not experienced any cost/staff savings (chapter 3), it is not surprising that there are no associations with those benefits.

Among the general areas of computing policies, technological development is correlated with a wider range of benefits than are either structural arrangements or socio-technical interface policies. Specifically, policies for advanced technological development are frequently related to benefits in the areas of management control, management planning, and community planning—the areas that result from more advanced applications of computing. These policies are related also, though to a much lesser extent, to benefits in the areas of speed and accuracy and service delivery effectiveness. Moreover, it is those technological policies that reflect the actual implementation of advanced technology, as represented by the degree of data linkage or report sophistication or on-line capability—as opposed to the intention to implement, as represented by the number of applications planned—that associate with the benefits from more advanced computing applications.

Structural arrangements and the socio-technical interface do not frequently associate with benefits, but where they do, they associate mainly with benefits that result from sophisticated applications in management and planning. The exception is centralization policy, which correlates with speed and accuracy benefits. The socio-technical interface policies of user training and assignment of programmers by user departments tend to be positively and consistently related to benefits in management and planning. But policies for structural arrangements are sporadic and mixed in their relation to benefits. For example, both policy board influence in EDP management and chief executive involvement are negatively related to management control benefits, and they are related to only that one benefit area, whereas department head involvement in EDP is positively related to community planning but negatively related to management decision-making.

In contrast to computing policy, computing environment variables tend to be associated with a narrow range of benefits. In particular, more advanced computing environments are mostly associated with benefits in the areas of management planning and community planning. Interestingly, greater experience with computing is associated with benefits in the areas of management planning while less experience with computing is associated with speed and accuracy benefits. This probably reflects the fact that cities with less experience in computing might be more sensitive to speed and accuracy benefits from automation in comparison to their previously manual operations, and also that such cities have not yet developed advanced applications which might produce management and planning benefits.

City environment parallels the relationships found between computing environment and benefits, especially in the relationship between experience with computing and benefits. Larger cities tend to have greater benefits in the areas of management and planning, whereas smaller cities tend to have greater benefits in the area of speed and accuracy.

OECD CITIES

The relationships of policies and environments with benefits in the OECD cities, shown in table 6.2,[4] are similar to those found in the URBIS cities.[5] Computing policy is associated with a broader range of benefits than is computing environment or city environment; the associations of policies and environments with benefits most frequently occur in the areas of management and planning; policies for advanced technological development are more frequently associated with benefits than are policies for structural arrangements or socio-technical interface; and advanced computing environments are associated with higher levels of benefits in the areas of management and planning.

Table 6.2 PEARSON CORRELATIONS OF COMPUTING BENEFITS WITH POLICY AND ENVIRONMENTAL CHARACTERISTICS OF OECD CITIES (N = 16)

	Computing Benefits						
	Speed/ accuracy	Cost/ staff savings	Service delivery effectiveness	Management control of staff	Management decision-making	Management planning	Community planning
MANAGEMENT POLICY							
Technological development							
Software							
Degree of data linkage	.32	.54*	.32	.18	.20	.72*	.26
Degree of report sophistication	.16	.59*	.05	.14	.17	.59*	.72*
Degree of sophistication of applications	.20	.49*	.27	.40	.27	.81*	.34
Total applications planned	.49*	.50*	.02	-.12	.32	.12	.14
Total applications to be modified	.32	.44	.04	.15	.32	.42	.35
Hardware							
On-line capability	-.26	-.21	.40	.07	.18	.24	.06
Number of terminals[a]	-.52	.21	-.07	-.04	-.31	.33	.06
Multiprogramming used	-.24	.11	.24	-.04	-.50*	.00	-.18
Structural arrangement							
Technology management							
Centralization	-.22	-.02	-.42	-.30	.17	-.42*	.13
Decisionmaking							
Decentralized control of priorities	-.33	-.37	-.22	-.49*	.04	-.23	-.09

Computing Benefits

	Speed/ accuracy	Cost/ staff savings	Service delivery effec- tiveness	Management control of staff	Management decision- making	Management planning	Community planning
Local policy board	-.25	.07	.04	.17	.12	.43*	.38
Chief executive involve- ment	.09	-.13	-.06	-.03	-.29	.00	.00
Department head involve- ment	.25	.02	-.12	-.19	.04	-.12	.19
Charging policy							
Charged for development	.29	.03	.10	-.08	-.18	-.12	-.21
Charged for use	.39	-.14	.48*	.15	.04	.04	.04
Socio-technical interface							
User-centered involvement							
User involvement in design	-.14	.08	.09	-.12	-.13	.08	-.02
Training/orientation							
Section head training	-.16	.11	-.09	.25	.30	.69*	.30
Department head training	-.43*	.04	.00	-.22	-.07	.13	-.25

COMPUTING ENVIRONMENT

Resource dedication						
EDP budget per capita	-.03	.09	.20	.10	.26	.40	.32
Percent EDP budget of total government budget	.32	.33	.22	.56*	-.23	.52*	-.17
Total EDP staff	-.56*	.03	.02	-.03	-.07	.47*	.13
Percent increase needed in 1976	-.27	-.82*	-.12	-.08	.12	-.36	-.35
Technology						
Degree of automation	-.01	.40	.33	.18	.20	.75*	.51*
Degree of functional automation	-.14	.33	.39	.00	.11	.60*	.33
Total core capacity	-.55*	.05	-.05	-.17	-.31	.25	.03
Percent computer used/week	-.21	.31	.32	-.09	.21	.50*	.46*
Experience with computing						
Year EDP began	.10	-.55*	.00	.14	-.07	-.56*	-.46*
CITY ENVIRONMENT						
Size of city	-.53*	.00	-.18	-.26	-.30	.29	.07
Size of government budget	-.59*	-.18	-.16	-.19	-.30	.02	-.02

[a] Only those cities with on-line capability were included, n = 9.

$*p < .05$

However, we can observe important differences in the OECD cities. First, policies for advanced technological development are associated with benefits in the area of cost/staff savings, whereas there were no such associations in the URBIS cities. Second, local control of EDP (as measured by centralization and local policy board) is related to benefits in the area of management planning but not community planning. However, the relative frequency and strength of local control associations with management planning is muchh less than that of various computing environment measures. Thus, benefits in the area of management planning might be more related to developmental stages of the computing environment than to the degree of local control (versus regional control) over data processing. Third, city environment as measured by size is related to speed and accuracy benefits, but not to other benefit areas. Smaller cities tend to have greater benefits in the area of speed and accuracy, whereas there tends to be no difference between smaller and larger cities in the other areas of benefits.

Policies, Environment, and Computing Problems

In chapter 4, we observed that computing problems are ubiquitous in both OECD and URBIS cities, although in most cases they are not overwhelming. We classified computing problems into six areas:

Staff problems: concerning the interface between the computing staff and user staff, and focusing primarily on inadequacies of the computing staff to deal with the needs of users.

Technical problems: primarily related to technical unreliability of the hardware and software systems in day-to-day operations.

Responsiveness problems: related to inflexibility of the city's computing resources in accommodating needs and changes of the user environment.

Resource problems: due to lack of sufficient monetary, staff, hardware, data, or other computing resources necessary to a successful computing operation.

Support problems: concerning unwillingness of the city organization to accept and support computing activity.

Knowledge problems: related to the lack of user understanding of the abilities and constraints of computing and the computing staff (not measured in URBIS cities).

As summarized in that chapter, it was found that the most serious problems in URBIS cities were related to EDP staff-user interactions, followed by technology problems, responsiveness problems, and resource problems. All these categories of problems were experienced in half or more of the cities. The fewest problems were reported in the area of support for computing. Despite other problems, local government officials in URBIS cities appear to be highly supportive of computing.

In OECD cities, problems appeared in a different mix. The most significant were resource problems (especially related to the high cost of computing) and responsiveness problems. These were experienced by one-half or more of the cities. Problems of EDP staff and of support for computing were reported by about one-third of the cities. The lowest classes of problems in OECD cities were technical and institutional, experienced in only about 10 percent of the cities.

Taken together, problems that seem serious in both URBIS and OECD cities relate to resources and responsiveness, and appear in over half of the cities in each group. URBIS cities show somewhat higher levels of problems than do OECD cities, but as noted earlier, given the differences in data collection methodology this difference might be accounted for by measurement alone. Responses to the URBIS problems were indicated on a pre-developed list, while the OECD problems were self-reported in an open-ended format, so it is possible that OECD cities under-reported their levels of problems. However, there is also the possibility that the URBIS cities, which on the average are somewhat more developed in use of the technology, do actually experience more problems. Unfortunately, it is impossible to definitively account for this difference given the data available.

Our method for examing the interaction of computing problems with policy and environment variables is essentially the same as that used in assessing the interaction of policy and environment with computing benefits. Pearson correlation analysis assesses the interrelation between each of the environment and policy variables and the full set of problems. Unlike the benefits list, the problems list remains the same as that used earlier (chapter 4). Again, we separate the discussion of URBIS and OECD findings, which are presented in tables 6.3 and 6.4.

URBIS CITIES

The analysis in table 6.3 indicates that computing policies, computing environment, and city environment are all significantly related to computing problems in the URBIS cities. Only support problems are not associated with policy and environment variables. We believe this exception is attributable to the high degree of support for computing among users, top management, and others in all of the URBIS cities.

Table 6.3 PEARSON CORRELATIONS OF COMPUTING PROBLEMS WITH POLICY AND ENVIRONMENTAL CHARACTERISTICS OF URBIS CITIES (N = 40)

	Computing Problems				
	Staff	Technical	Respon- siveness	Resource	Support
MANAGEMENT POLICY					
Technological development					
Software					
Degree of data linkage	.14	.06	−.01	.20	−.17
Degree of report sophistication	.40*	.19	.33*	.42*	.15
Total applications in development	.11	.35*	.16	.50*	.21
Total applications planned	.11	−.19	−.04	−.24	−.19
Change in development priorities	.07	.08	−.28	−.02	−.04
Hardware					
On-line capability	.16	.05	−.04	.06	.02
Number of terminals[a]	.30	.29*	.38*	.63*	.13
Multiprogramming used	.10	.04	−.07	.09	−.12
Hardware upgrading	.15	.37*	.14	.41*	.08
Structural arrangements					
Technology management					
Centralization	.08	.01	−.14	.23	−.04
Recent reorganization	.24	.38*	.23	.51*	.15
Decision making					
Decentralized control of priorities	.17	.20	.07	.23	.00

Table 6.3 cont.

	Computing Problems				
	Staff	Technical	Respon-siveness	Resource	Support
Policy board	.36*	.43*	.33*	.28*	.17
Board influence in appli-					
cations[a]	.49*	−.16	.08	−.09	−.14
Board influence in management[b]	.21	.02	−.17	.07	.00
Chief executive involvement	.12	.01	.09	.00	−.24
Department head involvement	.14	.40*	.17	.34*	.12
Charging policy					
Charged for use	.14	.00	.07	.20	.08
Socio-technical interface					
User-centered involvement					
User involvement in design	.38*	.27*	.13	.04	.13
EDP staffing assignment					
Programmers assigned by					
departments to EDP	.19	.36*	.12	.18	.24
Programmers assigned by					
EDP to departments	.01	−.27*	.12	.08	−.30*
Training					
User training	.36*	.12	.22	.30*	−.16
Department head training	.45*	.23	.19	.36*	.00
COMPUTING ENVIRONMENT					
Resource dedication					
EDP budget per capita	.21	.29*	.36*	.41*	.05
Percent EDP budget of total					
government budget	.04	.28*	.02	.18	.08
Total EDP staff	.20	.28*	.36*	.46*	.05
Technology					
Degree of automation	.30*	.14	.23	.39*	.00
Degree of functional					
automation	.27*	.17	.15	.21	.07
Total core capacity	.18	.33*	.34*	.53*	.04
Total clock hours per week	.34*	.42*	.35*	.53*	.14
Experience with computing					
Year EDP began	−.36*	−.33*	−.18	−.25	−.12
CITY ENVIRONMENT					
Size of city	.21	.34*	.32*	.31*	.19
Size of government budget	.14	.17	.33*	.25	.12

[a] Includes only those cities with on-line capability; n = 27.
[b] Includes only those cities with a policy board; n = 16.
*p < .05

The overall relationship between management policies and computing problems is surprising. Policies do not uniformly associate with the elimination of problems as might be expected, but, instead, many of the policies are positively associated with the presence of staff, technical, responsiveness, and resource problems. Specifically, advanced technological development is strongly related to greater problems, in direct contradiction to the common assertion that adoption of more powerful and sophisticated technology buys relief from computing problems. The degree of report sophistication, total number of applications in development, number of terminals, and recent hardware upgrading—all indicators of policy aiming towards advanced technological development—are positively and often significantly related to computing problems. Only one development policy— recent change in development priorities—is significantly related to fewer problems and, in this case, only to responsiveness problems. This relationship holds for structural arrangements and the sociotechnical interface policies as well. This unexpected finding undermines the assumption that adoption of "progressive" management policies will diminish problems with computing. For example, management policies for EDP policy boards (use of policy board and board influence in applications), participation of users in computing (department head involvement and user involvement in design), and provision of user training (user training and department head training) are positively related to the presence of computing problems in the URBIS cities. Only one policy—programmers assigned by EDP to departments—is related in the direction that one might expect, namely to the absence of technical and support problems.

Computing environment is also strongly related to the presence of problems. Computing environments that are characterized by high dedication of more resources, adoption of more technology, and longer experience with computing have more problems with staff, technology, responsiveness, and resources.

Finally, city environment is significantly related to computing problems in that larger cities tend to have more technical, responsiveness, and resource problems than do smaller cities.

OECD CITIES

Analysis of the OECD cities summarized in table 6.4 shows that management policies, computing environment, and city environment are all significantly related to computing problems. However, the pattern of these relationships in the OECD cities is critically different from that in the URBIS cities. The relationships are split systematically, with uniformly positive relationships for resource and technical problems and with nearly uniform negative relationships for responsiveness, staff, and support problems. Moreover, in contrast to the consistency among relationships in the URBIS cities, the OECD cities show inconsistent relationships between specific policies and environmental factors and support problems. The only significant relationship between policies and environments and the unique OECD category of knowledge problems is for centralization policy, which is strongly and positively associated.

In the area of management policies, advanced technological development (hardware and software development) policies are associated with the presence of resource and technical problems and with the absence of responsiveness, staff, and support problems. In particular, the sophistication of computer reports and applications and the volume of applications to be modified or developed are associated with greater resource and technical problems, whereas the sophistication of data bases (degree of data linkage), and applications, and computer hardware are associated with fewer responsiveness, staff, and support problems.

The pattern of relationships for structural arrangements is somewhat more complex than for technological development. Cities that participate in regionally controlled EDP facilities (centralization) have problems with responsiveness, staff, and knowledge, whereas cities with locally controlled facilities do not. Moreover, cities with decentralized decision-making structures (local policy board, chief executive involvement in EDP decision making, and department head involvement in EDP decision making) have more resource problems and fewer problems with responsiveness, staff, and support. Cities that charge for computer use have fewer responsiveness problems than those that do not.

Table 6.4 PEARSON CORRELATIONS OF COMPUTING PROBLEMS WITH POLICY AND ENVIRONMENTAL CHARACTERISTICS OF OECD CITIES (N = 16)

			Computing Problems			
	Resource	Tech-nical	Respon-siveness	Staff	Support	Knowledge
MANAGEMENT POLICY						
Technological development						
Software						
Degree of data linkage	.28	.24	−.43*	−.49*	−.42*	−.10
Degree of report sophistication	.17	.67*	.23	−.22	−.33	.30
Degree of sophistication of applications	.41*	.30	.15	−.55*	−.27	−.19
Total applications planned	−.23	.44*	.15	−.11	−.10	.23
Total applications to be modified	−.19	.51*	.11	−.30	−.33	.28
Hardware						
On-line capability	.00	.20	.08	.03	−.46*	−.22
Number of terminals[a]	.17	.29	−.39	−.58*	−.46*	−.36
Multiprogramming	.19	−.20	−.23	.21	−.21	−.04
Structural arrangements						
Technology management						
Centralization	−.13	−.01	.67*	.69*	.17*	.52*
Decision making						
Decentralized control of priorities	−.28	.06	−.08	.19	.10	.24
Local policy board	.58*	.16	−.14	−.34	−.42*	−.12
Chief executive involvement	.03	−.26	−.40	−.67*	.07	−.12
Department head involvement	.23	−.15	−.60*	−.07	.08	−.21
Charging policy						
Charged for development	−.33	−.05	−.33	−.37	−.37	.00
Charged for use	−.13	.00	−.42*	−.02	−.26	−.24
Socio-technical interface						
User-centered involvement						
User involvement in design	−.31	.11	−.38	−.44*	−.46*	.13
Training/orientation						
Section head training	.54*	.17	−.02	−.16	.09	−.12
Department head training	.58*	−.19	.01	−.10	−.30	−.28
COMPUTING ENVIRONMENT						
Resource dedication						
EDP budget per capita	.25	−.11	.12	−.44*	−.27	.06

	Computing Problems					
	Resource	Tech-nical	Respon-siveness	Staff	Support	Knowledge
Percent EDP budget of total government budget	.13	−.09	−.60*	−.33	.27	−.42
Total EDP staff	.30	.28	−.12	−.49*	−.56*	−.23
Percent increase needed in 1976	.37	−.38	−.16	.25	.05	−.27
Technology						
Degree of automation	.45*	.33	−.43*	−.32	−.29	−.15
Degree of functional automation	.37	.33	−.49*	−.19	−.46*	−.17
Total core capacity	.00	.17	−.14	−.40*	−.43*	−.14
Percent computer use	.08	.60*	.02	−.10	−.71*	.20
Experience with computing						
Year EDP began	.23	−.30	−.18	.47*	.20	−.39
CITY ENVIRONMENT						
Size of city	.01	.31	−.36	−.47*	−.37	−.01
Size of government budget	.19	.19	−.11	−.38	−.50*	−.03

[a] Only cities with on-line capability were included; n = 9.
*p < .05

Socio-technical interface policies are less frequently associated with computing problems than are policies for technological development or structural arrangements in OECD cities. Participative policies (user involvement in design) are negatively associated with staff and support problems whereas training and orientation policies (section head training and department head training) are associated with resource problems.

Computing environment exhibits the same general pattern of relationships as found in management policies. More developed computing environments (high degree of automation and high percent of computer use) tend to have resource and technical problems, whereas less developed computing environments (low automation, low functional automation, low core capacity, low percent of computer use, and low experience) tend to have responsiveness, staff, and support problems.

Finally, city environment is related to computing problems, but not significantly for most problems. Generally, smaller cities tend to have staff and support problems, but there is no significant relationship of larger cities to problems.

The Influence of City Size

Throughout this study, and in many other studies of organizations, size has been shown to be an important contingent variable for understanding differences in the ways organizations are structured and the ways they behave (Weber 1947; Blau and Schoenherr 1971; Meyer 1972; Child 1972; Kimberly 1976). Our earlier analysis in chapter 5 indicated that city size is closely related to computing environments but less related to computing policies. The analyses in this chapter also indicate that city size is associated with computing benefits and problems. It is important to examine which relationships among environments, policies, benefits, and problems change as a function of city size. To do so, we computed the partial correlations for these relationships, controlling for city size. The results of that analysis are presented in tables 6.5 through 6.8. The structure of these tables parallels tables 6.1 through 6.4 discussed above.

BENEFITS AND CITY SIZE

The effects of city size on the relationships of policy and environment with computing benefits differ in the URBIS and OECD cities. When city size is controlled, the computing environment in URBIS cities takes on less importance than policy in relation to computing benefits (table 6.5). Most of the previously discussed relationships between policy and benefits remain, and, indeed, some are heightened. But only two major relationships between computing environment and computing benefits remain. A high degree of functional automation continues to be related to benefits in the areas of management control, management planning, and community planning. And proportionately higher EDP spending (high EDP budget per capita) is related to management and community planning benefits, whereas proportionately lower EDP spending (low EDP budget per capita and low percent EDP budget to the total government budget) is related to speed

Table 6.5 PARTIAL CORRELATIONS OF COMPUTING BENEFITS WITH POLICY AND ENVIRONMENTAL CHARACTERISTICS OF URBIS CITIES CONTROLLING FOR CITY SIZE (N = 40)

	Computing Benefits						
	Speed/ accuracy	Cost/ staff savings	Service delivery effec- tiveness	Management control of staff	Management decision making	Management planning	Community planning
MANAGEMENT POLICY							
Technological development							
Software							
Degree of data linkage	.07	.16	.26	.30*	-.05	.40*	.36*
Degree of report sophistication	-.11	-.12	-.05	.44*	-.01	.07	.42*
Total applications in development	.08	-.09	.32*	.18	-.02	.08	.20
Total applications planned	.27*	-.05	.07	-.04	-.25	-.05	.08
Change in development priorities	.21	.05	.14	-.11	.07	-.07	-.23
Hardware							
On-line capability	.20	.04	.27*	.03	.17	.22	.07
Number of terminals[a]	-.12	-.24	-.07	-.08	-.43*	.01	.42*
Multiprogramming used	.25	.11	.34*	.01	.07	.28*	.13
Hardware upgrading	.09	-.15	.13	.27*	-.04	-.06	.02
Structural arrangements							
Technology management							
Centralization	.31	-.14	.12	.00	-.05	-.17	.13
Recent reorganization	.12	-.12	.19	.06	.03	-.06	.14

Computing Benefits

	Speed/accuracy	Cost/staff savings	Service delivery effectiveness	Management control of staff	Management decision making	Management planning	Community planning
Decision making							
Decentralized control of priorities	-.16	.05	.09	.03	-.29*	.02	.20
Policy board	-.21	-.01	.06	-.07	.18	.23	-.15
Board influence in applications[b]	-.25	.02	.07	.05	-.04	-.16	.53*
Board influence in management[b]	-.14	-.13	.10	-.57*	.03	-.11	.01
Chief executive involvement	-.07	-.16	-.15	-.27*	-.02	-.18	.03
Department head involvement	.03	.05	.12	-.04	-.31*	.05	.28*
Charging policy							
Charged for use	-.09	.12	.19	-.18	-.19	-.17	-.01
Socio-technical interface							
User-centered involvement							
User involvement in design	.24	-.03	.00	.23	.12	.03	.03

EDP staffing assignment							
Programmers assigned by departments to EDP	.11	.08	.17	.12	.28*	.11	−.05
Programmers assigned by EDP to departments	.20	−.25	−.14	.16	−.01	.01	.23
Training							
User training	.11	−.01	.02	.21	−.09	.27*	.33*
Department head training	.00	−.24	−.04	.00	−.01	−.03	.25
COMPUTING ENVIRONMENT							
Resource dedication							
EDP budget per capita	−.17	−.15	−.03	.10	−.13	.34*	.32*
Percent EDP budget of total government budget	−.27*	−.11	.01	.08	.18	−.05	−.07
Total EDP staff	−.01	−.07	.03	.06	−.07	.14	.12
Technology							
Degree of automation	.02	−.13	.03	.13	−.13	.19	.45*
Degree of functional automation	−.06	−.06	.02	.31*	−.01	.43*	.44*
Total core capacity	−.08	−.19	−.08	−.10	−.16	.20	.15
Total clock hours per week	−.21	−.17	.05	−.09	.19	.09	−.04
Experience with computing							
Year EDP began	.22	.11	.09	−.18	−.12	−.15	.02

[a] Includes only those cities with on-line capability; n = 27.
[b] Includes only those cities with a policy board; n = 16.
* $p < .05$

Table 6.6 PARTIAL CORRELATIONS OF COMPUTING BENEFITS WITH POLICY AND ENVIRONMENTAL CHARACTERISTICS OF OECD CITIES CONTROLLING FOR CITY SIZE (N=16)

	Computing Benefits						
	Speed/ accuracy	Cost/ staff savings	Service delivery effectiveness	Management control of staff	Management decision making	Management planning	Community planning
MANAGEMENT POLICY							
Technological development							
Software							
Degree of data linkage	.59*	.56*	.39	.28	.32	.69*	.25
Degree of report sophistication	.39	.62*	.11	.24	.28	.55*	.73*
Degree of sophistication of applications	.36	.49*	.31	.48*	.35	.80*	.33
Total applications planned	.35	.55*	-.07	-.26	.23	.27	.19
Total applications to be modified	.35	.44	.04	.14	.32	.45	.36
Hardware							
On-line capability	-.11	-.22	.50*	.17	.32	.15	.04
Number of terminals[a]	-.22	.32	.11	.25	-.13	.18	.02
Multiprogramming used	-.10	.12	.31	.04	-.45	-.09	-.21
Structural arrangements							
Technology management							
Centralization	-.72*	-.02	-.64*	-.55*	.00	-.33	.21
Decision making							
Decentralized control of priorities	-.34	-.37	-.21	-.49*	.07	-.27	-.09
Local policy board	.10	.08	.19	.43	.40	.34	.42
Chief executive involvement	.42	-.15	.02	.10	-.18	-.15	-.04

Department head involvement	.36	.02	-.10	-.17	.08	-.16	-.20
Charging policy							
Charged for development	.45	.04	.14	-.04	-.14	-.18	-.22
Charged for use	.50*	-.14	.50*	.17	.07	-.06	.04
Socio-technical interface							
User-centered involvement							
User involvement in design	.13	.09	.20	.00	.01	-.07	-.06
Training/orientation							
Section head training	-.02	.12	-.04	.35	.42	.66*	.29
Department head training	-.35*	.04	.05	-.16	.01	.05	-.28
COMPUTING ENVIRONMENT							
Resource dedication							
EDP budget per capita	.18	-.07	.25	.47*	.43	.50	.36
Percent EDP budget of total government budget	.46	.34	.25	.62*	-.20	.51*	-.18
Total EDP staff	-.26	.04	.33	.35	-.36	.43	.13
Percent increase needed in 1976	-.30	-.82*	-.12	-.07	.13	-.39	-.36
Technology							
Degree of automation	.27	.44	.45	.33	.37	.72*	.53*
Degree of functional automation	.14	.37	.53*	.13	.29	.55*	.34
Total core capacity	-.23	.09	.21	.10	-.11	.01	-.06
Percent computer used/week	.05	.35	.48	.04	.42	.43	.48*
Experience with computing							
Year EDP began	-.16	-.61*	-.09	.03	-.22	-.51*	-.48*

[a] Only those cities with on-line capability were included, n = 9.

* $p < .05$

Table 6.7 PARTIAL CORRELATIONS OF COMPUTING PROBLEMS WITH POLICY AND ENVIRONMENTAL CHARACTERISTICS OF URBIS CITIES CONTROLLING FOR CITY SIZE (N = 40)

	Computing Problems				
	Staff	Technical	Respon- siveness	Resource	Support
COMPUTING POLICY					
Technological development					
Software					
Degree of data linkage	.14	.06	−.01	.21	−.18
Degree of report sophistication	.37*	.12	.28*	.38*	.11
Total applications in development	.04	.27*	.06	.44*	.16
Total applications planned	.12	−.18	−.03	−.25	−.18
Change in development priorities	.08	.10	−.28*	−.01	−.03
Hardware					
On-line capability	.11	−.05	−.14	−.03	−.04
Number of terminals[a]	.25	.20	.30	.59*	.06
Multiprogramming used	.04	−.06	−.18	.00	−.19
Hardware upgrading	.10	.31*	.06	.35*	.03
Structural arrangements					
Technology management					
Centralization	.14	.11	−.07	.33*	.01
Recent reorganization	.20	.34*	.18	.48*	.12
Decision making					
Decentralized control of priorities	.15	.16	.02	.19	−.03
Policy board	.37*	.44*	.33*	.28*	.17
Board influence in applications[b]	.55*	−.11	.15	−.04	−.11
Board influence in management[b]	.20	.00	−.20	.05	−.02
Chief executive involvement	.15	.06	.14	.04	−.22
Department head involvement	.12	.39*	.15	.32*	.10
Charging policy					
Charged for use	.16	.02	.10	.23	.10
Socio-technical interface					
User-centered involvement					
User involvement in design	.36*	.24	.08	.00	.10
EDP staffing assignment					
Programmers assigned by departments to EDP	.13	.28*	.01	.08	.18
Programmers assigned by EDP to departments	−.01	−.33*	.09	.05	−.33*
Training					
User training	.32*	.01	.13	.23	−.24
Department head training	.45*	.22	.18	.36*	.01

	Computing Problems				
	Staff	Technical	Respon- siveness	Resource	Support
COMPUTING ENVIRONMENT					
Resource dedication					
EDP budget per capita	.17	.22	.29*	.36*	−.01
Percent EDP budget of total					
government budget	.05	.32	.04	.21	.10
Total EDP staff	.06	.05	.20	.36*	−.14
Technology					
Degree of automation	.24	.01	.12	.30*	. −.09
Degree of functional					
automation	.19	−.02	−.02	.06	−.05
Total core capacity	.12	.25	.27*	.48*	−.01
Total clock hours per week	.28*	.31*	.24	.46*	.06
Experience with computing					
Year EDP began	−.30*	−.20	−.04	−.11	−.02

ᵃ Includes only those cities with on-line capability; $n = 27$.
ᵇ Includes only those cities with a policy board; $n = 16$.
*$p < .05$

and accuracy benefits. Thus, the level of spending and breadth of automation are important features of the computing environment, and they are related to computing benefits in all URBIS cities regardless of size. Degree of automation, staff capacity, and computing (core) capacity are less related to benefits when size is controlled. Experience with computing is also less related to benefits when size is controlled, which corresponds to the finding in chapter 5 that size and experience with computing are strongly related.

Similar relationships are found for the OECD cities. Computing environment and management policy are related to the same areas of benefit as in table 6.2. However, the relationship of structural arrangements to benefits is strengthened. Specifically, locally controlled (versus centralized) computing facilities are related to benefits from both basic and advanced applications of computing; that is, in the areas of speed and accuracy, service delivery effectiveness, management control, and management planning. Without controlling for city size, the only relationship was with management planning.

Table 6.8 PARTIAL CORRELATIONS OF COMPUTING PROBLEMS WITH POLICY AND ENVIRONMENTAL CHARACTERISTICS OF OECD CITIES CONTROLLING FOR CITY SIZE (N = 16)

	Computing Problems					
	Resource	Tech-nical	Respon-siveness	Staff	Support	Knowledge
COMPUTING POLICY						
Technological development						
Software						
Degree of data linkage	.29	.17	−.36	−.42*	−.35*	−.10
Degree of report sophistication	.18	.64*	.37	−.10	−.25	.32
Degree of sophistication of applications	.41	.26	.24	−.53*	−.22	−.19
Total applications planned	−.25	.65*	.00	−.37	−.30	.25
Total applications to be modified	−.19	.55*	.10	−.37	−.38	.28
Hardware						
On-line capability	.00	.11	.23	.21	−.38	−.23
Number of terminals[a]	−.25	.09	−.20	−.39	−.30	−.53
Multiprogramming	.20	−.32	−.14	.41	−.11	−.04
Structural arrangements						
Technology management						
Centralization	−.16	.20	.60*	.58*	−.04	.62
Decision making						
Decentralized control of priorities	−.28	.04	−.06	.26	.14	.25
Local policy board	.73*	−.03	.10	−.09	−.27*	−.15
Chief executive involvement	.03	−.46	−.29	−.58*	.28	−.13
Department head involvement	.23	−.20	−.60*	−.02	.13	−.21
Charging policy						
Charged for development	−.34	−.11	−.30	−.33	−.34	.00
Charged for use	−.13	−.02	−.43*	.01	−.26	−.24
Socio-technical interface						
User-centered involvement						
User involvement in design	−.35	−.04	−.26	−.29*	−.36	.15
Training/orientation						
Section head training	.56*	.09	.09	−.03	.22	−.12
Department head training	.60*	−.30	.12	.03	−.22	−.29
COMPUTING ENVIRONMENT						
Resource dedication						
EDP budget per capita	.42	−.22	.27	−.31	.00	−.07

| | Computing Problems | | | | | |
	Resource	Tech-nical	Respon-siveness	Staff	Support	Knowledge
Percent EDP budget of total government budget	.13	−.14	−.60*	−.31	.34	−.42
Total EDP staff	.55*	.03	.37	−.20	−.50*	−.40
Percent increase needed in 1976	.37	−.41	−.16	−.30	.06	−.27
Technology						
Degree of automation	.49*	.24	−.33	−.16	−.17	−.16
Degree of functional automation	.41	.22	−.40	.03	−.36	−.19
Total core capacity	−.02	.19	.34	−.02	−.23	−.25
Percent computer use	.09	.55*	.23	.15	−.65*	.24
Experience with computing						
Year EDP began	.26	−.20	−.39	.34	.05	−.43*

[a] Only cities with on-line capability were included; n = 9.
*p < .05

PROBLEMS AND CITY SIZE

When city size is controlled, the computing environment becomes less related than policy to problems in the URBIS cities, and it remains equally important in the OECD cities (table 6.7). The major relationship between computing environment and problems that remain is in the area of resources, where cities with highly developed computing environments tend to have problems. In fact, the entire set of relationships between policy and environment and computing problems suggests that URBIS cities, regardless of size, are trying to cope with demands for computing services, but have too few resources to meet them.

In the OECD cities, the relationships of environment and policy with computing problems exhibit the same pattern, again regardless of city size (table 6.8). However, the relationships are much less clear than previously and there are fewer of them.

CONCLUSIONS ABOUT SIZE

As these analyses show, size does associate with benefits and problems in the use of computing, and controlling for size does alter some relationships between policy and computing environment variables and the outcome variables of benefits and problems. Size is clearly an important independent variable. The question that arises is whether size itself is a basic explanatory variable in its own right (i.e., those relationships that disappear when size is controlled for are merely manifestations of the more basic association between size and outcome), or whether size dominates these relationships because it relates consistently to certain other independent variables.

The evidence from the URBIS and OECD analysis, as well as from our reading of the case reports from the URBIS field work and the comments of interviewees in the OECD study, suggests to us that size is not a basic explanatory variable. Rather, it is artificially dominant in some relationships. The rationale for this conclusion is that those independent variables that change in association with outcomes in both URBIS (computing environment) and OECD (structural arrangements) are themselves closely but not necessarily related to size. It is reasonable to expect the computing environment in URBIS to vary as a function of size because city size and selected features of the computing environment do co-vary to a great extent. For example, the number of applications in an URBIS city associates very strongly with the size of the city. Larger cities have larger numbers of applications. This does not necessarily mean, however, that city size determines the quantity of applications. Rather, large city size is in turn associated with other variables (e.g., slack resources in budgets, economies of scale that provide opportunities for experiment, greater availability of in-house expertise), that enable the building of greater numbers of applications. Thus, it is possible that some combination of simple demand for applications (which could be a direct function of size) and these other enabling factors (that appear coincidentally with size) jointly result in greater applications development. Size is, therefore, a critical and underlying environmental variable that simultaneously creates an impetus and regulates the flow of resources for the development or lack of development of the computing environment.

Similarly, it is not surprising to find that the associations between structural arrangement policies and outcomes in the OECD cities are altered when controlling for size. Key structural arrangements, such as use of centralized (i.e., regional) computing centers as opposed to in-house computing by cities, are directly related to city size in the sample of cities included in the OECD study. While we know that cities that participate in centralized and regional consortia for computing service tend to be smaller and those with in-house computing tend to be larger, it is not clear that size determines that a city will use one or the other arrangement. Size, again, is an important summary variable, but not necessarily the underlying variable.

The objective of this analysis is to identify those independent variables, including size, that associate regularly with outcomes of computing use. We expect that some independent variables in themselves form "packages" that co-vary with one another, and hence with some outcomes, and that city size is a strong summary measure of one such package. However, because these are only associative analyses using cross-sectional data, the precise role of city size as well as the strength of that role remain subjects for further longitudinal research.

Relationships Between Benefits and Problems

Several common patterns can now be noted in the relationships among policies, environments, benefits, and problems. First, the relationships of policy and computing environment with benefits and problems are to some extent independent of the city environment as measured by city size, although the environment is an important factor.

Second, management policy and the computing environment are important in explaining relationships with benefits and problems. Generally, policy is related to a broader range of benefits and problems than is the computing environment. Yet, policy tends to show greater inconsistency in the relationships. Specifically, policies for structural arrangements, and to a lesser extent for socio-technical interface, tend to have inconsistent relationships with benefits and problems, whereas policies for technological development exhibit greater internal consistency.

Third, the computing environment exhibits two distinct patterns of relationships with benefits and problems. Highly developed computing environments tend to be related to benefits from advanced applications of computing (e.g., to benefits in the areas of management control, management planning, and community planning) and to the presence of multiple computing problems (e.g., in the areas of staff, technology, responsiveness, and resources). Less developed computing environments tend to be related to benefits from basic applications of computing (e.g., to benefits in the areas of speed and accuracy and cost/staff savings) and to no problems or to fewer problems (e.g., those related to start-up such as support or staff problems). Some additional support for these two distinct patterns of relationships is provided by factor analysis in table 6.9, which focuses on computing benefits in the URBIS cities. The table indicates that nearly three-fourths of the variation among cities is explained by two major "dimensions of benefits"—those resulting from "basic" applications of computing (speed and accuracy, cost and staff savings, service delivery effectiveness), and those resulting from "advanced" applications of computing for management (management control, management decision making) and for planning (management planning, community planning).

Fourth, computing environments and technological development policies show similar patterns of association with benefits and problems. Policies for advanced technological development and highly developed computing environments tend to be related positively to benefits from advanced computing applications and to problems that accompany such applications.

Table 6.9 FACTOR LOADINGS FOR DIMENSIONS OF BENEFITS

		Advanced	
Benefit Variables	Basic	Management	Planning
Speed and accuracy	.51*	−.19	−.16
Cost and staff savings	.62*	.02	.06
Service delivery effectiveness	.75*	.01	.08
Management control	−.08	.55*	.28
Management decision making	−.07	.90*	−.16*
Management planning	.17	.34	.59*
Community planning	−.09	−.11	.85*
Percent variance explained	25%	27%	19%

*p < .05

These latter findings suggest that there might be important relationships between benefits and problems. Based on conventional wisdom, one would expect negative correlations—that, in general, computing benefits would be highest in cities with the lowest levels of computing problems. To determine whether this hypothesis is confirmed, we analyze these correlations, first in URBIS and then in OECD cities.

BENEFITS AND PROBLEMS IN URBIS CITIES

Overall, the expectation that high benefits would be associated with low problems is not supported in the URBIS cities (table 6.10). Rather, the associations are systematically split between benefits resulting from either basic or sophisticated applications of computing. The benefits resulting from basic computing applications are associated with low problems in the benefit areas of speed and accuracy improvement and cost and staff savings and, to a lesser extent, service delivery effectiveness. In contrast, the benefits resulting

Table 6.10 PEARSON CORRELATIONS OF COMPUTING BENEFITS AND COMPUTING PROBLEMS IN THE URBIS CITIES (N = 40)

Computing Benefits	Computing Problems				
	Staff	Technical	Responsiveness	Resource	Support
Speed and accuracy	−.30*	−.53*	−.53*	−.20	−.24
Cost and staff savings	−.30*	−.28*	−.30*	−.08	−.06
Service delivery effectiveness	−.15	−.15	−.41*	.04	.08
Management control	.31*	.26*	.26*	.07	.24
Management decision making	.20	.11	.10	−.17	.20
Management planning	.09	.09	.09	.14	−.01
Community planning	.22	.08	.27*	.46*	.06

*p < .05

from more sophisticated applications tend to associate either with higher levels of problems (staff, technical, responsiveness, and resource problems), as in the case of management control and community planning benefits, or not much at all, as in the case of management decision making and management planning benefits.

These findings correspond to our earlier findings on the relationships among policies, benefits, and problems. The question of relationships between computing problems and benefits depends on which benefit areas are examined. Benefits stemming from less advanced applications of computing are associated with lower level problems; benefits from more advanced applications are associated with greater problems. Although these findings are at variance with conventional wisdom, they seem highly plausible on examination. We can assume that less advanced cities have automated recently and have automated only basic applications. They consequently could not have achieved benefits associated with more advanced applications. Such cities also would not be expected to have many computing problems because of their simpler applications and environments. On the other hand, more advanced cities adopted earlier and have more advanced applications operational. They exhibit the kinds of benefits that could be present only in sites with such applications. But these advanced cities also show greater levels of computing problems because the complexity of their applications and environments engenders more problems. Seen from this perspective, the associations found between benefits from advanced applications and problems and between benefits from basic applications and low levels of problems are believable.

BENEFITS AND PROBLEMS IN THE OECD CITIES

The relationships between benefits and problems in the OECD cities are shown by the data in table 6.11. The pattern of association in the OECD cities is similar to that of the URBIS cities, but it is far less clear. First, computing benefits associate negatively with problems in areas of basic application benefit and positively with problems in areas of sophisticated application benefit. Most of these associations are not statistically significant, but some of the statistically significant associations run directly counter to the general URBIS

Contingencies in Computing Management

Table 6.11 PEARSON CORRELATIONS OF COMPUTING BENEFITS AND PROBLEMS IN OECD CITIES (N = 16)

Computing Benefits		Computing Problems				
	Staff	Technical	Respon-siveness	Resource	Support	Knowledge
Speed and accuracy	−.32	−.19	−.16	.11	.23	−.29
Cost and staff savings	−.26	.48*	.15	.07	−.33	.25
Service delivery effectiveness	−.13	−.02	−.10	.32	−.33	−.63*
Management control	−.06	−.50*	−.21	−.03	.27	−.08
Management decision making	.21	.26	.28	.38	−.26	.02
Management planning	−.46*	.37	−.11	.36	−.25	−.13
Community planning	−.04	.61*	.33	.13	−.34	.31

*p < .05

pattern. Second, like the URBIS cities, the OECD cities also show greater benefit-problem association in the staff and technical problem areas, but again, certain statistically significant associations differ from the URBIS pattern. Thus, the most striking feature of the associations between impacts and problems in the OECD cities is the lack of a clear pattern to the interactions.

Integrating Our Findings

The analyses presented in this chapter indicate that different problems and benefits associate with different kinds of city environments, computing environments, and computing policies. Some of the patterns are the same in both URBIS and OECD cities, and some are different. This section integrates our findings and presents further analysis to clarify some of the relationships we have found.

In the URBIS cities, the problems and benefits of computing tend to vary uniformly between cities with more developed and less developed computing. Problems are common in URBIS cities that are larger, that have computing environments characterized by early adoption of computing, large computing capacity, high automation, policies that encourage development of sophisticated computing, a policy board for computing management, high client participation in computing, and high levels of management and user training. Such cities also exhibit low levels of computing benefits from the basic applications, but higher levels of benefits from more sophisticated applications.

In contrast, problems are less common in URBIS cities that are smaller, that have recently adopted computing, and that have moderate computing capacity, moderate levels of application development, policies that restrict high sophistication of computing, no policy board for computing management, low client participation, and low levels of management and user training. Such cities also have higher levels of benefits from basic application areas, and no benefit from sophisticated application areas. For all URBIS cities, the computing benefits from basic application areas associate with lower levels of problems, while the benefits from more sophisticated applications generally associate with greater problems.

We believe that the split in associations between less developed and more developed cities is significant. Less developed cities might have fewer problems with computing because the technology's use within the government is limited as yet to a few departments whose needs are adequately served by current capacity, and because relations between the computing professionals and the users are simple and direct. Often, the computing activity is actually located in the major user's department (i.e., the finance department). Also, users are less experienced with computing and their expectations are relatively modest. Computing has had relatively little benefit as yet, with the benefits occurring mainly in improvement in speed and accuracy and effectiveness of service delivery. At the least, it has not been disruptive.

The more advanced users might suffer from greater problems because computing has developed to the point that existing applications coupled with demand for new applications strain existing capacity. More departments use computing, and the relationships between the computer professionals and users are more complicated and strained. User expectations have grown considerably, but the capability of the computing department to deliver has not grown at the same pace. Benefits for basic areas have already been realized with more basic and simpler applications, so they are not as noticeable, or are more critically assessed. More advanced applications produce uncertain benefits for speed and accuracy or cost and staff savings, but do produce noticeable improvements in the more sophisticated tasks of planning and management.

It appears, then, that the level of computing advancement achieved by a city corresponds to the kinds of problems and benefits it experiences. The less advanced cities have relatively few problems from computing, but they also experience only the most basic of computing benefits. The more advanced cities experience greatly increased problems, but they also are able to experience computing benefits from more sophisticated applications.

A similar trend is evident in the OECD cities, but it is not as clear or as strong. Resource and staff problems are more common in larger cities with more experience with computing, larger staffs, policies encouraging high levels of application and sophistication, locally developed and controlled computing (i.e., city-level), high levels of management involvement but low levels of user involvement, and high levels of management and user training. As in URBIS, these cities also tend to experience few benefits from basic applications of computing but do experience benefits from more sophisticated applications.

Responsiveness, staff, support, and knowledge problems are more common in OECD cities that are smaller, that have small computing staffs, policies emphasizing low sophistication, shared computing arrangements and less local control over computing, and lower levels of management and user involvement and training. Again, as with the URBIS cities, these less developed OECD cities tend to have substantial computing benefits in areas stemming from basic applications, but little in areas stemming from sophisticated applications.

This difference between highly developed cities and less de-

veloped cities is as significant for OECD cities as it is for URBIS cities. We believe the more advanced cities experience greater resource and technical problems because they have high current demand
for computing and insufficient resources for satisfying that demand.
As a result, they experience problems with day-to-day service provision. They utilize client-oriented management policies (user boards,
user involvement, training, etc.), and these might be successful for
the OECD cities in mitigating problems of responsiveness, support, and
knowledge. Advanced cities do not appear to get as much benefit for
basic areas as for more sophisticated areas, probably for the same
reasons we suggest in the case of more developed URBIS cities: the
basic applications have already produced their major benefits, and it
is the more advanced applications that now are producing benefits.

  The smaller OECD cities experience problems that we feel are
related directly to their shared computing arrangement. As shown in
table 6.12, there is a strong correlation beween computing problems
and the presence of shared computing arrangements. Shared installations greatly increase the number of demands and the complexity
of relationships among all the actors party to the arrangement, which
makes responsiveness difficult. Shared installations are also often remote from users, which can cause problems of support and responsiveness, and probably increase the "social distance" between users
and computing professionals. Staff problems are likely to be higher
because computing staff is independent and more insulated from local managers and users and might be less sensitive to the needs of
the cities and departments they serve. Finally, many shared installations must implement large nation-wide or state-wide "standardized"
applications among cities, and thus have less time to work on development of "tailored" applications. Standard applications are not likely
to serve all cities equally well and are more likely to serve national
rather than local needs. This places the shared installation in the position of having to impose sometimes undesirable standardized applications on their clients, which can create ill will.

  The smaller cities do seem to experience considerable benefit
from computing in speed and accuracy and cost/staff savings. This is
to be expected, since these are the major benefits that standardized
applications are intended to produce. More advanced application

Table 6.12 COMPUTING PROBLEMS ASSOCIATED WITH SHARED INSTALLATIONS IN THE OECD CITIES

Type of Problem	Shared Installation
Staff	
EDP staff not sensitive to problems they create for users	.69*
EDP staff do not involve users sufficiently	.74*
Communication problems between EDP staff and users	.36
Responsiveness	
Inflexibility of systems	.42*
Inflexibility/inadequacy of national systems	.69*
Support/knowledge	
Lack of political pressure/support	.38
Staff adaptation	.59*
Resource	
Limited machine capacity	−.45*
Too few EDP staff	−.34

*Pearson correlations significant at the .05 level

benefits are not found; in part, because these cities cannot build the applications themselves, and because the shared installation is not likely to be able to afford to do the tailoring required to fit a sophisticated application to a user's environment.

Our data from chapters 3 and 4 suggest that not all computing environments vary in terms of the benefits they realize and the problems they experience. Our analyses in this chapter show that the variance among cities in their benefits and problems with computing is not attributable simply to the presence or absence of policies commonly held to be "helpful." For example, benefits are not linearly related to sophistication, extensiveness of development, or a high level of experience with computing. Instead, the relationship depends on the kind of benefit. Similarly, problems appear to be either curvilinearly related to benefits or related in a manner opposite to that suggested by conventional wisdom.

Computing benefits appear in a somewhat predictable pattern, in that the small, unsophisticated cities do not experience management and planning impacts, while the larger and more sophisticated cities do. Only the larger, more sophisticated cities have the kinds of applications that produce these benefits. The smaller, less developed cities show much stronger levels of benefit from speed and accuracy and service delivery effectiveness. It would seem that the more advanced cities would still be experiencing these benefits, and that there might even be an association of more development with greater benefit in these areas, but this does not seem to be the case. Centralization, which is a major structural policy (e.g., number of installations and use of policy boards) as well as a component in socio-technical interface policies (e.g., analyst/programmer deployment), plays a major role throughout the associations. Generally, centralized arrangements are associated with more basic benefits, while decentralized arrangements are associated with more sophisticated benefits. There is no theory from the literature on the management of computing to explain these findings.

The data further show that management policies commonly expected to *reduce* computing problems are frequently associated *with* problems in the cities. For example, a high-level technical sophistication of computing is significantly associated with computing problems, contradicting our assumption that such cities would have greater technical capacity for problem-free implementation of computing. Structural arrangements, particularly the use of policy boards and interdepartmental committees, also are positively associated with computing problems, even though these are a means for airing difficulties, developing priorities for dealing with them, and improving both coordination and communication between EDP staff and the operating departments. The socio-technical interface policies, especially extensive user involvement and intensive user training, are both positively and significantly associated with problems. This is again contrary to our assumptions that client participation in decision making would reduce problems by helping data-processing services to give greater attention to user needs.

Since these data are only cross-sectional, we are forced to ask in which direction the causal relationships lie. Do management policies cause computing problems? Or are the management policies found in the larger URBIS and OECD cities a *response* to computing problems, created in an effort to ameliorate them, but not very successful at doing so? In the final chapter we will review the evidence relating to problems and policies in light of our research and experience, as well as that of others, and develop a theory of the dynamics of computing that helps account for our findings.

Notes

1. The method of presentation and discussion of findings in this chapter is somewhat different from that in earlier chapters. Previously, our discussions have been organized around specific computing benefits or problems (e.g., speed and accuracy benefits or staff problems) with comparison of the URBIS and OECD cities oriented around a particular benefit or problem discussion. In this chapter, the discussions are organized around broad topics (i.e., computing benefits, computing problems) and the URBIS cities and the OECD cities are compared as a group.

2. An analysis of computing policies and computing problems was reported earlier in Kraemer and King (1981a).

3. The following changes were made in the benefit variables. The variables of Cost Saving and Staff Saving have been collapsed into a single variable called Cost and Staff Savings. Likewise, the variables of Accuracy Benefit and Speed Benefit have been collapsed into a single variable called Speed and Accuracy Benefits. The variables of Daily Decision Making and Major Decision Making have been collapsed to form a single variable called Management Decision Making Benefits. The variables of Service Delivery Effectiveness Benefits, Management Control of Staff Benefits, Management Planning Benefits, and Community Planning Benefits were unchanged.

4. The number of OECD cities studied was smaller than the number of URBIS cities studied, so correlation analysis here is somewhat more difficult to interpret (i.e., strong versus weak relationships are harder to determine). However, we are examining the associations between variables in the OECD cities in an effort simply to determine whether relationships found in the URBIS cities are also likely to be present in the OECD cities, or whether different relationships are likely. We are not using the associations found in the OECD data to test hypotheses as we are with the URBIS data. Consequently, the same methods of analysis used on the URBIS data can be used effectively on the OECD data.

5. The generally higher values of correlations in table 6.2 as compared to table 6.1 should not be taken as a sign of stronger relationships because they are a function of difference in sample size. The values in table 6.2 are roughly comparable in magnitude to those in table 6.1.

CHAPTER SEVEN
THE
DYNAMICS
OF COMPUTING

I N THIS chapter we re-
sume the second of our
two stories—that of change in computing over time—begun in chapter 1. Our findings from the previous chapters are somewhat counter-
intuitive and at variance with much of the prescriptive literature on
the management of computing. A close examination of our findings,
coupled with consideration of existing theories about the growth of
computing over time in organizations, provides us with an opportunity
to refine our understanding of the dynamic aspects of computing in
a manner that allows explanation of our research results.

Here we consider some alternative ways of explaining our
findings and conclude that the most constructive approach is to incorporate a longitudinal perspective rather than the cross-sectional
perspective we have held in chapters 2 through 6. We do this through
examination of "stage" theories of computing growth that provide useful
insights into the factors that contribute to the conditions we see in
our study cities. We then use data from the URBIS study to examine
mixes of policies that associate with various stages derived from this
study of the literature. The results of these analyses suggest that there
are indeed stage-like features identifiable from policies, benefits, and

problems experienced by the URBIS cities, and, further, that a broad theory of the dynamics of stages can be constructed around the concepts of freedom and constraint for organizational actors in pursuit of computing development decisions. We integrate our theoretical constructs into our basic model, first presented in chapter 1, and develop a more refined model that might serve as a basis for further research.

Alternative Views on Our Findings Thus Far

Our findings, especially those presented in chapter 6, run contrary to our preconceptions, which were based on prescriptive literature. Some discrepancies in relationships among policies, benefits, and problems were expected, but we assumed that there would be a noticeable association between the presence of "advanced" policies and high levels of computing development on the one hand and substantial computing benefits and low levels of problems on the other. Instead, we found these policies associated with indications of fewer basic computing benefits and more computing problems in the cities studied. In short, those policies suggested in the literature as likely to produce payoffs and to mitigate problems were often associated with diminished payoffs and unanticipated problems.

We can see three possible sources of explanation for these results: the characteristics of the data base; the cross-sectional nature of the study; and the peculiarities of computing that make it complex and difficult to manage. The first we do not adopt, but the second and third we consider.

The first source of explanation—that the findings are due to the characteristics of our data base—is plausible but we must reject it. The data for this study were primarily self-reports by respondents to attitudinal and factual questions. We do acknowledge the possibility that these reports do not correspond to what is actually taking place in the organization. For example, respondents who claim that their city uses a particular policy might not be making the important distinction between the promulgation of a policy and full compliance with the policy by organizational actors. If a policy exists in name only, and the respondent reports that the policy is in use, our analyses will assume that the policy is actually implemented. There is no absolute defense against this question given the data we used. However, these problems were anticipated in the design and execution of the URBIS and OECD studies by eliciting responses to the same question from individuals occupying different positions within the city. The sample of respondents in the cities was purposively selected to obtain data on the computing environment from those who were most knowledgeable, and efforts were made to collect multiple responses for each question asked. We reject this first possible explanation, then, because we trust the data base to be reflective of the actual conditions in the cities studied.

The second source of explanation—the cross-sectional nature of the study—raises an interesting question regarding change over time. Since the data were collected at a single point in time, might not the studies have collected their data during an unusual period in the history of computing in cities? For example, if we view computing as a complex technology only recently adopted by cities and assume that most cities are still trying to cope with managing the technology, we could say that we had sampled during a period of "growing pains" in many of the cities. Policies to deal with these problems might be in place, but have not had time to take effect. Our cross-sectional data do not permit us to test whether policies precipitated problems or vice-versa because we cannot make causal inferences without at least one more panel of data recording conditions at a different time. However, we can indirectly study theories of causality using cross-sectional data to test for the presence of conditions that would verify or disconfirm earlier predictions made in the literature. This approach was used in chapter 6, and we continue its use in this chapter.

The third source of explanation—that our data correctly measure a chronic condition of difficulty in the management of computing—also raises the issue of change over time. If constant changes occur in major forces behind computing in organizations, the complexities of managing this change might increase as the use of systems increases. We might argue that the difficulties of the task of managing such complexity and constant change are inherent, and that more advanced cities have passed into a persistent state of difficulty in the management of computing. If this is so, the attempt to formulate effective general policies for computing management could be a hopeless effort. Once again, our cross-sectional data make this impossible to test directly, but we can test the predictions of previous theories to help shed light on this possibility.

These latter two possible explanations reintroduce the important issue of change over time raised in chapter 1—that computing changes over time is confirmed by statistics on the growth of computing use. The expectation of change is implicit in all of the literature on the management of computing in the sense that policies are enacted specifically to influence the nature of changes that occur. The model we present in figure 1.3 of chapter 1 is fundamentally a model of the processes of change in the computing phenomenon in cities. That model is reintroduced in this chapter, used to help explain our findings, and elaborated in light of theory-building presented below.

Stage Theories of Computing Change in Organizations

If change over time is a common condition of computing in organizations, what are the reasons behind the changes? This question becomes especially relevant if the data on changes show unwanted trends. Assuming that change is not random, the characteristics of change might be identified by cataloging and analyzing changes over time in actual organizations. If these changes follow particular observable patterns, one can develop a theory to account for the changes and, possibly, some means of controlling change more effectively.

A common method for factoring changes over time is to divide the observed history of changes into stages that are demarked by the coincidence of major changes in a number of different, important factors. When stages follow a particular direction toward a particular end, one can develop a general model to account for change. For example, Walter Rostow (1971) developed a general stage theory of economic growth in societies around the observation that growth tends to follow a particular pattern: beginning with the traditional society lacking modern technology, through the initial adoption of modern technology in agriculture and the incorporation of compound interest rates in capital formation, to the expansion of technically advanced industries producing a broad range of products and services. Eventually the economy reaches the stage of full maturity, in which economic production focuses on the creation of durable consumer goods and services and support of the welfare state.

Stage theories have been common in several fields of study, including history and the social sciences (Moore 1967; Nisbet 1969; Braudel 1981; Nelson and Winter 1982).[1] There have been a number of substantial critiques of such theories, and even of the use of stages as an intellectual tool for describing change. As noted by van Parijs (1981), stage theories often require adoption of certain unfounded assumptions about the mechanics of change and seldom contribute much to understanding the truly evolutionary nature of change. Such criticisms are supported by the fact that the majority of stage theories of social and economic change propounded during the nineteenth century by such enlightened minds as Compte, Spencer, Marx, and Spengler have proved to be weak predictive theories when judged against subsequent events (Moore 1967). The problems with stage theories and with the stage approach to explaining change are important for our analyses here. If the very foundations of theory-building techniques are flawed, what good can theories thus constructed be to us? We are mindful of the problems of stage theories, but many of the notions embodied in stage theories of computing change are useful for categorizing the kinds of change processes that might be operating (Tornatzky et al. 1983). In any case, most writing dealing with computing change over time has adopted some form of stage approach as a basic analytical tool. Our objective in this section is to assess these theories to determine which of their aspects might be helpful in explaining our findings and constructing a more refined theory of change.

EARLY STAGE THEORIES OF COMPUTING GROWTH: THE NOLAN LINE

Stage theories on the growth of computing in organizations have been advanced by Churchill, Kempster, and Uretsky (1969), Uretsky (1973), Nolan (1973a, 1977a, 1979), Gibson and Nolan (1974), and Glaser, Torrance, and Schwartz (1983). Nolan's work is the most representative in this stream, and we refer mainly to his theory in this examination.[2] These theories were first promulgated in the early 1970s, and have been elaborated since. The early theory was based in part on observations drawn from brief case studies in three large firms (Nolan 1973a); the elaborated theory reportedly draws on additional observations in an unspecified number of firms (Nolan 1979).

Nolan's early theory claims that changes in computing budgets over time can be used to identify the stages of computing development in organizations. Budgetary changes serve as surrogate indicators of change in the organization and in its use and management of computing. Budget increases are traced by the "S-shaped" logistic curve. Each major change in the curve signifies a change in stage (i.e., three changes and four stages). It suggests that when organizations reach a period of budget growth represented by the asymptote of the logistic curve, they will have reached the end state of "maturity" where the expected payoffs will be realized and where problems with computing will be under control (see figure 7.1).

The first critical empirical assumption of this early theory and its elaboration in the literature (Gibson and Nolan 1974) is that the growth curve of budgets for data processing accurately reflects changes in the major situational or environmental variables that affect the organization and its use of computing (nature of the industry, sales growth, organizational strategies, management practices, technological change) (Nolan 1973a). The second assumption is that the four stages identified by the "S curve" capture the tendencies of three major tasks involved in the management of computing: planning, organizing, and controlling.

The four stages identified in the early Nolan model can be summarized briefly. Computing technology comes into the organization because it is needed or desired ("Initiation" stage). Controls are lax with respect to containing costs and ensuring appropriate growth

Figure 7.1 NOLAN'S 1973 STAGES OF COMPUTING BUDGET GROWTH

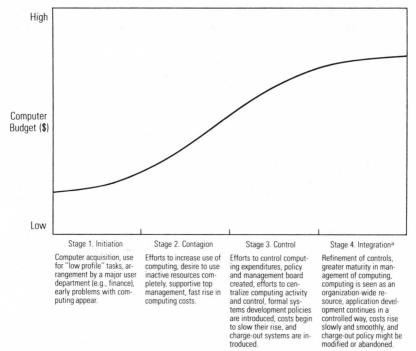

Stage 1. Initiation	Stage 2. Contagion	Stage 3. Control	Stage 4. Integration[a]
Computer acquisition, use for "low profile" tasks, arrangement by a major user department (e.g., finance), early problems with computing appear.	Efforts to increase use of computing, desire to use inactive resources completely, supportive top management, fast rise in computing costs.	Efforts to control computing expenditures, policy and management board created, efforts to centralize computing activity and control, formal systems development policies are introduced, costs begin to slow their rise, and charge-out systems are introduced.	Refinement of controls, greater maturity in management of computing, computing is seen as an organization-wide resource, application development continues in a controlled way, costs rise slowly and smoothly, and charge-out policy might be modified or abandoned.

SOURCE: Adapted from Nolan 1973a.
[a]In late stage theory writing Nolan has expanded the stages to six, adding "Data Administration" and "Maturity." However, these two additions do not substantially change the concept except to account for ever-increasing computing c᷉⁺ˢ that have been incurred (See Nolan 1979; King and Kraemer 1983).

to serve organizational interests. The power of the computing manager to make needed reforms is inadequate because the manager's job is too low in the organizational hierarchy. Lax controls plus great demand for computing leads to increased use and higher costs ("Contagion" stage). Rising costs cause top management to institute strong controls on growth (chargeout policies, priority settings), raise the status of the computing manager (e.g., to make the data-processing function a separate staff department closer to top management) and initiate serious planning ("Control" stage). These control measures often are too strict, constraining productive growth. This is recognized by top management, and the experience gained in managing the computing resource and planning for the future leads to a refinement of controls. Refined controls result in a balance between the "contagion" and "control" forces acting on the growth of computing. This end state is called the "Integration" stage in Nolan (1973a), and the "Maturity" stage in Gibson and Nolan (1974). In the end state computing costs are predicted to grow at a much slower rate, problems are to diminish, and the productivity gains will increase. The theory as expressed by Gibson and Nolan (1974) suggests that a few organizations have reached the state of maturity, but that new technological changes might spur entirely new S curves.

Nolan elaborated upon this theory late in the 1970s (Nolan 1977a, 1979). This elaborated theory attempted to account for the fact that computing expenditures have continued to grow rapidly (i.e., the earlier prediction failed). In this new version of the theory the first three stages (initiation, contagion, and control) remain intact from the earlier version. However, since the integration stage did not result in a decline in growth of computing costs, the stage theory was modified to add the stages of "Data Administration" and "Maturity," creating a six-stage model.

The rationale for the addition of new stages runs as follows. The controls imposed in the integration stage are focused mainly on controlling the computer as a resource, not on control and management of data. Two powerful new technical developments (data communications and data base management) have emerged that change the course of growth. These technologies provide users and the organization with the opportunity to increase exploitation of computing and data for non-routine data-processing purposes. This stimulates additional computing growth. Technological advancement also brings greater external knowledge (i.e., knowledge about technical opportunities), while the experience gained in the control and integration stages brings greater internal knowledge (i.e., knowledge about how to use and manage computing). Enhanced internal knowledge allows the assertion of improved organizational control capabilities. The new stage of data administration is reached in which the focus of organizational control is on managing the data rather than on managing the computer. Once the benefits of the "data resource management" perspective are in place, policies are refined sufficiently to lead the organization into the state where "slack" (relaxed constraints enabling innovation) and "control" (tightened constraints to increase efficiency) are balanced for the overall well-being of the organization. This, in Nolan's 1979 model, is the state of maturity.

NOLAN'S THEORY EVALUATED

This theory rests on several important assumptions. First, it assumes that changes in most of the important variables governing the growth of computing can be captured by plotting either the absolute growth in level of DP budgets (Nolan 1973a), or the "normalized" level of DP budgets as a function of sales growth (Nolan 1979). Second, it assumes that the primary driving feature behind stage migration is change in information processing technology and the opportunities it brings to the organization (Gibson and Nolan 1974:88; Nolan 1979:116). Third, it assumes that there exist clear-cut organizational goals for the appropriate use of computing technology. Fourth, it assumes that education and experience (external and internal knowledge) will enlighten management and users alike and provide them with the means to control the technology and exploit it effectively in light of organizational goals. Fifth, it assumes that the primary function in maintaining effective control is to "balance" two variables, slack and control, such that innovation is nurtured while costs are controlled and quality of computing services is kept stable.

Some of these assumptions pose difficulties for this theory's use in explaining the patterns found in our data. The first and most serious problem with the theory is its empirical foundation. It seems unlikely that a single variable such as expenditures for computing could capture the influence of such important and different variables as organizational environment and managerial strategies for control of computing. There is an inherent danger of circularity in this definition, as well: changes in expenditures are said to signify changes in key environmental and managerial variables; yet changes in these variables result in changes in the expenditure curve. Even if we assume that Nolan's budgetary data do describe the behaviors of these variables in the firms he studied, it is unlikely that budget data can be relied on to identify stages among our cities. Lucas and Sutton's (1977) study of computing expenditures in California local governments revealed that growth of expenditures tended to be linear rather than curvilinear (a phenomenon recognized in Nolan's 1979 paper), and that more powerful explanators than Nolan's stage theory would account for the pattern of budget growth in local governments. Goldstein and McCririk (1981) and Drury (1983) had similar difficulty validating the empirical bases of Nolan's claims in their studies of over 200 organizations.

This problem with the empirical basis of Nolan's model restricts its acceptance as a validated theory in the scientific sense of that term. Nevertheless, can the theory's account of computing growth help to explain our data? Here, again, we run into difficulties with the theoretical bases of Nolan's model. Assumptions two through four listed above reflect a basic ideology about management and the process of technological change in organizations that may be a mistaken one. The assumption (#2) that technological change is the primary driving force behind the growth of computing through the stages could overstate the importance of this force. Technological change plays a role in the complex of forces that results in change, but there are important additional factors that should be considered. Most important are the "demand-pull" features that create a ripe environment for technological changes to be considered and adopted. At least three such forces seem appropriate for consideration here. One we call "institutionalized demand," created by the extant presence of computing in the organization. Computing systems must be maintained and, typically, must undergo major maintenance and upgrading over time. These changes add to the costs of computing and to the need for additional computing changes (e.g., hardware upgrades, more disk storage). Another is what we call "affective demand" for computing services due to powerful but frequently overlooked aspects of computing as a technology that is desirable for users to adopt, expand, and control. Computing not only offers a hope for improving productivity in current operations, but it generates the possibility for new capabilities that are appealing to some users. Computing provides departments with opportunities to increase their share of organizational resources, since the presence of a computer can help justify additional capital, personnel, and space demands. Finally, computing is for many people an entertaining and status-increasing enterprise, making it desirable. If these institutional and affective demand-pull forces are powerful drivers of change, it is likely that they might take precedence over the supply-push factors of technological change that result in increased technological capabilities and declining price/performance ratios for the technology in certain circumstances. For example, the fact that new capabilities exist in the computing technology marketplace might have no effect on the growth of computing in organizations due to low demand to adopt the new advances.

The assumption (#3) that there are clear-cut organizational goals to be realized through application of the technology might apply to some organizations, but it certainly does not apply to all. The question of whether organizational goals are uniform and consistent guides for the behavior of organizational actors, as opposed to dynamic and changing targets that result from competition and conflict among organizational actors has been extensively discussed in the literature (Cyert and March 1963; Lawrence and Lorsch 1967; Kling 1979; Danziger, Dutton, Kling, and Kraemer 1982). This research suggests that the setting and maintenance of organizational goals is a dynamic process in which internal disagreements on strategy are only temporarily resolved through goal-clarifying processes, and that organizational norms that result might last only for a short time. If the organizational goals for the application of computing are themselves undergoing change, there can be no lasting consensus on how "best" to manage the computing activity. This would undermine the expectation that organizational management will know what it is searching for in its quest to master the technology. Perhaps the very general goals of the organization can be assumed to be clear and consistent (e.g., organizational survival, making a profit or avoiding a deficit, sustained organizational growth). But establishing a linkage between use of computing and the achievement of these goals requires the specification of much more detailed sub-goals directed specifically at the application of the technology to particular tasks and needs. Given demand-pull factors mentioned above, agreement on sub-goals cannot be assumed *a priori,* and the assumption that the differing goals of organizational actors will have unitary correspondence with agreed-on organizational goals cannot be made at all.

The assumption (#4) that increased external and internal

knowledge will eventually lead to effective and efficient control over computing (i.e., achievement of "maturity") presents difficulties because it assumes that the "right" knowledge is available, and that organizational actors will acquire this knowledge and act appropriately as a result of having it. External knowledge, which in Nolan's model comes into the organization in the form of new technological capabilities and ideas about how to exploit them, varies greatly in its utility. There are many competing theories about how best to exploit computing, and there are no proven tests by which a manager can tell which theories are correct and appropriate to his organization.

Nolan claims that his stage theory offers "a generic and empirically supported theory of the evolution of a DP acitivity" (Nolan 1979:125), but this claim is overstated. In fact, there is little external knowledge to help the manager determine which policies should be adopted. Internal knowledge, which is based on experience, also has its drawbacks. Experiences with the use of computing technology in organizations vary greatly. Some have been more successful than others in adopting and managing the technology. According to Nolan's theory, those who are successful have learned how to deal with technology, while those who are not successful have not learned what they need to know. But what accounts for these differences in learning? Nolan's theory does not suggest any answers to this question. The explanation of how organizational knowledge is brought to bear on solving problems with computing is lacking, leaving little insight as to how appropriate policies for the integration, data administration, and maturity stages will be found and applied.

We question several aspects of the assumption (#5) that the task of effective management of computing is to strike a balance between "slack" and "control," although in this assumption we find an important insight (discussed below). Our problem is with the assumption that top management, which has the prerogative to implement "slack" or "control" policies, will be able to know when each of these policies is appropriate. Policies are deliberately chosen from someplace along the "slack" to "control" spectrum. This raises a difficulty noted above regarding the assumptions that there are clear-cut organizational goals and means to incorporate external and internal knowledge into effective decision making. There is no guarantee that organizational actors can know how to manage computing activities in terms of "slack" and "control" given organizational conditions. More important for our purposes, a completely different interpretation of the dynamics of computing growth is suggested if we assume that policy actions of top management falling on the "slack" to "control" continuum are not proactive at all, but rather are highly reactive. Policies, in this sense, are adopted in reaction to issues that come to the attention of managers and about which they have little knowledge to guide them in adopting the "appropriate" course of action.

Aside from the problems with Nolan's theory, the notion that "slack" and "control" constitute ends of a spectrum of policy options has utility for our purposes. This concept has been proposed in the literature in various forms (Cyert and March 1956), and it has a certain intuitive appeal and utility. As Nolan (1979:116) uses the concept, a "slack" environment of computing policies provides more resources to the computing activity than are strictly necessary to accomplish objectives. This nurtures innovation, presumably resulting in at least some applications that improve the welfare of the organization. "Control" environments use sophisticated controls over resource allocation for computing that are tied to performance assessment. Planning, budgeting, project management, personnel performance reviews, and chargeback or cost-accounting systems are used to ensure that DP activites meet implied standards of effectiveness and efficiency.

Nolan's use of this concept reveals a basic assumption of his theory: that the adoption and expansion of computing technology and use in an organization must eventually reach a threshold and level off. The supply-push forces and demand-pull forces will continue to encourage expansion in use of the technology, so the forces acting to control the rate of expansion must come from within the organization itself. To Nolan, these forces are the actions of top management. Nolan's theory is thus a dialectical model of change, in which managers regulate organizational change by balancing the mix of freedom and constraint in their policies.[3] Freedom yields a laissez-faire or laissez-innover condition in which technology and new techniques are easily adopted and innovations are not discouraged. Constraint is selectively used to avoid consequences of unbounded freedom (e.g., rapidly rising costs without readily observable benefits, difficulties in maintaining central organizational control). By this construction, of course, freedom is a default state (i.e., the absence of constraint is freedom). The admonition of the Nolan model is that the task of top managers is to strike a balance that provides enough freedom to encourage innovation and enough constraint to mitigate unwanted consequences of unbridled growth.

The strength of Nolan's model is in three observations. First, that growth in the expansion of the technology's use in the organization must eventually reach a plateau or equilibrium state when constraint is used to inhibit the freedom to innovate. Second, there is no guarantee that future disturbances (e.g., new technological advancements) might not disrupt this equilibrium, but equilibrium is reestablished by management action. Third, the actions of managers are most effective where they incorporate a balance between freedom and constraint. This last idea, in particular, is a powerful one, and one we adopt in the development of our own theory.

Using the data from our cities, we construct a somewhat different theory of computing growth in organizations. We adopt the underlying tenet of Nolan's model that growth occurs as a series of steps, in which the freedom for adoption and innovation is eventually constrained by actions of policymakers within the organization. We build the remainder of our theory by analyzing our data using measures of the variables Nolan represented by the growth in computing budgets. This model takes the data collected on these variables at one point in time and attempts to establish relationships among the different variables. From this analysis we construct an interpretation of these relationships in light of the basic tenet of Nolan's model.

AN ALTERNATIVE STAGE THEORY

This study was undertaken with the assumption that "advanced" policies (e.g., use of sophisticated technology, greater user involvement in design) would be associated with greater payoffs of computing and with fewer computing problems. The analyses presented in chapter 6 indicate that the more "advanced" computing sites tend to have higher levels of problems than did the less advanced sites. Moreover, detailed analysis of policies and their relationship to computing benefits indicates an unexpected relationship: compared to the less advanced sites, the more advanced sites show less computing payoffs (i.e., speed, accuracy, and service delivery improvements) from more routine tasks, but greater payoffs from more sophisticated applications to management and planning. These findings might be partially explained by the fact that lower staged cities simply do not have these policies, but they do tend to disconfirm the assumption that "advanced" management policies will result in the benefits claimed for these policies. Moreover, they suggest that there is a struggle between the forces of freedom and constraint we noted above.

Our interpretation of these relationships yields a stage model containing three stages.[4] Each stage is marked by certain thresholds, including large-scale hardware changes (e.g., change in generation of machine in use), the expansion of computing's application beyond a single function to other governmental functions, the shift from more routine applications (i.e., calculating, printing, and recordkeeping) to more sophisticated applications (i.e., information retrieval, sophisticated analytics, and record restructuring); the introduction of computer policy boards; and, the centralization of computer services. Figure 7.2 illustrates the three stages developed from our analyses. The stages are described as follows.

STAGE I: INTRODUCTION AND CONQUEST

This stage is illustrated by the URBIS and OECD cities that are using shared computing arrangements, service bureaus, or are in the early phase of in-house computing. Stage I cities are recent adopters with little or no local computing capacity and staff expertise, although they might get such resources through a shared computing installation or service bureau. These cities have basic-mode computer applications centered primarily around the needs of the resource controllers (usually finance and administration). They experience slow application growth, due to limited development funds and lack of local knowledge about the technology, and have low demand for computing. These cities have problems generating support for the technology due to lack of knowledge of potential application, and/or past failure of computing service providers to adequately tailor appli-

Figure 7.2 STAGES OF EDP GROWTH INDICATED BY URBIS AND OECD DATA

Growth Stage	Computing Environment	Computing Benefits	Computing Problems	Management Policies	Illustration
1 Introduction and Conquest	Recent adopters Low local computing capacity and staff expertise Few applications, usually batch, in a few departments Slow application growth Computing located in finance department, a shared facility, or a service bureau Functional decentralization	Some benefits of improved speed and accuracy in routine data-processing applications, and in cost avoidance	Moderate to major problems with responsiveness, staff, support, and knowledge	No local policy board Low or "remote" manager and user involvement Low orientation and training for managers and users Control of computing is in the hands of the "owner" of computing resources Use shared facility, service bureau, or small local installation	Smaller OECD cities with shared computing
	Middling adopters Moderate local computing capacity and staff Slack computer resources	Established improvements in speed, accuracy, and cost avoidance in routine applications New capabilities for improving service	Moderate to major problems with EDP staff, technology, responsiveness, and resources	No local policy board Low to moderate involvement of users Low to moderate orientation and training of managers and users	Small and moderate sized URBIS cities

Stage	Applications	Impacts	Problems	Management and technology	Examples
2 Experimentation and Expansion	Rapid application growth and expansion to many departments Computing located in finance or independent department	delivery being explored Very early management and planning applications yield minor improvements in decision making		Technology expanded and moderately upgraded Control of computing under the chief executive	
3 Competition and Regulation	Early adopters Large sophisticated computing capacity and technical staff; computing and staff capacity is overloaded Many sophisticated applications in many departments Application growth is marginal, in areas already developed Extensive demand for maintenance and modification of equipment, software, applications Computing located in an independent department	No new improvements in speed, accuracy, or cost avoidance for routine applications, and in some cases reduced payoffs due to system obsolescence; impacts on decision making and planning more common from management and planning applications as applications expand	Moderate to major problems with EDP staff, technology, responsiveness, and resources No support problems	Use policy board or interdepartmental committee Centralize computing in a local installation High management and user involvement Intensive management and user orientation and training Control of computing shared between chief executive and policy board Advanced technology is used	Larger URBIS and OECD cities

cations to local users' needs. They have staff problems from inability of EDP staff to communicate with users, from lack of users' orientation and training, or from their physical remoteness from users (as in the case of shared regional computing centers or service bureaus). They also have problems of low responsiveness to users by EDP staff who are inexperienced and unable to respond to users' requests for special information or for modification to applications, and who themselves are unfamiliar with the applications that often have been designed and built elsewhere (e.g., in a regional center). The primary payoffs of computing in Stage I are routine improvements in speed and accuracy of operations and, secondarily, in cost avoidance (elimination of the need to hire new staff to meet a growing workload). There is no benefit for planning or management because few, if any, applications for these tasks are operating.

STAGE II: EXPERIMENTATION AND EXPANSION

This stage is illustrated by the small- and medium-size OECD and URBIS cities. Stage II cities have moderate local computing capacity and staff expertise, recently upgraded hardware capacity, slack computing resources relative to current demand, extensive applications development underway in many departments, and often utilize a newly formed independent computer department instead of a computing operation based in the finance department. These cities have relatively few major problems. Stage I problems have been worked out, experienced users are satisfied with service, new users are enthusiastic and promotional about their developing applications, and slack computing resources are sufficient to handle some increase in demand. User involvement and training policies are instituted or continued, but control of computing decisions remains in the hands of the chief executive. The technology is expanded and upgraded moderately in sophistication. Major benefits are from routine applications that have been fully integrated into operations, and initial applications for planning and management are beginning to produce benefits.

STAGE III: COMPETITION AND REGULATION

This stage is most often illustrated by larger URBIS and OECD cities. Stage II cities possess large, sophisticated computing capacity and technical expertise, usually located in a single central computing installation, with many sophisticated applications serving most city departments. Computer and staff capacity are likely to be overloaded, both by maintenance demands of the existing applications that consume an increasing share of computing resources, and by competition among departments for scarce development resources for new applications. Communication problems develop between EDP staff and users given the complexity of operations and the tension among departments. EDP staff often insulate themselves from user demands and problems and thus do not respond well to users' needs. Technical problems arise due to equipment and procedural adjustments to increase efficiency. To deal with these problems a policy board or interdepartmental committee will likely be established to resolve conflicts in priority among the departments and to deal with problems between EDP staff and users. Managers and users become more involved in decision making about computing arrangements and in application design, while training for computer use is expanded. Analysts and programmers might be decentralized to departments to improve responsiveness and staff relations, and technological fixes, such as multiprogramming and upgrading the CPU, might be installed to cope with shortfalls in capacity. Major benefits are from the more advanced and newer applications designed for planning and management. The routine application benefits, such as speed and accuracy improvements or cost avoidance, do not accrue as frequently, because these payoffs have already been realized in earlier stages and are less noticeable, or because older applications that produce such benefits suffer from age and the need for maintenance or redevelopment.

Basic to our stage theory are three features: each stage is a discrete step; the stages proceed in sequential fashion; and all cities pass through this sequence, although the pace of passage might vary among cities. The stage of any particular city's computing activity will be determined in large part by characteristics of its computing environment, such as its level of computing resources, degree of automation, and application demand. Different computing benefits and problems are associated with different computing environments and, therefore, with different stages of growth. Management policies are introduced into this "environment benefits problems" setting in a proactive or reactive effort to control the computing environment. It is hoped that control will maximize the payoffs and ameliorate the problems, but the data indicate that this is not always the case. At best, we expect that the appropriateness and effectiveness of particular policies will depend on the stage of computing growth. Our analysis in the next section suggests that this is the case.

POLICY MIXES ASSOCIATED WITH STAGES

Are there mixes of policies that appear at different stages in response to problems that arise from computing? To investigate such a possibility we can utilize the URBIS city data to identify whether there are associations of particular policies with benefits and problems that fit the stage theory. For this purpose we constructed a set of "policy-benefit mixes" and "policy-problems mixes" that consist of the statistically important associations among a highly distilled set of policy, benefit, and problem variables used for analysis in chapter 6. It is important to note that this analysis does not "test" for such relationships; we cannot do that because these are the same data used to build the theory, and because the data were not collected with such an analysis in mind. But this analysis does permit us to see whether clusterings of policies, benefits, and problems occur in patterns that fit the characteristics of our stage theory.

The analysis presented here utilizes regression analysis of the policy variables and the benefit and problem outcome variables. We also include in our analysis environment variables, to identify those outcomes that are more heavily dependent on environmental characteristics than on policies. In both tables 7.1 and 7.2, where the results of our regression analysis are presented, the environmental variables that are shown are bracketed so they can be easily distinguished from the policy variables. The discussion of the policy mixes, which follows, summarizes the regressions, constructs an interpretation of the findings, and suggests which stages of computing development would be indicated by cities with particular mixes of policies and environmental characteristics. Policy-benefit mixes are discussed first, followed by policy-problem mixes.

POLICY-BENEFIT MIXES

Table 7.1 shows the regression results of the independent variables and the seven kinds of computing benefits utilized in chapter 6. First, speed and accuracy benefits are most noticeable in cities that use centralized installations, that leave computing management up to the computing department (i.e., no policy board), that are relatively recent adopters of computing, and that have ambitious development plans. This describes cities that have made a strong, focused commitment to computing development under central control. Such cities correspond to Stage I and early Stage II.

Second, policies are not strong predictors of cost and staff savings. These benefits accrue most in cities with programming centralized but not assigned to departments, with less department head training, and with some integration of systems and data (data linkage). This describes cities with a centralized computing arrangement oriented toward straight service provision (e.g., no custom programming and no user department training). These cities correspond to Stage I and early Stage II.

Third, service delivery effectiveness benefits are strongest in cities that have adopted computing relatively recently, but that already have advanced hardware capability to service users (e.g., multiprogramming), involve users in applications development, and charge user departments for computer use. This describes cities that are moving toward a period of new application development and that have found it necessary to introduce controls on computing demand through use of charging mechanisms and to establish greater user orientation through user involvement in system design. They might also soon undergo a period of hardware expansion to accommodate new users and applications. These are Stage II cities.

Fourth, cities with the greatest benefits of computing on management control are those with more advanced applications usage (i.e., sophisticated reports), cost-free computing from the standpoint of user departments, little involvement of top management in computing management, and considerable computing experience. These cities are likely to be at a plateau in computing development where there is little need for (and possibly pressure against) centralized top

Table 7.1 REGRESSION RESULTS FOR COMPUTING BENEFITS BY INDEPENDENT VARIABLES IN THE URBIS CITIES

Dependent Variable	Independent Variable	Zero-Order Coefficient	Path Explained	Variance Explained	Total Variance Explained	R Square
Speed and accuracy benefits	Centralized installation (Year EDP began in city)	.36	.49	13%	42%	.65
	Policy board involvement in applications sophistication	.32	.24	12%		
		.43	.33	9%		
		-.23	-.37	8%		
		.40	.30			
Cost and staff savings benefits	Programmers assigned to departments from EDP	-.25	-.24	6%	18%	.43
	Degree of data linkage	.16	.31	5%		
	Department head training	-.25	-.30	7%		
Service delivery effectiveness benefits	Multiprogramming	.29	.42	9%	26%	.51
	Departments charged for computing (Year EDP began in city)	.19	.27	5%		
	User involvement in design	.13	.32	7%		
		.18	.23	5%		
Management control benefits	Degree of report sophistication	.47	.45	23%	44%	.66
	Departments charged for computing	-.19	-.35	8%		

Management decision-making benefits	CAO involvement in management of computing	−.29	−.31	8%	
	(Year EDP began in city)	−.28	−.24	5%	
	Programmers assigned by departments to EDP	.32	.59	10%	
	Department head involvement in management of computing	−.29	−.53	13%	48% .69
	Total applications planned	−.25	−.32	9%	
	Departments charged for computing	−.20	−.37	9%	
	User involvement in design	−.04	.32	8%	
Management planning benefits	Degree of functional automation	.53	.62	28%	
	Department head training	−.02	−.43	8%	49% .70
	Policy board	.23	.30	8%	
	Multiprogramming	.35	.26	6%	
Community planning benefits	Degree of functional automation	.60	.70	36%	
	Recent structural reorganization	.22	.34	9%	52% .73
	(Percent of EDP budget of government operating budget)	−.09	−.28	7%	

managerial control or intervention, but where there is sophisticated computing activity and well-developed computing uses. These cities are likely to be in Stage II and early Stage III.

Fifth, management decision-making benefits accrue most strongly in cities with decentralization of both technical staff (i.e., programmers are located in user departments but are assigned to the EDP department) and systems design (i.e., user involvement), less managerial involvement in or control over computing activity (i.e., little department head involvement and less charging policy), and a generally stable applications profile (few new applications in development). Although the regressions do not indicate it, these conditions usually occur in larger cities with multiple installations, large numbers of applications, substantial user demands for computing, and few mechanisms for management to exercise central managerial control. These are likely to be Stage III cities.

Sixth, management planning benefits occur most in cities with a high degree of automation (degree of functional automation), decentralized control (i.e., use of policy board), sophisticated hardware (multiprogramming) and a service orientation that does not encourage user department training. These conditions tend to describe the largest and most advanced cities using computing. Users have gained considerable control over computing, often having access to their own or a nearby installation. They also have highly developed hardware and software capability. These are probably Stage III cities.

Seventh, cities with the greatest levels of community planning benefits are highly automated, have turbulent computing environments (structural reorganization), and spend somewhat less than normal on computing as a proportion of city budgets. These tend to be the most advanced cities in use of computing and are often (but not always) the cities that have been using computing the longest. These are probably early Stage III cities.

POLICY-PROBLEM MIXES

Table 7.2 presents the findings from the regression of a set of independent variables on the five kinds of computing problems discussed in chapters 4 and 6. First, EDP staff-user interface problems tend to be associated with computing environments that have imple-

Table 7.2 REGRESSION RESULTS FOR COMPUTING PROBLEMS BY INDEPENDENT VARIABLES IN THE URBIS CITIES

Dependent Variable	Independent Variable	Zero-Order Coefficient	Path Explained	Variance Explained	Total Variance Explained	R Square
Staff-user interface problems	Department head training	.45	.26	21%	38%	.62
	Policy board involvement in applications	.43	.33	9%		
	Degree of report sophistication	.40	.30	8%		
Technical problems	Policy board	.43	.31	18%	47%	.69
	Recent reorganization	.38	.37	11%		
	Programmers assigned to department from EDP	-.27	-.36	7%		
	(DP budget per capita)	.29	.34	11%		
	(Total EDP staff)	.53	.48	29%		
Responsiveness problems	Policy board involvement in applications	.33	.30	8%	35%	.59
	Change in software development priorities	-.28	-.33	8%		
	Recent structural reorganization	.23	.26	7%		
	(Total clock hours)	.53	.48	29%		
Resource problems	Recent structural reorganization	.51	.45	22%	67%	.82
	On-line capability	.06	-.36	5%		
	(DP budget per capita)	.41	.27	6%		
	Hardware upgrading	.41	.24	5%		
Support problems	Programmers assigned to departments from EDP	-.30	-.22	9%	43%	.66
	Programmers assigned by departments to EDP	.24	.41	8%		
	User involvement in design	.29	.49	11%		
	Degree of data linkage	-.17	-.32	7%		
	CAO involvement in management	-.24	-.30	8%		

mented training for managers in the operating departments, have a policy board involved in decisions about applications development and priority, and have sophisticated computerized reporting. These policies might have been implemented as a response to staff problems (which are more likely to arise in places that have sophisticated computing), and in cities that adopted computing early and have more extensive and complex relationships between the operating departments and the computing department. These cities are probably in Stage III.

Second, technical problems are more likely to be present in a policy environment where structural and socio-technical policies are being used. Technical problems occur where there is a recent reorganization of computing, centralization of technical personnel (analysts and programmers) but decentralization of computing control (i.e., through policy boards), and large budgets (a size indicator). Such cities are usually larger and more sophisticated, with more automation. Policy boards are used to deal with computing issues, but decentralizing EDP staff, another strategy suggested for reducing problems, is not. Reorganizations can contribute to technical problems during the period in which the organizational changes are being effected. These cities are likely to be in transition from Stage II to Stage III.

Third, responsiveness problems occur in computing environments that have stable and decentralized control over computing applications (policy board and no changes in development priorities), but that have undergone recent structural reoganization. It is possible that dislocations caused by major changes in structural arrangements upset the equilibrium in such cities with large staffs, policy boards, and well-determined development priorities. It is not clear what stage such cities would be in, but they are most likely to be in transition from one stage to the next.

Fourth, resource problems occur in relatively unsophisticated computing environments operating at stretched capacity and undergoing major change. Resource problems relate to around-the-clock operation (number of hours per week that the computer operates), substantial investment in computing, structural and technical changes (reorganization and hardware upgrades), and little technical sophistication (few on-line applications). Thus, resource problems appear to occur in computing environments that have relatively little technical and organizational development but are spending considerable resources on computing. These cities appear to be in transition from Stage II to Stage III.

Although support problems are not common problems in URBIS cities, the data show that support problems do follow a particular pattern. These problems occur most in cities with the following characteristics: decentralized computing operations in which programmers are not assigned by the EDP department to users but are assigned from operating departments to EDP, little top-level management of computing, user involvement in design, and few integrated systems (low data linkage). Such cities are probably relatively new to computing, and functional user departments (e.g., finance, police, etc.) are doing their own development when they can (possibly because of weak support from a centralized computing shop). These would appear to be Stage I cities.

SUMMARY

It appears that we can identify some policy mixes that correspond to different stages of computing. The testing of such a relationship requires causal analysis using longitudinal data, so we do not feel our analyses verify the causal explanations we have provided. Nevertheless, the regressions suggest that policies indicative of cities at different stages do relate to certain benefits and problems. The more routine benefits of computing for cost and staff savings, speed and accuracy of operations, and improvement in service delivery tend to be higher in cities with policies that correspond to the earlier stages of computing evolution (late Stage I and early Stage II). Benefits for more advanced application areas of management and planning tend to occur in cities with policies associated with later stages in evolution (late Stage II and Stage III). Problems, on the other hand, tend to be more intense in later stages of development. More significantly, problems seem to be related to periods of transition between stages, such as the movement from Stage II to Stage III.

The policy mixes associated with our stages do not prove that our stage theory correctly represents the pattern of computing growth in the study cities. However, the theory does provide a working hypothesis whereby we can construct a plausible scenario of the patterns and processes of change.

From Nolan's model we adopted the theoretical postulate that growth of computing use in an organization must eventually level off, or reach a threshold, and that the threshold is established, reestablished, and often maintained at equilibrium by the balancing of freedom and constraint in policy actions of management. Our stage theory is agnostic about the "end state" to which computing use is headed (e.g., "maturity" in Nolan's model), and concentrates instead on the possible driving forces of change based in the motives and behaviors of organizational actors. In our model, the fundamental driving forces behind computing growth are the demand-pull forces within the organization. In a state of relative freedom (i.e., lack of constraint on development), decisions to adopt and expand computing use are left to organizational subunits. New uses for the technology are explored and existing systems are enhanced. Rapid, uncontrolled growth cannot go unchecked for long, however, because of rising costs and problems of integrating the various developments into a pattern that serves larger organizational objectives, as defined by central leaders. Growth is constrained and channeled, but in the process competition increases among various subunits, each of which seeks to consolidate or increase its share of computing resources. Refinement of constraining policies might help attenuate competitive problems and enable continued exploitation of the technology, but as our findings about policy-benefit and policy-problem mixes suggest, few if any cities have found the policy key to "maturity" in computing use.

The primary claims of our stage theory are that: (1) computing use has a natural tendency to expand in organizations because of strong demand-pull forces, (2) computing will expand to some threshold level of use and expenditure, (3) the threshold is artificially imposed by the constraining actions of management policy, and (4) management policies are often marginally effective at constraining cost growth and nurturing computing environments that provide high levels of benefit and low levels of problems. In particular, the more advanced and sophisticated environments will be characterized by significant benefits but high levels of problems with computing. As with many other aspects of management in complex, modern organiza-

tions, the effective management of computing is a difficult challenge
to meet.

The Dynamics of Computing

To this point we have concentrated on development of a descriptive
theory of the pattern of change in the cities. We do not yet have a
model of the processes whereby change takes place. In this section,
which is the "title section" of our book, we integrate our stage model
with our earlier theoretical model of the process of computing change
(chapter 1) to produce an elaborated model that constitutes the basis
of our conclusion. Our stage model suggests a pattern of computing
growth over time. This pattern of growth emerges as a result of
changes in a policy/implementation/use/feedback cycle. This cycle,
which we first presented in figure 1.3, encompasses both the formal
processes of organizational procedure and policy as well as the in-
formal behaviors of various actors in the environment of computing
provision and use.

      Examining figure 1.3, we can observe that key features of our
stage theory are not adequately accounted for. In particular, the
feedback cycle between the outcomes of computing (benefits and
problems) and the organizational political/administrative system is too
vague. What are the processes by which the outcomes of computing
eventually affect changes in computing policies and computing environment? In our initial model, these processes are simply embedded
in the organizational political/administrative system. But this system,
while it includes the users of computing, is mainly the policymaking
and controlling component of the organization. The specific options
for change in computing it deals with must arise as articulated requests or demands for change from various organizational actors, including computer users. Our refined model, which is shown in figure
7.3, incorporates a new category we refer to as "demands of change."
Also, we have separated and elaborated one aspect of the extra-
community environment (technicological change in the marketplace)
to include direct influence on both demands for change and on the
organizational political/administrative system.

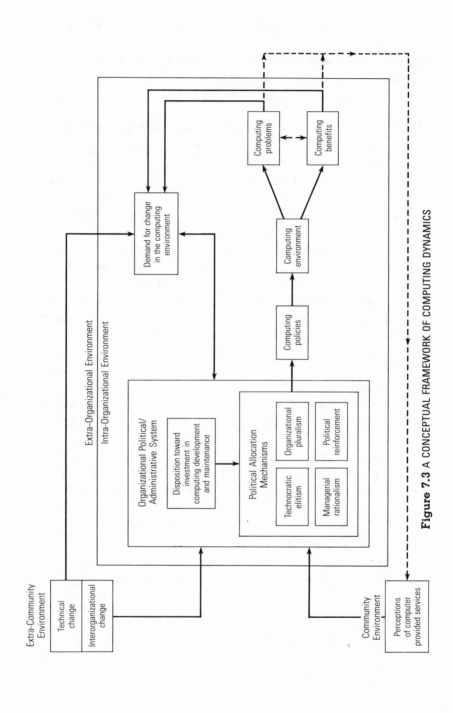

Figure 7.3 A CONCEPTUAL FRAMEWORK OF COMPUTING DYNAMICS

The new model in figure 7.3 recognizes several levels of variables influencing both computing benefits and problems, and suggests a more detailed process of the ways in which reactions to benefits and problems are dealt with to produce alterations in computing policy. We will discuss the basic elements of the model, moving counterclockwise, beginning with the boundary between extra-organizational and intra-organizational variables.

As in our model from chapter 1, the first basic distinction is between the intra-organizational and extra-organizational environment. The boundary between the two is the formal boundary of the city corporation. The extra-organizational environment includes the local community environment (e.g., characteristics of the city, its local economy, and political processes) as well as the extra-community environment (e.g., state and federal governments, the computing technology offered by vendors). Both the community and extra-community environments affect the internal environment of the local government through the political/administrative system of the organization, in terms of such characteristics as the local government's size, wealth, professionalism of management, organizational structure, reform orientation, and control mechanisms (e.g., centralized vs. decentralized government organization). We add to our earlier model the influence of technological change (a variable in the extra-community environment) on our new variable, demands for change, which is discussed below.

Within the political/administrative system of the organization is the government's disposition toward investment in technological development, as well as the underlying biases concerning what kinds of computing applications need to be developed and maintained. These dispositions are exercised through the several political decision modes that allocate resources described in chapter 1. These allocation modes arbitrate the resource divisions and the decision process whereby policy for computing development is made. However, the influence of the political/administrative system need not be direct or explicit. A set of clearly articulated expectations of top management can serve to maintain and modulate the policymaking process, such that groups and individuals act under these general guidelines. Top managers and policymakers in such cases intervene only when computing becomes very problematic and trouble-prone, whereupon they usually impose top-down solutions. The threat of such top-down intervention reinforces the intentions of top managers, and works to ensure that the desires of the political/administrative system are met. Thus, it is not necessary that top management continually be involved with computing decisions, and, indeed, in most cities they are not.

The political/administrative system controls computing through computing policies. This control comes both through "directive" policy (e.g., a policy that all users must be charged for use of the computer) and "enabling" policy (e.g., where the computing department is given freedom to acquire whatever equipment it needs to satisfy demand). These kinds of policies set the context in which computing development takes place. Policies can have the effect of constraining development and use of computing, as for example, chargeout policy, or of "freeing" opportunities for development.

Policy action leads to creation of the computing environment and works through it once it is created. The computing environment consists of the technical, resource, and experiential commitment the government has invested in computing. It is the vehicle whereby pressures for expansion, through policies for development of specific computing applications, are translated into actual applications, thus producing computing outcomes. Computing policies create the computing environment in the sense that policies, such as a decision to adopt computing or to acquire a particular kind or size of computer, provide the physical foundation of the computing environment. Computing policies also work through the computing environment to carry out mandates of the political/administrative environment regarding application development.

The outcomes of computing are divided into two classes: benefits and problems. Benefits consist mainly of the welfare-improving effects of computing use on routine organizational concerns, such as speed of operations, accuracy of data, staff and cost economies, and service delivery effectiveness, as well as on more specialized tasks, such as planning and management. Computing problems consist of those unintended consequences arising in the use of computing that adversely affect the benefits derived from computing use. These include such problems as staff-user interaction difficulties, technical

breakdowns, and user negativism toward computing. Computing outcomes have direct effects on the operations of the local government,
and they interact with one another in the sense that problems can
inhibit benefits, and a lack of benefits can cause problems (for example, support for computing might fall if computing benefits do not
meet expectations). Outcomes also affect the community environment
in two ways. They affect the operation of the local government, and
hence its effectiveness in carrying out its mandates for service, which
is recognized indirectly by the community (i.e., citizens do not perceive the role of computing in such effects). Sometimes, outcomes of
computing directly affect citizens through systems such as automated citizen-complaint monitoring, voter registration systems, and
various kinds of billing and citizen-notification systems. However, such
strong connections between outcomes of computing and the extra
community environment are limited at present because computing is
seldom used in direct service delivery.

Computing outcomes also have important effects for the nature of computing in the local government, because outcomes give
rise to a new dimension we call demands for change in the computing environment (figure 7.3). Demands arise in two ways. In one, benefits from computing create expectations and desires for more (and
more sophisticated) applications, both among current users and among
those who desire to break into computing use. Demands for change
are also influenced by the extra-organizational factor of technical
change in which improved computing capability and economics create new opportunities. However, existing applications that produce
benefits require continued maintenance to remain productive, and,
typically, maintenance costs grow as systems age. Those applications that do not produce the benefits hoped for usually must undergo
modification, which produces strong demand for resources. Uncontrolled expansion and its consequence of rapid growth create computing problems that can interfere with successful computing use and
detract from the advantages that applications do provide. This produces a second kind of demand: for changes to rectify problems.
Usually, such demands focus on the need for greater financial resources (e.g., to get a machine with bigger core memory or to hire
more programmers), or on the need for policy to overcome users'

problems (e.g., demand for establishment of a computing policy board to help unserviced users obtain service they desire).

Demands for change feed directly back into the political/administrative environment as requests for more resources, new applications, new equipment, more staff, improved user access to computing resources, more training for users or for technical staff, decentralization of computing activity, or a host of other possible changes. These demands are filtered by the political/administrative environment, possibly undergoing modifications as the constraints imposed by the political/administrative environment are dealt with, and the results of the filtering and arbitration are new policies for computing. New policies, in turn, alter the computing environment, which produces altered outcomes followed by new sets of demands.

The cycle is not quite complete, however, because the intra-organizational environment is continually influenced by the extra-organizational environment. The extra-organizational environment has a strong influence on computing growth in the cities. This influence occurs two ways. First, technical promotion increases the propensity toward expansion by promoting a demand for change in the form of greater use of computing technology. This demand results in policies for development of sophisticated computing capability, which in turn results in a more diverse and sophisticated computing environment and more extensive applications development. This, in turn, brings changes in computing benefits and problems, stimulating new demands for change. Second, outside funding sources, such as federal and state government agencies, can affect the political/administrative system's propensity to allow computing growth by providing funds to adopt and expand computing. Outside resources also can alter the equilibrium of the political decision modes for allocating computing resources by subsidizing particular interests (e.g., law enforcement or city planning), thereby affecting the pattern of growth (Perry and Kraemer 1979).

The community environment influences the political/administrative system by providing (and changing) the top political leadership of the local government through the electoral process. Computing can and sometimes does become a political issue in local elections, usually because it is perceived that some change needs to be made. Regardless of whether computing is an election issue, the outcomes of local elections can dramatically alter the policies for computing by altering priorities for systems and services, and thus the whole process of interaction among environment, outcome, and demand factors.

This completes the cycle of computing development and growth. This model for understanding the computing milieu in local governments is a counterclockwise flow, from the political/administrative system to policies for computing that both build and act through the computing enviornment to produce benefits and problems of computing. These benefits and problems in turn feed back to the political/administrative system through demands for resource commitment to support greater development and requests to alter computing policies to mitigate problems. Benefits and problems also affect the community environment, indirectly through the service delivery mechanisms of the local government and directly in the form of computer applications that actually reach citizens. The community environment in turn affects the political/administrative system and changes it through the political process. The extra-community environment affects computing within the city through technical change, which affects the economics of investment in computing, and through inter-organizational change, which affects the requirements and incentives for investment in particular application areas (e.g., reporting requirements and financial grants from federal or state agencies).

Our theory suggests that local governments have grown in their use of computing through a series of stages, brought about by changes demanded as a result of external technical development, intergovernmental relationships, and the outcomes of computer use. To summarize the theory, the earlier stages of computing growth are characterized by initial computing adoption, dedication of computing to automation of previously manual portions of routine tasks, vague and nonspecific policies for computing management, speed and accuracy benefits, cost and staff savings, and in some cases benefits from improved service delivery. They also experience problems in gaining support from potential users, acquiring skilled staff, and gaining knowledge of what computing can and cannot do. The constraints on computing are usually alleviated due to pressure for growth of computing into new functional areas as potential users become desirous of obtaining computing capability. This begins a move to the middle stage.

The middle stage is characterized by established, routine uses, with increasing embellishment of those uses, and growing application to more complex tasks such as management and planning. In the middle stage there is development of increasingly specific management policies to control and constrain computing, such as more formal central management control of computing. Computing growth is not tightly constrained, however, and there is a willingness to support development of new systems. There are some continued increases in benefits from improved speed and accuracy, cost and staff savings, and enhanced service delivery. There might be some early benefits from simple analytical and reporting systems for planning and management. These middle-stage cities have relatively few problems. Continued growth, coupled with simultaneous resource restrictions and increasing user department pressure to decentralize control and systems development, prepares the installation for a move toward the later stages of development.

The later stages of computing growth (as of the time we collected our data) are characterized by long-established routine applications and rapidly increasing application to management and planning tasks. There is a mix of policies for centralized computing services, but decentralized computing for systems development and policymaking through mechanisms such as policy boards and management and user training, as well as continued efforts to apply advanced technology to meet demands. There are decreasing benefits from automation of routine tasks, but increasing benefits from management and planning tasks that have been automated. Problems are increasing with obsolescence in older routine applications, complexities of the technology, difficulty in finding and keeping highly trained staff needed to cope with the complex environment, and growing reluctance on the part of the organizational policymakers to continue to come up with the resources needed to cope with the rapidly escalating costs of computing. This stage, which characterizes the more advanced computing installations, might be followed by yet another stage with properties that are not yet observable.

Our stage model indicates several important features of computing growth and describes the difficulties in controlling the computing phenomenon. Growth seems to be endemic to computing environments thus far. Few if any organizations that adopt computing remain long at a low level of use. Even when new applications development is curtailed, older systems are usually being augmented and enhanced. Another feature of the evolution of computing is its cyclical character, even though the overall process can be described in terms of stages. The cyclical nature of evolution takes place through the cycle of problem and need recognition, policy formulation or change, modification of the computing environment, the appearance of the outcomes of such changes, and the recognition of new problems and needs. This begins the cycle again by generating demands for change. This cycle might revolve through several iterations for each major component of computing activity: systems development, hardware upgrades, reorganization of the computing operation, and so forth. Finally, it seems likely that policies for computing are often reactive rather than proactive in their origin. That is, they are often formulated and adopted in attempts to try to resolve recognized problems and needs, rather than in the hope that some ideal state of computing will materialize. Policies tend to be coping strategies, designed to deal with problems that appear in the computing and user environments at given points in time.[5] Policy changes eventually result in changes in the computing environment and outcomes of use, which in turn create new mixes of needs and problems that must be dealt with.

IMPLICATIONS OF OUR THEORY
    There are two alternative implications of this theory. First, we could speculate that computing is a dynamic phenomenon in which change is so rapid that nearly all computing environments are beset with problems and shortfalls in expected benefits. In such circumstances it is doubtful that management policies can fully remedy this situation. Our model does not predict a stage of "maturity" in which benefits are highly positive and problems fully under control. Thus we posit no policy pathway to computing maturity. Rather, the best organizations can hope for is to come up with "coping strategies" to attenuate the negative and accentuate the positive outcomes of computing use.
    The alternative implication of our theory is that computing de-

velopment is highly dynamic, but ultimately is controllable through concerted and informed policy action. Widespread problems in computing at the present result from the slow "learning curve" that organizations must follow in developing appropriate policy that can bring this complex technology under control. As changes in the technology itself slow down and as experience is gained in application and management of computing, advanced computer-using organizations probably will achieve some greater state of control, and possibly a state of maturity.[6]

Both of these are plausible implications of the theory articulated in this chapter, but neither can be tested using our data bases. Further research must be done to determine whether proactive computing policies can be developed that will determine the course of computing development and the outcomes of computing use. In the final section we conclude with a discussion of research strategies that will aid in this task.

Toward Better Theories of the Evolution of Computing in Organizations

This book has told two stories. One story deals with the ways in which computing is utilized in city government organizations and with what effects. The second deals with the patterns of change over time that might account for the findings of our study of computing use and effects. This final section discusses these stories in the light of a basic motivation that led us to write this book: a desire to explain the relationships between the characteristics of computing use and effects in organizations and the strategies adopted to help direct that use toward different ends. At this point we can step back and assess where the two stories fit into the broader pattern of intellectual inquiry on the subject of computing's place in organizations.

The stage theories described above attempt to account for change in computing over time. They assume that the changes follow some identifiable pattern or patterns. They are therefore theories of the evolution of computing in organizations and thus fit within the general form of evolution explanations in the social sciences. Evolution theories in the social sciences take two general forms (van Parijs 1981). The first is the "evolutionist" form, which concentrates on identifying the direction of change, usually in the context of some expected end state toward which change proceeds. Evolutionist theories of change in the social sciences are commonly constructed as successions of stages leading to the end state. Among the better-known stage theories of social evolution are those of St. Augustine, Compte, Hegel, Spencer, and Newman (Ponsioen 1969). Well-known stage theories of change in economics are found in the works of Marx (1867), Kuznets (1965) and Rostow (1971). In such theories the direction taken by the evolving entity (e.g., a social group, a firm, an economy) is determined by the mechanisms that reenforce the change toward the end state, and discourage change away from the end state. In most cases, such theories do not provide comprehensive explanations of the mechanisms of change, or details on how such mechanisms function on a regular basis.

The second general form of evolution theories is the "evolutionary" form, which attempt to explain in detail the mechanisms of change that result in orderly (i.e., not fully random) change. Evolutionary theories generally do not presume any end state toward which change is proceeding. Rather, they assume that changes occur through mechanisms that generally, but not always, result in improved welfare for the evolving entity given prevailing environmental conditions. The directionality provided by the sum of the changes is determined through the consequences the changes have on the entity. Evolutionary changes that reduce an entity's welfare are either "corrected" by selection of new and more advantageous states, or result in the demise of the entity. A key component of evolutionary theories is that, to some extent, the mechanisms of selection must choose randomly among their selection choices.[7] This makes an expected end state illogical, and evolutionary theories generally do not lead easily to predictions.

The stage theories presented in this chapter are not evolutionary theories. The Nolan theory is a classical evolutionist theory, in which the changes in computing in the organization move in the direction of the state of "maturity." Technical advancement stimulates change, while the intervening force of regulatory action balances freedom and constraint to produce policies that contribute to the eventual achievement of maturity.

Our stage theory adopts a modified version of this conflictual model involving freedom and constraint, but we do not assume the presence of an end state as Nolan's theory does. Our theory implies only the possible presence of an equilibrium state in which a balance is effected between tendencies for computing to grow and the constraining actions of management. This state is unstable over time because of continuing changes in the supply-push and demand-pull forces that stimulate computing growth. Our theory concentrates less on the likely end state of computing than on the processes by which changes through the stages take place. In this sense our theory fits someplace between evolutionist and evolutionary theories, in a category that can be called theories of dynamics (Sorokin 1957; Moore 1967; Ponsioen 1969; Klein 1977; Nelson and Winter 1982; van Parijs, 1981). Theories of dynamics are attempts to describe the actual processes of continual change in an effort to identify those patterns that show some consistency over time. They stop short of describing the exact mechanisms whereby "selection" takes place, so they are not evolutionary theories. However, their agnosticism about the presence of true end states sets them apart from evolutionist theories.

Evolutionist theories often precede evolutionary theories (van Parijs 1981). They are accounts of possible interactions among variables thought to be significant in accounting for ordered change. They might be better called "hypotheses," and, indeed, Nolan called his early stage theory a hypothesis (Nolan 1973a). But evolutionist theories have a singular drawback in the realm of scientific research. Their characterizations of the mechanisms of change are so broad that they are difficult to test empirically. Tests of such theories are possible only in the broad sense of watching to see whether predictions based on them prove to be correct. All evolutionist theories embody predictions, the eventual achievement of an end state being the most obvious. Nolan's early theory (1973a) failed on this test of prediction when the predicted end state of "integration," incorporating reduced cost growth, failed to materialize. The theory was modifed (Nolan 1979) to account for this failure by addition of new stages. This later theory made another prediction that an end state (this time called maturity) would be achieved, and further predicted that growth in costs would decline after a new stage ("data administration") was completed.[8]

Our own stage theory does not predict the emergence of an end state, so it cannot be tested by its predictions. However, it incorporates greater specification of the variables involved and the relationships among them. It can be tested by comprehensive study of the changes that take place with computing in organizations over time. Such a detailed longitudinal study would determine more precisely the ordering of the key events in the process of change, thereby establishing the likely causal connections among the variables incorporated in our theory.

What, then, do we suggest as a fruitful path for future research on the evolution of computing? Further research incorporating Nolan's model might focus on determining whether there is a "true" direction being taken in computing growth in organizations, leading to some inevitable end state. This has not been done as yet, and it is not clear that it can be done successfully. There is the possibility that no identifiable end state can be ascertained from a study of past and present experiences. There may be in fact no such end state, or it may be impossible to uncover it if there is one. Unless a purposive direction behind changes in computing in organizations is empirically identified, theories about the direction and any end state toward which it is headed must remain speculative. Nevertheless, important insights emerge as a result of constructing evolutionist theories like Nolan's.

Our own inclination is somewhat different, however. We think it will be fruitful to continue to explore the actual experiences with computing in organizations over time. In this we seek to explore the dynamics of computing in greater detail in a consistent manner, over a period of years, and within the same organizations. Ideally, such research would be undertaken as a long-term monitoring study using a scientifically selected sample of organizations. Unfortunately the constraints of time and budget that accompany most research in this field will likely preclude such an ambitious study. Nevertheless, detailed scenarios of computing change can be constructed for a set of organizations using retrospective accounts and cross-sectional data collected at two or more points in time (e.g., every five or ten years).[9] Such a study might collect data in two ways: it could record the "status" value of key variables at different points in time; and it could historically trace the processes and events that participants in the changes believed to be important.

Whether a genuine evolutionary theory of computing change in organizations can be constructed and tested remains to be seen. No such theory has emerged as yet. The next step in research leading to such a theory must concentrate on specifying the exact mechanisms by which the changes occur. It is to this end that we will turn our attention in our own research, and we encourage others to do so.

Notes

1. Extensive discussion of the use of stage theories in accounting for the diffusion of innovations can be found in Tornatzky et al. (1983:17–48).

2. The descriptions of Nolan's theory presented here are drawn from Nolan (1973a), Gibson and Nolan (1974), and Nolan (1979). A systematic comparison and critique of these theories is presented in King and Kraemer (1983).

3. Our use of the terms "freedom" and "constraint" as substitutes for Nolan's terms "slack" and "control" is intended to generalize the description of the basic forces behind change in his model. We believe freedom and constraint are less purposive than the terms slack and control because the latter imply deliberate policy intention: that is, to allow slack or to introduce control. In our basic rendering of Nolan's model we reduce slack to the more general term freedom in order to show that freedom can arise as the absence of policy. We reduce control to constraint to indicate that constraint, while often a component of control, can also be present by default when conditions become self-constraining.

4. An earlier articulation of this model can be found in Kraemer and King (1981a), and in a theoretical paper by Kraemer (1980).

5. Lucas (1982) has also commented on this possibility, and indeed, titles his book *Coping with Computing*.

6. This is very much like the implication Nolan (1979) draws from his theory. The successful balancing of slack and control (freedom and constraint) is a skill that can be acquired by managers over time, although Nolan does not specify how the skill is acquired or how long it should take.

7. A completely random set of changes would result in any evolution, since the notion of evolution entails that there is order in change. On the other hand, evolutionary selection must to some extent be a random process. Without randomness change is either "inevitable," in which case there is no use constructing a mechanistic theory to account for variance in changes, or it is fully "actional," resulting from the deliberate actions of some all-powerful entity. This is fully explained in van Parijs (1981:128–173).

8. According to Nolan's 1979 prediction, the decline in cost growth should occur in three to five years, making the "test period" of the prediction 1982–1984 (Nolan 1979:122).

9. We, together with Debora Dunkle, have recently begun two studies that will attempt to refine our understanding of how computing changes in organizations over time. One consists of a set of detailed case studies in ten cities, in which the detailed histories of computing evolution will be traced using a combination of retrospective analyses involving knowledgeable informants in the sites and the comparison of current and prior data from the sites collected in studies over the past fifteen years. The second study will replicate key portions of the 1975 URBIS Project census survey of U.S. cities in order to establish a second panel of data on the character, uses, and policies and outcomes related to computing in cities.

DETAILS
OF THE
RESEARCH

1.0 Overview

THIS RESEARCH project utilized two existing data bases: the URBIS Project data base on computing in U.S. cities and counties, developed by the Public Policy Research Organization (PPRO) in 1976; and the Organization for Economic Cooperation and Development data base on computing in cities in nine member nations of the OECD (not including the United States), also developed in 1976. This appendix describes the genesis of this comparative study, the research methodologies employed in conducting the comparative analyses presented in this book, and the measures used in analysis in both data bases.

The URBIS and OECD studies were conceived independently, but they were brought together through the efforts of Dr. Ruth Davis (then at the National Bureau of Standards), a member of the URBIS Project National Advisory Committee and the U.S. representative to the OECD Committee for Science and Technology. The URBIS project staff established communication with the Steering Committee of the

OECD Panel on Information Technology and Urban Management, which was responsible for the OECD study that resulted in the exchange of project plans, questionnaires, and reports. These cooperative efforts culminated in a formal submission to OECD by the authors of a request for the completed inquiry forms (the raw project data) from the OECD study, which was granted through the efforts of Hans Peter Gassman, OECD Secretariat.

Support for combined analysis of the URBIS and OECD data was provided by a grant from the National Science Foundation. An International Advisory Committee comprised of people who had participated in the OECD study was formed that provided guidance and reviewed the project's reports. The Committee members were:

Dr. Mogens Rømer, Chairman of the OECD Panel and Director of Kommunedata, Denmark

Dr. Barry Wellar, Department of Urban Affairs, Ministry of State, Canada

Mr. George Gaits, Department of Environment, United Kingdom

Dr. Wolfgang Hartenstein, DATUM, Federal Republic of Germany

Mr. Eric Lefèvre, Mission a l'Informatique, Ministère de l'Industrie, France

Mr. Paul Kenneth, OECD Secretariat

2.0 Methods

This research used secondary analysis of preexisting data bases collected for specific purposes that did not exactly correspond to the purposes of our research focus. Such analysis required reformulation of the data bases such that our research questions could be analyzed. In some cases this meant selecting out the responses from certain respondents for analysis and combining and scaling variables into constructs not originally envisioned by those who created the data bases. The fact that this research depended on secondary analysis emphasizes its focus on hypothesis-generation rather than hypothesis-testing.

This research was also a comparative analysis, utilizing responses to research questions taken from different samples. Respondents were from 56 cities in 10 nations: 40 from the United States studied in the URBIS project, and 16 from 9 other nations studied in the OECD study. There is sometimes a problem of low comparability among seemingly identical indicators because of differences among the samples in such studies. We minimized these by use of a schema whereby the responses from the OECD survey could be reliably considered comparable to responses from the URBIS survey. This schema is explained in section 2.4 below.

2.1 DESCRIPTION OF THE URBIS AND OECD DATA BASES

2.1.1 DATA COLLECTION IN THE URBIS PROJECT

The URBIS Project began in 1974 at the Public Policy Research Organization of the University of California at Irvine, supported by a grant from the National Science Foundation. The goal of the project was to "determine how information technology can be used more effectively to improve the performance of local governments in the areas of decision making, services delivery, and work environment" (PPRO 1974).

The project took place in two phases. Phase I, an extensive census survey of all 403 U.S. cities with over 50,000 population, was used to develop a profile on the state-of-the-art in local government computing operations and to gather preliminary information about the impacts of computer technology from responses of local government chief executives (mayors, city managers, etc.). Data were collected from approximately 80 percent of the governments surveyed.

These data were input to a stratification algorithm for selection of 40 cities arrayed along six dimensions of computing characteristics produced by various policies for computing management: degree of automation, degree of sophistication of data processing, degree of data integration, degree of decentralization of computing resources, and degree to which users are charged for computing services. This stratified selection produced a sample of 20 cities located at each of the high and low ends of each characteristic (Kraemer, Danziger, Dutton, Mood, and Kling 1976).

Phase II focused on a set of "information processing tasks"

(IPTs) for selecting respondents, gathering data, and assessing impacts. An IPT is an activity with a specific objective that explicitly involves information processing and that might be automated. Examples of ITPs would be payroll processing, which involves translating records of hours worked, pay rates, and payroll deductions into a payroll check, and utility customer inquiry, which involves searching a file of utility customers for unpaid bills or other information. A large number of possible IPTs have been identified for city governments, but for practical purposes only six major IPTs were utilized in our study. These are summarized in figure A.1.

URBIS data collection utilized structured interviews, self-administered questionnaires, secondary data obtained from published reports and the U.S. Census, and extensive site reports written by the investigators. Structured interviews were used to obtain data on the six IPTs. Respondents were selected based on their role in city government and their relationship to at least one of the IPTs. The interviews were conducted with approximately forty people in each city by two members of the research team during two-week site visits to each city. In addition, each interviewee plus an average of 45 other city personnel filled out self-administered questionnaires in each city. A total of 2,637 such questionnaires were obtained from a set of respondents ranging from top city management to clerks and patrol officers.

Each computer installation servicing each city was surveyed using a self-administered questionnaire regarding facility policies, equipment in use, staffing, the amount of money budgeted for computing, the organizational arrangements of the computing facility, and the number and kinds of applications operational within the computing facility. This was completed by the manager of each installation.

Finally, extensive contextual information was collected by the research team and incorporated into detailed case study reports for each city.

Phase II of the URBIS Project provided the primary input to this comparative study because it collected the information necessary to develop an understanding of the important policies affecting performance impacts of alternative computing arrangements in cities under varying conditions.

Figure A.1 TYPES OF INFORMATION PROCESSING TASKS AND ASSOCIATED APPLICATIONS

Type	Characterization	Applications Chosen
Record-keeping	Activities which primarily involve the *entry, updating, and storage of data,* with a secondary need for access; the computer facilitates manageable storage and easy updating for nearly unlimited amounts of information.	Traffic ticket processing
Calculating/Printing	Activities which primarily involve *sorting, calculating, and printing of stored data* to produce specific operational outputs; utilizes the computer's capabilities as a high-speed data processor.	Budget control (reporting)
Record-searching	Activities where *access to and search of data files* are of primary importance; by defining parameters, relevant cases can be retrieved from a file with speed and comprehensiveness; on-line capability of computer is particularly useful.	Detective investigative support Patrol officer support
Record restructuring	Activities which involve *reorganization, reaggregation, and/or analysis of data;* the computer is used to link data from diverse sources or to summarize large volumes of data as management and planning information.	Policy analysis
Sophisticated analytics	Activities which *utilize sophisticated visual, mathematical, simulation, or other analytical methods to examine data;* the special capabilities of computers make possible the manipulation of data about complex, interdependent phenomena.	Patrol manpower allocation
Process control	Activities which approximate a cybernetic system; *data about the state of a system is continually monitored and fed back to a human or automatic controller* which steers the system toward a performance standard; the computer's capability for real-time monitoring and direction of activities are utilized.	Budget control (monitoring)

2.1.2 DATA COLLECTION IN THE OECD PROJECT

The OECD project began in early 1974 under the Panel on Information Technology and Urban Management of the Computer Utilization Group of the Organization for Economic Cooperation and Development (OECD). Nine member nations of OECD participated in this study: Austria, Canada, Denmark, Finland, France, Germany, Japan, Sweden, and the United Kingdom. The sixteen cities chosen to participate in the project (listed in chapter 1) were selected by the panel's representatives according to a set of guiding criteria: 1) the cities selected must have had sufficient computer experience for the investigator to discern impacts from that use, 2) both cities with locally-based computing arrangements and cities with regional/national computing arrangements were to be represented, and 3) different sizes of local governments were to be selected. Because of the complexity and variety of cities located within each nation in the study, the panel felt that the use of statistical techniques for site selection would not be practical (Gaits 1978). Instead, a purposive sampling of cities in the participating nations was used to obtain a sample that provided variation not only in terms of computer policies and arrangements, but in terms of the size of the populations served as well.

The OECD study used a combination of methods for data collection: review of existing studies and secondary data, administration of prestructured interviews, and examination of existing documents and contextual materials gathered from site visits. Four areas of computing impacts were selected for intensive study: impacts on the city population, impacts upon the efficiency of local administration, impacts upon planning and provision of services, and impacts on the work of municipal employees (Gaits 1978). The investigators interviewed a variety of sources within the local government using structured, open-ended interviews with position holders in different levels of the local government. Respondents ranged from the top city management down to the users of EDP applications, as well as EDP management. Special interview schedules were used for the chief executive, department heads, section heads, the EDP managers, and EDP personnel who worked on applications used by the section heads. The interview schedules were open-ended to enable the interviewer to take into account local variations. The interviews were conducted in the language of the respondents, but the responses (except those of the French cities) were recorded in English. All interviews were conducted by the national experts from the OECD panel.

In addition to interviewing respondents, the researchers filled out a fact sheet (Form A) designed to obtain basic economic, sociological, and governmental-administrative characteristics about each site city visited. The researchers also prepared extensive site reports detailing, summarizing, and elaborating the computing activity within each city.

Research and data collection took place in late 1975 and early 1976. Reports were prepared by the nine participating nations' delegations, and several summary papers dealing with topical issues such as management of data processing in the cities studied were written. These materials were published as report number 12 in the OECD Informatics Studies series (OECD 1978). However, it was not possible for the panel to conduct the extensive empirical analyses originally planned because of constraints of time and analytic resources (OECD 1978). Therefore, the raw OECD data provided the OECD input to this research report.

2.2 SIMILARITIES BETWEEN THE URBIS AND OECD PROJECTS

Both studies were conducted independently, but there were striking similarities between the two data bases. Figure A.2 summarizes these similarities.

First, the *theoretical orientation* of the two projects was similar. Computing was seen in both studies both to affect the organization and to be affected by the organization. Thus, both studies concentrated on collecting a wide array of data about the organizations themselves as well as their computing activities.

Second, data were collected from *similar position holders* within each local government: chief executives, department heads, and section heads. The URBIS Project included many government personnel, but it was possible to select out only those respondents in each URBIS city who held positions similar to those in the OECD cities. Tables A.1 and A.2 display the number of respondents for each position in the OECD and URBIS cities. Except for the city of Leeds, the num-

Table A.1 DISTRIBUTION OF RESPONDENTS IN URBIS CITIES

City	CAO	Department Heads	Section Heads	EDP Managers	Total
Montgomery, Ala.	1	4	3	1[a]	9
Little Rock, Ark.	1	3	6	1	11
Burbank, Calif.	1	7	2	1	11
Costa Mesa, Calif.	1	5	5	1	12
Long Beach, Calif.	0	2	4	1	7
Riverside, Calif.	1	7	5	1	13
Sacramento, Calif.	1	8	6	1	16
San Francisco, Calif.	1	10	4	1	16
San Jose, Calif.	1	2	3	1	7
Stockton, Calif.	1	6	6	1	14
Fort Lauderdale, Fla.	1	6	2	1	10
Miami Beach, Fla.	1	3	5	1	10
Tampa, Fla.	1	8	14	1[a]	24
Atlanta, Ga.	1	1	8	1	11
Evansville, Ill.	0	3	1	1[a]	5
Louisville, Ky.	1	7	10	1	19
New Orleans, La.	1	4	6	1[a]	12
Baltimore, Md.	0	2	8	1[a]	11
Brockton, Mass.	0	3	2	1	6
Newton, Mass.	1	6	4	1[a]	12
Grand Rapids, Mich.	1	9	9	1	20
Warren, Mich.	0	6	7	1	14
Florissant, Mo.	1	3	4	1	9
Kansas City, Mo.	1	9	11	1[a]	22
St. Louis, Mo.	1	8	6	1[a]	16
Lincoln, Neb.	1	9	3	1	14
Las Vegas, Nev.	0	9	3	1[a]	13
Paterson, N.J.	1	3	7	1	12
Albany, N.Y.	1	7	0	1[a]	9
Cleveland, Ohio	1	7	11	1	20
Tulsa, Okla.	0	6	9	1	16
Lancaster, Pa.	1	4	4	1	10
Philadelphia, Pa.	0	6	10	1[a]	17
Chesapeake, Va.	1	11	1	1[a]	14
Hampton, Va.	1	9	7	1	18
Portsmouth, Va.	1	9	5	1	15
Seattle, Wash.	1	9	6	1[a]	16
Spokane, Wash.	0	4	2	1	7
Milwaukee, Wis.	1	5	5	1[a]	12
Oshkosh, Wis.	1	3	3	1	8
Total	32	233	217	40	522

[a] Multiple installations within the city.

Table A.2 DISTRIBUTION OF RESPONDENTS IN OECD CITIES

Country City	CAO	Department Heads	Secion Heads	Appli- cations	EDP Managers	Total
Austria						
Vienna	1	4	3	4	1	13
Denmark						
Vaerloese	1	5	8	8	1	23
Aarhus	1	5	9	9	1	25
Finland						
Helsinki	1	2	3	2	1	9
France						
Gagny	1	1	3	4	1	10
Montpellier	1	1	3	4	1	10
Toulouse	1	2	3	7	1	14
Germany						
Backnang	1	3	6	0	1 [a]	11
Duisberg	1	1	1	1	1	5
Nurtingen	1	2	2	2	1 [a]	8
Sweden						
Jonkoping	1	3	3	5	1 [b]	13
United Kingdom						
Leeds	1	1	0	0	1	3
Torbay	1	1	7	7	1	17
Canada						
Calgary	1	4	5	0	1	11
Japan						
Maebashi	1	5	9	7	1	23
Nishinomiya	1	5	8	10	1	25
Total	16	45	73	70	16	

[a] The EDP manager and installation surveyed is Stuttgart (the regional installation). Hence, the responses for Backnang and for Nurtingen are identical on this file.

[b] Only limited information is known about Jonkoping. Form E was filled out by the local linkage with Kommunedata.

ber of respondents proved to be adequate for representing the computing efforts in the OECD cities. In the case of Leeds, the site report was extensive enough to score Leeds on a number of indicators and to check the responses of the single department head interviewed. In nine of the URBIS cities, the chief appointed (executive) officer did not respond to the questionnaire, which somewhat weakened the major indicators of computing impact being measured for this level. However, sufficient data from the other cities were available for this purpose.

Figure A.2 MAJOR SIMILARITIES BETWEEN OECD AND URBIS PROJECTS

Similar Theoretical Orientation
Computing is embedded within an organization, e.g., local government.
Surveys of Similar Position Holders
Chief executives, department heads, and section heads were surveyed.
Similar Areas of Investigation
Data collected on impacts of computers on local government performance, the relative economies of computer usage over manual usage, and the problems related to the use of computing in local government.
Surveys of EDP Managers
Computing policies were reported by EDP managers.
Similar Applications Studied
Applications studied were common to both studies.
Site Reports Prepared
A detailed site report was prepared for each city in both studies.
Approximately the Same Time of Investigation
Both projects conducted in the period 1975–1976.

The OECD and URBIS data bases also had similar distributions in respondents, with approximately one-third of department and section heads based in the central administrative departments, and the other two-thirds in the operating departments. There is a major difference, however, in the high percentage of police departments represented among the URBIS cities that is not found among the OECD cities. Similarly, there is a higher representation of social welfare departments in the OECD cities than in the URBIS cities. Police functions are generally performed by American local governments, but are performed by other levels of government in most of the OECD study nations. More functional agencies in the area of social welfare are found in the OECD cities than in the URBIS cities. Tables A.3 and A.4 show the types of departments in which the department heads and section heads were located.

Third, both surveys included *similar areas of investigation.* For example, both surveys included questions on the impacts of computers on local government performance, the relative economies of computer usage over manual usage, and the problems related to the use of computing in local government. Investigation of these areas of interest involved querying similar position-holders in both studies. Chief executives and department heads were surveyed regarding impacts

Table **A.3** DISTRIBUTION OF DEPARTMENTS FOR URBIS CITIES

Department	Department Head Level (N = 287)	Section Head Level (N = 159)	Total (N = 446)
Top management			
CAO's office	2%	0%	1%
Central Administration			
Finance	4	20	10
EDP	–	2	1
Accounting	–	7	3
Budget	18	0	11
Purchasing	3	0	2
Personnel	6	1	4
Clerk/recorder	2	0	2
Controller	–	8	3
Operating			
Police	7	29	15
Planning	3	1	2
Traffic	3	12	6
Courts	5	9	6
Fire	4	2	4
Treasury/collection	4	0	3
Assessment	3	1	2
Tax	1	1	1
Central garage/motor pool	–	1	–
Housing and urban renewal	1	0	1
Licensing and code			
enforcement	2	1	2
Engineering	1	0	1
Streets and highways	2	1	2
Transportation	2	0	1
Public works	3	2	3
Sanitation	1	0	1
Water supply	3	2	3
Utilities	2	2	2
Public health/hospitals	2	0	2
Public welfare, human			
resources, social services	3	0	2
Parks and recreation	4	0	2
Libraries	2	0	1
Communications	1	0	–
Public safety	1	1	1
Election commission	1	0	–
Management research	–	0	–
	100	100	100

Note: Dash (–) denotes less than 1 percent but not zero.

Table A.4 DISTRIBUTION OF DEPARTMENTS FOR OECD CITIES

Department	Department Head Level (N = 55)	Section Head Level (N = 71)	Total (N = 126)
Top Management			
Council	2%	0%	1%
Mayor's office	4	1	2
Central Administration			
Finance	7	4	6
Accounting	9	11	10
Budget	0	1	1
Purchasing	0	1	1
Personnel	5	6	6
Administrative services	20	1	10
Controller	0	1	1
Operating			
Police	4	1	2
Planning	2	3	2
Treasury/collection	2	4	3
Assessment	0	1	1
Tax	5	10	8
Central garage/motor pool	0	1	1
Housing	0	6	3
Engineering	2	1	2
Streets and highways	4	3	3
Transportation	4	1	2
Water	4	4	4
Utilities	4	3	3
Public health/hospitals	4	6	5
Public welfare, human resources, social services	9	15	13
Libraries	0	1	1
Election commission, voter registration	0	1	1
Management research	2	0	1
Education	4	3	3
Agriculture	2	1	2
Population registry	0	3	2
Technical services	4	1	2
	100	100	100

of computing on management policy making in both URBIS and OECD cities. This made it possible to utilize responses from similar position-holders in the two surveys.

Fourth, in both surveys the *EDP managers were surveyed* about policies and characteristics of the computing installation servicing each local government, resulting in collection of data on EDP operations, asking similar questions from respondents of equivalent perspective.

Fifth, in both surveys, *similar applications* for government operations were investigated. The OECD data contained detailed information on specific information-processing tasks similar to those in the URBIS project. However, the same tasks were not investigated in every OECD city, which precluded comparisons of information-processing tasks between the OECD cities and the URBIS cities. This book does not present the analysis of similar application areas, but preliminary analysis and clarification of certain relationships found in later analysis were aided by the capability of comparing similar applications used in local governments.

Sixth, investigators in both surveys drew up extensive *site reports* on each city that they visited. These provided the contextual information necessary for conducting a comparative study using both data bases.

Finally, both surveys were conducted around the *same time period,* 1975–1976, which lessened the effect of differing time periods in the comparison of the two data bases.

2.3 METHODOLOGICAL DIFFERENCES BETWEEN URBIS AND OECD

Despite the important similarities between the two databases, there were differences between the two samples that raised methodological questions. Figure A.3 summarizes these differences.

First, different *data collection instruments* were used. Most of the URBIS data used in this book were obtained through a forced-choice questionnaire (the User Core questionnaire) distributed to a wide variety of city employees in the 40 URBIS Phase 2 cities. For OECD, the data were obtained from the responses of city employees to a series of open-ended questions with very few forced-choice questions presented to each respondent. This difference is important because responses can be affected by the type of stimulus presented (Edwards 1957; Selltiz, Wrightsman, and Cook 1976). Variations in response could be attributed to differences in data collection methods instead of to real differences between the URBIS and OECD cities.

Figure A.3 MAJOR DIFFERENCES BETWEEN URBIS AND OECD PROJECTS

URBIS	OECD
Data collection method	
Forced-choice mail-back questionnaire	Semi-structured interviews
Sampling method	
Stratified random sample by U.S. cities with at least minimal computing	Purposive sampling by national experts
Respondent selection	
Nonprobability sampling of respondents from all departments within city	Non-probability sampling of respondents from departments using computing within a city
Sampling frame	
Only U.S. cities	Cities located in nine nations

For example, URBIS respondents were provided with a series of straightforward questions with all possible responses listed. The respondent merely circled the response closest to his own attitudes, opinions, or knowledge of the topic of the question. Hence, the URBIS data contained standardized responses to specific structured stimuli. In the OECD case, impacts of computing were obtained from semi-structured, open-ended questions, in which the respondent was asked to list the specific impacts of computing. No list of impacts was presented, thereby leaving the frame of reference open to the respondent. The fact that an impact was not discussed does not necessarily mean that it had not occurred; perhaps the respondent forgot about it. In general, then, our analyses were both a comparison of OECD and URBIS responses and differences in data collection method (open-ended compared to close-ended survey formats).

Second, the *method of sampling cities* differed between the two projects. URBIS used a multi-stage, stratified sampling technique to select the cities. Cities varied according to the six characteristics, but as a group they were representative of these different characteristics. OECD used a purposive sampling technique in which the researchers selected sites representative of varying types of computing arrangements. OECD cities were therefore not necessarily representative of either their particular nations or of the particular computing arrangements in question.

A third difference between URBIS and OECD was the method used for the *selection of respondents* within the cities. URBIS respondents were selected either because they were affiliated with a specified IPT or were part of the total group of departments within the city. Not all respondents were heavily involved in computer usage within their respective departments, and in some cases the departments surveyed were only minimally automated. OECD interviews were conducted only with department heads and section heads who were located within departments that utilized computing. In most of the cities it was the more intensive users of computing that were interviewed.

Finally, the URBIS and OECD projects differed in terms of the *intranational vs. international sampling frame* used. URBIS sampled cities located within one nation, the United States. OECD cities were selected from nine different nations. National differences were not an issue in URBIS cities, but national and cultural differences were inevitable in the OECD cities. We were thus faced with comparing a homogeneous data base with a heterogeneous data base where variations could be due to national differences rather than differences of computing environment, city environment, or management policies.

The major differences between URBIS and OECD, therefore, were concentrated around data collection methods and sampling methods. These are problems faced by many researchers attempting secondary comparative analysis. Prior to discussing the analytical approach we took with the data, we will briefly describe the methods used to resolve the differences between data sets.

2.4 METHODS USED IN COMPARING URBIS AND OECD

2.4.1 UNIT OF COMPARISON

Given the small number of cities within each national boundary (usually two per nation) in the OECD survey, a decision was made to group together all OECD cities as a single analysis unit, ignoring the fact that these cities were located within different nations. This approach was based on several considerations of the data bases. First, the original OECD selection of sites focused on representation of cities across national boundaries. Hence, cities selected within national boundaries were not necessarily representative of that nation. Most likely it would have compounded errors to do a within-nation analysis. In addition, preliminary intra-nation analysis indicated that national differences were less important than differences of computing environment among the surveyed cities.

2.4.2 RESPONDENT SELECTION

The URBIS data base contained many more position-holders than the OECD data base. To attain comparability of the respondents in the two data bases, the URBIS data base was reduced to include only those respondents who held positions as the chief executive, a department head, or a section head. All other personnel were eliminated from the URBIS sample. Furthermore, since the respondents within the OECD sample were primarily located within departments or sections in which computing was used, the URBIS sample was similarly reduced by eliminating all department heads and section heads located within departments or sections that did not utilize computing in performing their duties. Excluding these repondents also limited the possibility of noninformed opinion by respondents who had little or no experience with computing (Converse 1964).

2.4.3 UNIT OF ANALYSIS

While most of the data in both studies were obtained from individual respondents, the city was selected as the unit of analysis. All respondents within the city were considered representative of the computing community within the city, and their responses were aggregated to represent the computing endeavor within that city. City-level analysis was chosen for several reasons. Our major interest in the research was in ascertaining cities' overall benefits and problems in both the use of computerized applications and policies for computing management. Most cities' computing policies do not vary from level to level or department to department, but are instituted throughout the local government (Kraemer, Dutton, and Northrop 1981). City-wide computing management policies affect the impacts from computing, so all data were aggregated to the city level.

2.4.4 COMPARATIVE CODING PROCEDURE

URBIS interviews and questionnaires used a pre-coded format for data collection, and all coding and file building had been completed by the start of the analyses presented in this book. The OECD project interview forms were in a raw, uncoded state that required the design of a coding procedure that classified the open-ended responses of individuals into a scheme that would permit comparison within OECD as well as with URBIS. The coding format had to include both comparable and theoretically-based variable categories and also allow us to discern an absence of responses in either the URBIS or the OECD sample (Selltiz et al. 1976: 469). The codebook used for coding the various OECD questionnaires was designed to create comparable measures with the URBIS study where possible, and also to capture any unique patterns in the responses made by the OECD respondents. By "unique" we mean both responses not likely to be found in the URBIS context and responses to questions not asked in the URBIS survey.

The OECD interview schedules were coded by recording each open-ended OECD question in the appropriate codebook response category. The category of "other" was included, and the coders were encouraged to use this category to make it possible to pick out those responses that were "unique" to OECD. Questionnaire items in which the category of "other" was frequently used were then identified and subjected to further refinement into additional categories for the responses.

These additional new categories were listed in the codebook, and such questions were then recoded by a different coder to check the reliability and comparability of the original coding effort. In the few cases where there were few indicators or responses on some single interview forms, an aggregate city-level score was created using several interview forms. In such cases, all responses for a single questionnaire item common to all the OECD questionnaires (for example, "What are the constraints on computing?") were listed for each city. Two researchers then independently created coding categories for the responses. Comparison and discussion of the coding categories resulted in a final categorization.

2.4.5 CONSTRUCTION OF VARIABLES AND INDICES

Our goal, like that of other comparative researchers (Scheuch 1968; Verba 1969; Przeworski and Teune 1970), was to select indicators that were "functionally equivalent" items for each concept.

Functional equivalence means that the same variable may be measured by a variety of different indicators, all of which have some bearing on the concept. This helps control for contextual and methodological differences between the two data bases and limits the extent to which indicators are selected on a face-validity basis only. This requires dependence on the researcher's determination of equivalence, which can bias selection. Our choices were strengthened by two conditions: the investigators for this study were intimately knowledgeable on the URBIS indicator and the "meaning" of each indicator, so ambiguous indicators could be easily screened; and the OECD responses to open-ended questions provided extensive information that enabled problematic indicators to be eliminated from the indexes constructed.

2.4.6 METHOD OF AGGREGATION

Aggregation of multiple responses to city-level scores depended on the manner in which the responses were obtained. Three different methods of aggregation were used on the data bases.

For forced-choice items, a mean value aggregation to the city level was performed. This method was used for all URBIS measures from the User Core questionnaire and for OECD forced-choice items. With the forced-choice, mail-back questionnaire design, the investigator loses control of the knowledge of how the questionnaire was completed. Such factors as mood, knowledge, and intent of the respondent were not known (Leege and Francis 1974: 193–198). While filtering of the respondents in terms of the extent to which they were involved in computing on the job had been done, there still remained the possibility of idiosyncratic or uninformed responses. Averaging was used to smooth out such anomalies.

For those items taken from the responses to the OECD open-ended questions, a "maximum value" method was employed; that is, if any department head or section head made reference to the area of interest, the city was scored as possessing that characteristic. While such a method conceivably could give too much weight to idiosyncratic responses, the extended comments of the respondents were available to lessen this possibility. Care was taken not to code responses that appeared to be completely unique to the respondent.

Whenever responses were questionable, the coder would check the site reports and other department head or section head responses in that city for further guidance.

A third aggregation method was used for the construction of the URBIS installation-level variables in those cities with multiple computer installations. Certain characteristics of personnel within an installation will affect computing impacts on performance as well as the extent of problems experienced by users of the installation, so it was inappropriate to simply aggregate the responses of all EDP managers to produce an average city-level variable. Multiple-installation cities can differ considerably from single-installation cities. For example, in a two-installation city in the United States it is often the case that one of the two installations will be devoted to police department use, while the other installation will be designated for all other city department uses. These two different installations tend to devise different approaches to provision of services, so the use of any aggregation method would result in distorted recording of installation characteristics. We therefore selected only one of the installations within a city to "represent" that city, based on the responses of the EDP managers about the kinds of operational applications and about the general users of the data-processing services of the installation. The installation that provided the most significant service to the largest number of users within the city was chosen as the representative installation.

2.5 THE ISSUE OF COMPARABILITY

Different measures can result in incomparability of the concepts being investigated, so the focus of our comparisons was primarily on the interrelationships within each sample rather than across the URBIS and OECD samples. The reader is advised that even though we do present the percentage of cities for each dependent variable within the text of the report, we are not comparing the actual frequencies between the URBIS and OECD samples in terms of "higher than" or "lower than." Rather, we compare the second-order relationships: the extent to which similar relationships between independent and dependent variables can be observed in the two samples. If similar relationships between variables exist in both samples, we have provided substantial evidence that the relationship is in fact there. Our approach, therefore, was to analyze the URBIS and OECD samples separately but within a conceptually similar framework. Each data base was viewed as both a means of replication of the findings of the other data base and a means of specification of relationships between the independent and dependent variables investigated. At times, missing information from one or the other data base restricted our analyses to a single data base. In such cases, one of the data bases served as a generator of hypotheses that could be examined using the other data base.

Throughout the analyses we used construct validation to increase our confidence that we were indeed measuring that which we thought we were measuring. Construct validation tests the adequacy and validity of a construct in terms of its theoretically hypothesized relationships with other variables. For example, the correlations of several different measures of computing benefit with a specific computing policy according to our hypothesized associations would suggest that our measures did represent the variables they were believed to represent.

The differences between the two data bases placed limitations on our analyses, and some of our findings and conclusions cannot be stated as strongly as we would wish. Still, these limitations do not preclude comparison. The relationships found between characteristics of computing policy and computing environment on one hand and computing benefits and problems on the other increase our confidence in the interaction among organization, policy, and computing. Each data base was found to enhance the contribution of the other data bases to our understanding of computing in the cities studied.

3.0 Specific OECD Measures

This section describes the specific measures used for the OECD cities in this book. The various measures were obtained from the following sources:

Form A: Site Profile—Basic Facts
Form B: Format Questions for Interview with "Chief Executive"
Form C: Format Questions for Interview with "Major Depart-
ment Heads"
Form D: Format Questions for Interview with "Section Heads"
Form E: Format Questions for the DP Department
Form F: Applications Enquiry Form (DP)
Site report written by interviewer(s) for that city

3.1 DESCRIPTION OF OECD SAMPLE

The OECD survey consisted of interviews with a variety of local government officials in different local government positions. Variables were selected from the responses to questions located in the
different interviews. The methodology utilized provided data at the individual level and the city level. All analysis was done at the city level.
In order to obtain city-level scores the responses from the department head and section head were aggregated. The exact wording of
the questions used for measuring each variable in OECD, the variable
constructed, the questionnaire used, and the method of aggregation
(if any) used are discussed for each variable.

3.2 INDEPENDENT VARIABLES

3.2.1 CITY ENVIRONMENT

Size of city: the total size of the population of the city, obtained from Form A (see table A.5). The population figures are not
standardized in terms of the source (e.g., census, official estimate,
etc.) but are a good approximation of city size.

Government budget: the total city operating expenditures in
millions of dollars, obtained from Form A and converted to U.S. dollars based on the rate of exchange for March 31, 1976 (table A.5). In
cases where the 1976 figures were not available, the 1975 total operating expenditures were substituted.

3.2.2 COMPUTING ENVIRONMENT

Total EDP budget: 1976 budget obtained from Form E and converted to U.S. dollars at the March 31, 1976, exchange rate (table A.6).

Table **A.5** DISTRIBUTION OF CITY ENVIRONMENT VARIABLES

	Mean	Standard Deviation	Range	(N)
Size of city	366,688	399,046	17,000–1,614,000	(16)
Size of government budget	$214,885,428	$316,227,992	$14,622,000–$1,065,504,000	(14)

DP managers were queried concerning the budgetary expenditures for the following seven areas: all hardware including annual rental costs and maintenance costs; leased and/or purchased software; staff costs including staff overheads; building costs including heating, cleaning, and repairs; consumables such as materials, paper, tapes; external services purchased; plus all other expenditures. The 1974–75 budget total was used when 1975–76 data were not available. For those cities providing services to other sites (e.g., Aarhus), the percentage of income derived from regional/other cities' processing was subtracted from the EDP budget in order to obtain the city-level budget.

Percent of government budget allocated to EDP: the percentage of the total government operating budget allocated for EDP operations, obtained by dividing the total EDP budget by the total government operating budget (table A.6).

Table **A.6** DISTRIBUTION OF COMPUTING ENVIRONMENT VARIABLES

	Mean	Standard Deviation	Range	(N)
Percent of government budget allocated to EDP	.82%	.60%	.24%–2.10%	(14)
EDP budget per capita	$2.96	$1.70	$1.20–$6.53	(16)
Total EDP staff	64.2	67.4	4–204	(13)
Percent computer use	59.5%	24.0%	23%–100%	(14)
Percent increase needed in 1976	35.7%	45.9%	0%–130%	(15)
Year EDP began in city	65.6	4.6	58–72	(16)
Degree of automation	24.0	20.4	4–85	(15)
Degree of functional automation	9.0	4.1	3–19	(15)
Total core capacity	576.6K	585.0K	5K–2048K	(15)

Total EDP staff: the summation of all full-time staff in six categories (managerial, analysts, programmers, data-input operators, clerical support services, and operations) obtained from Form E (table A.6). Part-time staff were not included in the calculation.

EDP budget per capita: the amount of money per city resident spent on EDP, calculated by dividing the total local EDP budget allocation by the size of the population (table A.6).

Percent computer use: the percent level of utilization of the computer per average week, obtained from Form E (table A.6). The base percent figures used were "20×8 hours shift $= 100\%$; 1×8 hours shift $= 5\%$" so all respondents applied identical bases for the percent given.

Percent increase needed in 1976: the increase needed in the following year to provide the same rate of service, excluding inflation (table A.6).

Year EDP began in city: the year the city began using computers (not ADP equipment) obtained from Form E (table A.6). In questionable cases, the site reports were used to obtain the value of this variable.

Degree of automation: the total number of computer applications operational in the city (table A.6). This variable had to be constructed from a variety of sources (e.g., site reports, supporting documents sent from the site, and personal letters), so the inventory of applications can be considered as only an approximation of the degree of automation within the city. For regional sites, only those applications used by the site city were counted.

Degree of functional automation: the list of applications for each site city, classified into the thirty-one functional areas of government operations used in the URBIS Project and listed in figure A.4 (table A.6). The score is the sum of functional areas in which at least one application is operational. The list of applications was obtained from several different sources (site reports, supporting documents, letters), so this variable is an approximation.

Total core capacity: Total core capacity is summing the total core size of all the machines used by the city (table A.6).

Figure A.4 URBIS CLASSIFICATION OF FUNCTIONAL AREAS OF AUTOMATION

Public Safety	Community Development and Public Works
Police protection	Planning and zoning
Fire protection	Housing and urban renewal
Courts	Licensing and code enforcement
Emergency preparedness	Engineering
Finance/Administration	Transportation
Accounting	Streets and highways
Treasury/collection	Sanitation
Assessment	Water supply
Budgeting and management	Utilities
Purchasing/inventory	Human Resources
Personnel	Public health/hospitals
General Government	Public welfare
Data processing	Parks and recreation
Geoprocessing	Vital statistics
Public information	Libraries
Public buildings	Voter registration
Clerk/recorder	
Central garage/motor pool	
Other general government	

3.2.3 TECHNOLOGICAL DEVELOPMENT

Degree of data linkage: the extent to which there is a capability to integrate and link data between files, obtained from the Form E questions: "Do you link data between files?" and "Is your authority developing integrated data bases?," combined into a single index with the following scores and their descriptions:

1. No linkage of data between files and no development of integrated data bases.
2. Sometimes linkage of data between files but no development of integrated data bases.
3. Sometimes linkage of data between files and development of integrated data bases.
4. Linkage of data between files but no development of integrated data bases.
5. Linkage of data between files and development of integrated data bases.

Degree of report sophistication: the degree to which local officials use sophisticated computerized reports in the area of planning, obtained from chief executive and department head responses to the question: "In what ways have computers been used in planning for the future?" (table A.7). Four kinds of responses were found: use data on present situation in conjunction with manual planning methods; use simulations/models in planning; use it for regression projections, forecasting in planning; use survey research and other statistics in determining public opinion for planning purposes. Both the chief executives and department heads could be coded for more than one use type, according to the following scoring pattern: 1) use data with manual planning and/or survey research and other statistics to determine public opinion for planning purposes; 2) regression projections, forecasting; and 3) use simulations/models in planning. Each respondent's answer was given a value from 1–3, depending on the highest mode of use. The city score for degree of report sophistication is the maximum value for all department heads and the CAO in the city. Hence degree of report sophistication scores can range from 0–3.

Number of terminals: the total number of terminals attached to the computer installation obtained from Form E (table A.7). Only those cities with on-line capability were scored on this variable; batch system cities were assigned a missing value score.

On-line computing capability: whether the computing installation provides on-line computing capability, obtained from Form E (table A.7). Four choices were provided (batch, remote-batch, on-line, on-line-real-time) and responses were recoded into one of two categories: batch or remote-batch; and on-line or on-line-real-time.

Degree of sophistication of applications: the highest degree of sophistication of applications used by the local government, obtained from Form C (table A.7). Respondents were asked: "What does your department use computer technology and services for?" Responses were categorized by four types: calculating/record-keeping/record searching, record restructuring (score of 1), process control (score of 2), and sophisticated analytics (score of 3). City-level measures were obtained by aggregating all responses using the maximum value method, so the variable measures the highest level of sophisticated use among departments within the city.

Total applications planned: the number of applications planned

Table A.7 DISTRIBUTION OF TECHNOLOGICAL DEVELOPMENT VARIABLES

	Percent of Cities	(N)
Degree of data linkage		
No linkage	7%	(1)
Some linkage but no development	33	(5)
Some linkage and development	13	(2)
Linkage but no further development	33	(5)
Linkage and further development	13	(2)
	100	(15)
Degree of report (planning) sophistication		
None	12%	(2)
Use data with manual planning	19	(3)
Regression projections/forecasting	44	(7)
Simulations/models	25	(4)
	100	(16)
Degree of sophistication of applications		
Record-keeping/calculating	38%	(6)
Restructuring	12	(2)
Process control	12	(2)
Sophisticated analytics	38	(6)
	100	(16)
On-line computing capability		
No	25%	(4)
Yes	75	(12)
	100	(16)
Multiprogramming capability		
No	29%	(4)
Yes	71	(10)
	100	(14)

	Mean	Standard Deviation	Range	(N)
Total applications planned	2.9	2.0	0–8	(14)
Total applications to be modified	4.0	3.1	1–10	(14)
Number of terminals	25.2	19.2	3–56	(10)

for the city obtained from Form D (table A.7). The total applications planned for the city is the summation of responses to the item, "New major applications under consideration (please list)," making the scores a rough estimation of the plans for future applications. Given that the interviews conducted within each city were done with the heaviest users of automation, the number of applications planned within each city is probably an adequate indicator of application development.

Total applications to be modified: the number of applications undergoing modification obtained from the Form D question, "Major extensions to existing systems (please describe)" (table A.7). The city score is the summation of responses to this item, providing a rough estimation of modifications among the heaviest users of automation. The city score is probably representative of application development for the city.

Multiprogramming: obtained from responses to the Form E item: "Mode of processing: single/multi/real-time/on-line/remote-batch/batch" (table A.7). Responses to "single/multi" were coded: 1) multiprogramming not circled; 2) multiprogramming circled.

3.2.4 STRUCTURAL ARRANGEMENTS

Technological centralization: whether the computer installation is shared by a number of cities (regional) or is located solely within a single city (table A.8). Aarhus was scored specially as a local installation although it serves as a regional installation because it is located within the city.

Decentralized control of priorities: the degree to which user departments are involved in the decisions regarding the use of computers (table A.8). Cities were scored based on the responses to the question on Forms B and C: "How do you set priorities in your authority (department)?" Those cities in which either the DP manager at the regional level or an intergovernmental committee set priorities were scored as "1"; those cities in which the DP manager at the city level or the CAO or the local legislature and mayor or an interdepartmental committee set priorities were scored as "2"; and those cities where the user department heads set priorities were scored as "3."

Policy board: the use of a local policy board for computing (table A.8). This variable was scored by the researchers after reading the site report and Form E responses to a series of items related to use of a formalized group mechanism for the making of EDP decisions on applications development or EDP management. Cities using

Table A.8 DISTRIBUTIONS OF STRUCTURAL ARRANGEMENTS VARIABLES

	Percent of Cities	(N)
Technological centralization		
Local installation	62%	(10)
Regional installation	38	(6)
	100	(16)
Decentralized control of priorities		
Centralized	19%	(3)
Moderately centralized	56	(9)
Decentralized	25	(4)
	100	(16)
Policy board at local level		
No	80%	(12)
Yes	20	(3)
	100	(15)
CAO involvement in management of computing		
Passive	14%	(2)
Cooperate with DP	29	(4)
Team effort with DP	43	(6)
Active	14	(2)
	100	(14)
Department head involvement in management of computing		
Passive	13%	(2)
Cooperate with DP	19	(3)
Team effort with DP	38	(6)
Active	30	(5)
	100	(16)
Charging policy for development		
EDP department pays	64%	(9)
User department pays	36	(5)
	100	(14)
Charging policy for system operation		
EDP department pays	40%	(6)
User department pays	60	(9)
	100	(15)

a regional installation were scored as having a policy board only if the policy board consisted entirely of local members.

CAO involvement in the management of computing: the degree to which the chief executive participates in the management of the changes in computing, based on responses of the CAO to the following questions: "What changes do you anticipate in the use of computers in your department five years from now?" and "How do you intend to manage these changes?" (table A.8). A score of "1" indicated that the CAO expected to be completely passive and allow the DP to manage any changes; a score of "2" indicated that the CAO primarily expected to cooperate with DP, although DP would take the lead; a score of "3" indicated that the CAO expected team effort with DP as a co-equal partner; a score of "4" indicated that the CAO expected to be completely active and taking the lead in managing changes in computing.

Department head involvement in management of computing: the degree to which the department heads participate in the management of the changes in computing, based on the responses of the department heads to the questions: "What changes do you anticipate in the use of computers in your department five years from now?" and "How do you intend to manage these changes?" (table A.8). A score of "1" indicated that the department head expected to be completely passive and allow DP to manage any changes; a score of "2" indicated that the department head expected to cooperate with DP, although DP would take the lead; a score of "3" indicated that the department head expected team effort with DP as a co-equal partner; a score of "4" indicated that the department head expected to be completely active and to take the lead in managing changes in computing. The city-level score was obtained by computing an average of all department head responses within the city.

Charging policy for development: whether development charges are assumed by the user department or by the EDP department, obtained from responses to the Form C question: "How are budgeting and personnel matters involving computer services accounted for in the department for developing systems?" (table A.8). City-level scores were obtained by comparing all responses for consistency and checking site reports and other accompanying documents when different responses were noted.

Charging policy for system operation: whether operating charges are assumed by the user department or by the EDP department, obtained from responses to the Form C interview item: "How are budgeting and personnel matters involving computer services accounted for in the department for operating system?" (table A.8). City-level scores were obtained by comparing all department head responses and checking site reports and other accompanying documents where different responses occurred.

3.2.5 SOCIO-TECHNICAL INTERFACE

User involvement in design: the degree to which users are actively involved in the design of applications for their particular departments, obtained from Form E responses (table A.9). Responses were coded into seven initial categories: 1) no involvement at all (i.e., we just use it; 2) reviewed and adopted the application as is; 3) extensively modified the application as presented; 4) participated in the design of the application; 5) participated in the design and programming of the application; 6) managed the project and assisted in the design and programming of the application, and 7) completely managed, designed, and programmed the application. The variable was then recoded into three categories: 1) low (scores 1–3); 2) moderate (scores 4–5); and 3) high (scores 6–7). Finally, the mean score by city, over all applications surveyed, for each section head, was then calculated.

Orientation of department heads: the extent to which department heads have attended computer appreciation courses, based on the report by each department head (table A.9). City-level scores were obtained through mean aggregation of all department head responses in each city.

Orientation of section head: the extent to which section heads have attended computer appreciation courses. City-level scores were

Table A.9 DISTRIBUTIONS OF SOCIO-TECHNICAL INTERFACE VARIABLES

	Mean	Standard Deviation	Range	(N)
User involvement in design	1.72	.56	1.00–3.00	(14)
Orientation of department heads	1.72	.32	1.00–2.00	(16)
Orientation of section heads	1.59	.31	1.00–2.00	(13)

obtained by mean aggregation of responses of all section heads in each city.

3.3 DEPENDENT VARIABLES

3.3.1 BENEFITS

Efficiency Index: the extent to which computing has resulted in increased speed of operations and accuracy of data in local government operations (two dimensions of efficiency) (table A.10). This index was built from "no" (score = 0) and "yes" (score = 1) responses to three questions on Form D related to each application used: 1) "Has the introduction of the application as compared to previous system, if any, led to more efficient transaction of business?"; 2) "Has the introduction of the application as compared to previous system, if any, led to increased capacity to handle workload?"; and 3) "Has the introduction of the application as compared to previous system, if any, led to reduced error rate?"

City-level measures were obtained by averaging the section head's response to each item across the applications being assessed, then creating a mean aggregation across section head respondents within each city. The Efficiency Index is therefore the average of the three city-level efficiency measures.

Savings Index: the extent to which cost savings and staff savings have been realized due to computing (table A.10). This index was built from "no" (score = 0) and "yes" (score = 1) responses to the question on Form D for each application in use: "Has the introduction of the application as compared to previous system, if any, led to staff savings?" An average of the assessments for each application was calculated, and a city-level score was obtained by mean-aggregating all responses within the city. A measure of cost savings was obtained from responses to the question: "What are the annual savings/costs when compared to (previous, manual) alternatives?" Responses were originally coded: 1 = much more costly, 2 = more costly, 3 = no difference, 4 = less costly, and 5 = much less costly. These responses were recoded such that 0 = much more costly to no difference and 1 = less costly and much less costly, and a city-level score was obtained by the mean aggregation of all section head

Table A.10 DISTRIBUTION OF BENEFITS AND PROBLEMS VARIABLES

Index	Mean	Standard Deviation	Range	(N)
Efficiency	.54	.22	0–.82	(15)
Savings	.45	.21	0–.76	(13)
Service delivery effectiveness	.47	.24	0–.88	(15)
Staff problems	1.06	1.48	0–5	(16)
Technical problems	1.19	1.28	0–4	(16)
Responsiveness problems	1.19	1.38	0–4	(16)
Resource problems	2.25	1.48	0–5	(16)
Support problems	.94	1.06	0–3	(16)
Knowledge problems	1.06	1.18	0–4	(16)

	Percent of Cities	(N)
Management control over staff		
Not used	67%	(10)
Used	33	(5)
	100	(15)
Management decision-making		
Not used	60%	(9)
Used	40	(6)
	100	(15)
Management planning		
No impact	56%	(9)
Some impact	38	(6)
Impact	6	(1)
	100	(16)
Community planning		
No impact	50%	(8)
Some impact	44	(7)
Impact	6	(1)
	100	(16)

responses within the city. The Savings Index is the average of the city-level staff savings score and the city-level cost savings score.

Service Delivery Effectiveness Index: the extent to which computing has improved operations in terms of provision of better service delivery (table A.10). None of the OECD interview forms directly addressed this issue, so the indicators used are indirect. The index was built from "no" (score = 0) and "yes" (score = 1) responses to the following Form D questions about each application in use: 1) "Has the introduction of the application as compared to previous system, if any, led to greater ability to cope with nonstandard situations?"; 2) "Has the introduction of the application as compared to previous system, if any, led to provision of better analysis?"; 3) "Has the introduction of the application as compared to previous system, if any, led to provision for more integrated presentation of data?"

Section heads could assess up to four different applications. Average scores over the multiple applications were calculated, and a city-level score was obtained by the mean aggregation of all section head average scores within the city. The Index is the average of the three city-level scores.

Management Control Over Staff: the extent to which management control over staff is increased by computing use (table A.10). The Form C open-ended question, "How do you use computer technology in performing your official duties?" had a possible response of increased management control with respect to staff and operations within the department. If any department heads interviewed within the city mentioned management control uses, the city was scored as utilizing computing for management control. This variable represents the presence or absence of the use of computing for management control purposes within any interviewed department within the city, but does not measure the degree to which management control is utilized.

Management Decision Making: the extent to which computing is used for management decision making (table A.10). Two possible responses to the Form C open-ended question, "How do you use computer technology in performing your official duties?" were used for this measure: "used for daily decision making" and "used in major decisions." If any department head mentioned utilizing computing for making daily decisions or for making major decisions, the city was scored as utilizing computing for these respective uses. These variables represent the presence or absence of the use of computing for daily and major decision making, but do not measure the degree to which computing is used for these types of general decision making. The variable Management Decision Making is a summary variable in which a city was scored as using computing for management decision making if any department head utilized the technology in making daily or major decisions.

Management Planning Impacts Index: the extent to which managers (CAO and department heads) utilize computing effectively in long-range planning within departments and city-wide (table A.10). The cities were scored by the investigators based on a composite listing of the responses to various items in the Form B and Form C interview schedules, plus reading of the site reports written during the interviews in the cities. All 16 cities were arrayed and clustered into 4 categories with 0 = no impact and 3 = high impact. Cities were therefore compared with one another in assigning scores.

Community Planning Impacts Index: the extent to which managers (CAO and department heads) utilize computing effectively in planning within the community (table A.10). The cities were scored by the investigators in a manner identical to that for Management Planning Impacts Index above.

3.3.2 PROBLEMS

The set of city-level Problems Indices were obtained by hand-coding each city based on the responses of the CAO, department heads, and section heads to the question in Forms B, C, and D: "What constraints do you have upon fuller exploitation of the computer's potential for your department?" This method was necessitated because various responses were elicited within each level of the government hierarchy. Given that respondents at different levels would be involved in computing differently, combining all responses, assigning equal weights to each response, and summating the responses within each category provided a "representative sampling" of problems. Summation of the number of times a particular problem category occurred provided some differentiation (although crude) to which each category of problems is experienced. Six categories were developed.

Staff Problems Index: the extent to which the city is experiencing problems in the interface between the computing staff and user staff, focusing primarily on inadequacies of the computing staff to deal with the needs of users.

Technical Problems Index: the extent to which the city is experiencing technical reliability difficulties of the hardware and software systems in day-to-day operations.

Responsiveness Problems Index: the extent to which the city is experiencing difficulties arising from inflexibility of the computing resource of the city to accommodate needs and changes of the user environment.

Resource Problems Index: the extent to which there are problems involving shortages of monetary, staff, hardware, data, or other computing resources within the city.

Support Problems Index: the extent to which there is an unwillingness by the city organization to accept and support computing activity.

Knowledge Problems Index: the extent to which there is a lack of user understanding as to what the abilities and constraints of computing and computing staff are in the city.

4.0 Specific URBIS Measures

This section describes the specific measures used for the URBIS cities in this book. The various measures were obtained from the following data files:

> Secondary data on the cities from the U.S. Census
> "Local Government Data Processing Installations, 1975" (Phase 1)
> "Management Oriented Computing (MOC) Interview" (Phase 2)
> "User-Core Questionnaire" (Phase 2)
> Site Report written by interviewer(s) for that city (Phase 2)

4.1 DESCRIPTION OF THE URBIS SAMPLES

Both phases of the URBIS project produced data at the individual level, the city level, and the installation level. In comparing the URBIS data with the OECD data, only city-level measures were used. Certain decisions concerning the aggregation of the URBIS data were made, which we will briefly describe.

User Core data base. Analysis of the relevant variables in the User Core data base required selection of certain respondents with roles similar to those surveyed in the OECD cities. The three role types selected were: chief executives, department heads, and section heads.

Several decision criteria were used in the selection process. For chief executives, either the CAO or the Mayor in each URBIS city was selected. The priority was to select the CAO from the city, but if no CAO was available (non-respondent or no CAO) the selection was then the Mayor. No Mayor or CAO substitutes were allowed (i.e., staff from the Mayor's or CAO's office were not used in place of the chief executive). Missing data is high for this role type; 9 of the 40 cities' executives did not complete the User Core questionnaire. Department heads were included if their task codes were one of the following: Traffic Ticket Director, Planning Director, Department Head. Section heads were included if their task codes were one of the following: Manpower Allocation Supervisor, Traffic Ticket Supervisor, Head of Balance Report Unit, Central Budget Unit Staff Analysts, Head of Budget Monitoring Unit, Division Head.

Since only those departments that used computing were included in the OECD survey, only URBIS department heads and section heads who worked in departments that used computing were included in the respondent pool. This selection criterion also helped to minimize the "non-attitude" responses to the User Core questions. (Attitude scales—most of the User Core—presume that the respondent has some feeling or attitude concerning the question. If the respondent is not involved in the area of questioning, the likelihood of random response increases.)

All User Core variables were aggregated to the city level by computations of means.

Installation data base. One of two different methods was used to aggregate data from those cities with multiple installations. In most cases, only one of the installations within the city was selected to "represent" that city. Based on previous research, we found it most successful to choose the installation that provided service to the largest number of users within the city (Kraemer, Dutton, and Northrop 1981). In some cases, however, we used aggregations of all installations within the city. This was the case for variables that related more to city policymaking and city characteristics than to operations of the installation. For example, the total EDP budget was obtained from all installations within the city as was the number of functional areas automated within the city. Similarly, the year in which the installation began servicing was also considered a city-level characteristic, and, in this instance, the earliest installation year was selected to provide an approximate indicator of when EDP processing first began within the city.

In the descriptions below the method of aggregation or selection is indicated.

4.2 INDEPENDENT VARIABLES

Listed below are the URBIS independent variables. These variables are similar to those for the OECD data base, but certain variables are unique to the URBIS data base.

4.2.1 CITY ENVIRONMENT

Size of population: the total size of the population (in thousands) of the city, from U.S. census reports for 1975 (table A.11).

Government budget: the total city operating expenditures in millions of dollars, obtained from the following MOC interview question: "Could you please provide the total amount expended during the last fiscal year (1975–76) by this city?" (table A.11).

4.2.2 COMPUTING ENVIRONMENT

EDP budget: obtained by summing the responses to the 1976 Installation Questionnaire inquiry of current budget amounts for the following categories: personnel (all salaries and fringe benefits); hardware; maintenance contracts, software purchases (including consultants); expenses associated with training and education of programmers and analysts; expenses associated with training users; materials and supplies; all other (such as travel, utilities, etc.). *EDP budget per capita* was then calculated by dividing the EDP budget by

Table A.11 DISTRIBUTION OF CITY ENVIRONMENT VARIABLES

	Mean	Standard Deviation	Range	(N)
Size of city	309,050	332,706	52,000– 1,862,000	(40)
Size of government budget	$150,919,000	$246,449,000	$6,000,000– $1,288,000,000	(37)

the city population, and *percent EDP budget of total budget* was calculated by dividing the EDP budget by the total city operating expenditures (table A.12). Both of these are city-level scores, not the scores of single installations.

Total EDP staff: obtained from responses to the 1976 Installation Questionnaire query: "Please provide the current number of full-time-equivalent positions for each of the following at your installation" for the EDP manager, assistant managers, managers of systems-analysts and programmers, managers of computer operations, supervisors of tab operations and keypunching, systems-analysts, combined systems-analysts and application-programmers, systems-programmers, application-programmers, computer operators, and data entry personnel. Total EDP staff is the summation of full-time equivalents in all positions listed. In cities in which there are multiple installations, the primary (major) installation was selected. EDP staff is thus the total number of EDP staff for the major installation within the city (table A.12).

Total clock hours per week (computers operational): an indicator of the degree of hardware usage in the installation, obtained from the 1975 Installation Questionnaire. For multiple installation cities, the primary (major) installation was used to represent the city (table A.12).

Year EDP began in city: obtained from responses to the 1976 Installation Questionnaire item: "Which year did your installation be-

Table A.12 DISTRIBUTION OF COMPUTING ENVIRONMENT VARIABLES

	Mean	Standard Deviation	Range	(N)
EDP budget per capita	$3.98	2.49	$.68–$11.15	(37)
Percent EDP budget of total budget	1.3%	.9%	.11%–4.0%	(36)
Total EDP staff	36.7	41.3	4–212	(40)
Total clock hours per week	97.5	45.3	20–168	(30)
Year EDP began in city	65.8	4.9	55–74	(40)
Degree of automation	62.6	34.3	4–152	(40)
Degree of functional automation	16.4	5.7	2–28	(40)
Total core capacity	577.7K	911.8K	8K–4324K	(40)

gin servicing?" (table A.12). For multiple installation cities, the earliest year among the installations was selected.

Degree of automation: the total number of computer applications operational in the city, which is a summation of the total number of applications circled by the EDP manager from an inventory of computer applications listed in the 1976 Installation Questionnaire (table A.12).

Degree of functional automation: a measure of the extensiveness of computerization within the city created by classifying applications for each city into the thirty-one functional areas of government operations listed in figure A.4. The total score is the sum of functional areas in which at least one application is operational in at least one installation (table A.12).

Total core capacity: the sum of total core capacity in kilobytes of the central processing units within the primary (major) installation in each city (table A.12).

4.2.3 TECHNOLOGICAL DEVELOPMENT

Degree of data linkage: a measure of the extent to which there is the capability to integrate and link data between files, created from the responses to the 1976 Installation Questionnaire item: "Do you have the capability for linking data coded on the basis of one geographic base, such as an address, to other geographic bases, such as census tract or land parcel?" (1 = "no," 2 = "yes"). In multiple installation cities the primary (major) installation was used (table A.l13).

Multiprogramming capability: an indirect measure of the sophistication of the hardware within the installation, obtained from the 1975 Installation Questionaire item: "Does your installation have the capability of processing multiple jobs concurrently in the same CPU (multiprogramming)?" In multiple installation cities the primary (major) installation was used (table A.13).

Degree of report sophistication: the degree to which local officials are using sophisticated computerized techniques, based on the classification of reports generally sent to city-level officials according to the presence of the following kinds of analyses: marginal or frequency tables; bar graphs, histograms, frequency polygons; bivariate correlations or cross-tabulations; maps; multivariate correlation,

Table A.13 DISTRIBUTION OF TECHNOLOGICAL DEVELOPMENT VARIABLES

	Percent of Cities	(N)
Degree of data linkage		
Do not have capability	44%	(17)
Have capability	56	(22)
	100	(39)
Multiprogramming used		
No	29%	(9)
Yes	71	(22)
	100	(31)
Degree of report sophistication		
Not in evidence	3%	(1)
Marginal or frequency tables	3	(1)
Bar graphs	25	(9)
Geobased analysis by fixed geographic areas	20	(7)
Bivariate correlations	20	(7)
Multivariate analyses	21	(8)
Geobased analyses involving changing geographic areas	8	(3)
	100	(36)
On-line capability		
Batch	30%	(12)
On-line	70	(28)
	100	(40)
Change in development priorities		
No	75%	(30)
Yes	25	(10)
	100	(40)
Hardware upgrading		
No upgrading	48%	(19)
One change	12	(5)
Two changes	18	(7)
Three changes	22	(9)
	100	(40)

	Mean	Standard Deviation	Range	(N)
Total applications in development	17.6	17.6	0–76	(34)
Total applications planned	36.2	29.2	0–111	(34)
Number of terminals	44.2	60.1	0–269	(28)

regression, factor analysis, cluster analysis; geobased analysis by fixed geographic area, i.e., census tract, district; geobased analyses involving geographic areas (data clearly aggregated at multiple levels of analysis). Guttman produced the following ordering (easiest to hardest) of these kinds of analyses (C.R. = .90): 1 = marginal or frequency tables; 2 = maps; 3 = bar graphs, 4 = geobased analysis by fixed geographic areas (e.g., census tract or district); 5 = bivariate correlations or cross-tabulations; and 6 = multivariate correlations, regression, factor analysis, cluster analysis, and geobased analyses involving data aggregated at multiple levels of analysis in changing geographic areas (table A.13).

On-line capability: whether the computing installation is capable of providing on-line computing (i.e., at least one application within the primary city installation was on-line and operational)(table A.13).

Change in development priorities: whether the primary city installation had experienced within the previous year a major change in priorities among systems that are in development, obtained from the 1976 Installation Questionnaire item (table A.13).

Hardware upgrading: an index of hardware changes within the previous year in the primary city installation, classified according to the following types of changes: 1) a change of major equipment vendors (switching from one to another), 2) a change in generation of machine, 3) a major change in sophistication of operating system, 4) a change in the number of CPU's, 5) a significant upgrading in size of CPU (table A.13).

Number of terminals: the total number of terminals attached to the primary city computer installation, an indirect measure of the extent of sophistication of the computer installation, obtained from responses to the 1976 Installation Questionnaire item: "Please indicate how many cathode ray tube terminals and remote time-sharing typewriter terminals are used by your installation." Total number of terminals is the summation of both cathode ray tube terminals and remote time-sharing typewriter terminals (table A.13). Only those cities which have an on-line capability were given a score for the number of terminals.

Total applications in development: the total number of applications being developed in all city computing installations in 1975, obtained from the 1975 Installation Questionnaire (table A.13).

Total applications planned: the total number of applications planned in all city installations during the next two years, obtained by the 1975 Installation Questionnaire (table A.13).

4.2.4 STRUCTURAL ARRANGEMENTS

Technological centralization: whether a computer installation is shared by a number of departments (single installation) or is primarily department-based (multiple-installation city). Each URBIS city was scored as either a single-installation city or a multiple-installation city, and single-installation cities were considered shared-computer-installation cities (table A.14). Note that "technological centralization" in the OECD cities meant "sharing" among local cities, while for in the URBIS cities "sharing" meant sharing among departments within a single city.

Recent reorganization: the number of structural changes experienced by the primary city installation in the previous year, based on responses to the 1976 Installation Questionnaire item regarding three kinds of changes: 1) a change in the physical location of the installation, 2) a change in EDP departmental location or status within the city government, 3) a change in relationship between computer installations, such as consolidation or division of EDP installations, or the establishment of new installations (table A.14).

Decentralized control of priorities: the degree to which user departments using the primary city installation are involved in the decisions regarding the use of computers, using responses to the following 1976 Installation Questionnaire item: "Which one of the following individuals or groups has the major influence over whether or not a new set of computer applications will be adopted: data-processing manager; department head over data processing; user department heads; chief appointed official; local legislature and mayor; an interdepartmental board or steering committee; an intergovernmental board or steering committee?" Cities were recoded as follows: 1 = centralized control (data-processing manager, department head over data processing, chief appointed official, local legislature and mayor, intergovernmental board or steering committee); 2 =

Table A.14 DISTRIBUTIONS OF STRUCTURAL ARRANGEMENTS VARIABLES

	Percent of Cities	(N)
Centralization		
Multiple installations	25%	(10)
Single installation	75	(30)
	100	(40)
Recent reorganization		
No changes	83%	(33)
One change	12	(5)
Two changes	5	(2)
	100	(40)
Decentralized control of priorities		
Centralized	73%	(29)
Moderate	12	(5)
Decentralized	15	(6)
	100	(40)
Charged for use		
Free	60%	(22)
User department pays	40	(15)
	100	(37)
Policy board used		
No	58%	(23)
Yes	42	(17)
	100	(40)

	Mean	Standard Deviation	Range	(N)
Board influence in applications	1.6	.4	1–2	(17)
Board influence in management	1.4	.4	1–2	(17)
Chief executive involvement	3.9	1.9	0–6	(38)
Department head involvement	2.9	1.3	0–5	(40)

moderate centralized control (interdepartmental board or steering committee); and 3 = decentralized control (user department heads)(table A.14).

Charged for computer use: whether or not departments are charged for their use of the primary installations of the city's computer (as opposed to receiving free computing), obtained from a 1976 Installation Questionnaire item (table A.14).

Policy board used: whether the major installation within the city uses a policy board, based on the 1976 Installation Questionnaire item: "Does your government have a user board or committee which recommends policies that affect the design and development of applications?" (table A.14).

Board influence in application development: the degree to which interdepartmental boards or steering committees are influential in application development, within the primary city installation, obtained from the responses ("yes" or "no") to the Installation Questionnaire items listed in table A.15. These items were factor analyzed, producing a two-factor solution. The index of the first, "board influence in applications," was constructed by summating the three highest-loading items on the factor and dividing by three (table A.14).

Board influence in management: the second factor identified above; the influence of interdepartmental boards or steering committees in policymaking in the primary city installation, from the items in table A.15. The three highest-loading items on the factor were summed and divided by three (table A.14).

CAO involvement in management of computing: the degree to which the chief executive participates in the management of the changes in computing in the primary city installation, based on responses to the 1976 Installation Questionnaire query about the CAO's influence in: deciding whether or not a new set of computer applications will be adopted; setting priorities for the development of new applications; approving budget requests for major equipment purchases; approving requests for new peripheral equipment in user departments; evaluating the services provided by the installation; and approving major reorganizations (e.g., changing the EDP departmental status or location) (table A.14).

Department heads involvement in management of computing: the degree to which department heads participate in the management of the changes in computing in the primary city installation, based on the evaluation of department head influence on the items listed above (table A.14).

Table A.15 FACTOR LOADINGS FOR BOARD ACTIVITY INDEXES: URBIS

	Board Involvement in Management	Board Involvement in Applications
Must approve requests for new peripheral equipment in user departments	.92	.08
Must approve major reorganizations, such as changing the departmental status or location of EDP	.90	.04
Must approve budget requests for major computer equipment purchases	.75	.32
Highly influential in deciding whether or not a new set of computer applications will be adopted	.19	.97
Highly involved in setting priorities for the development of new applications	.01	.79
Responsible for evaluating the services provided by the installation	.56	.63

4.2.5 SOCIO-TECHNICAL INTERFACE

User involvement in design: the degree to which users are actively involved in the design of applications provided to their particular departments by the primary city installation, obtained from the 1976 Installation Questionnaire item: "Considering applications developed in the last two years, how frequently did users of your data-processing unit perform each of the following tasks?" (listed in table A.16). The response categories were: never, for less than half of applications, for more than half, for almost all applications. The index (table A.17) was calculated by averaging the responses to the four highest loading variables on the first factor in the factor analysis. The factor labled "user involvement in EDP management" was not used for further analysis.

Programmers assigned by EDP to departments: the extent to which decentralization of EDP staff personnel is occurring within the primary city installation, based on responses to the Installation Questionnaire item: "Please indicate the number of EDP personnel employed by and paid by your installation that are assigned to user departments for applications development and assistance". "None" received the value "1," and any value of one or more received a "2" (table A.17).

Table A.16 FACTOR LOADINGS FOR USER INVOLVEMENT

	User Involvement in Design	User Involvement in EDP Management
Review designs for a new application	.77	.28
Provide test data for an application	.65	−.01
Sign off, accepting an application	.65	.11
Work as a member of a technical group in designing an application	.60	.13
Sit on a policy board overseeing the computer unit	.12	.79
Participate in assigning priority to data-processing projects	.13	.78

Programmers assigned by departments to EDP: similar to that above, but in responses to the question: "Please list the number of EDP personnel (other than those on your own staff) currently located within and paid by any agencies and departments using this installation": "None" received the value "1," and one or more received the value "2" (table A.17).

Training of department heads by EDP: whether the primary city installation provides training for department-level managers, based on response to the Installation Questionnaire item: "Approximately what percent of the department heads took EDP training courses, seminars, or conferences at your installation in the last year?" If the percent was 0, the city was scored as "1," providing no training. If the percent was greater than 0, the city was scored "2" (table A.17).

Training of users by EDP: identical to the above, except with respect to provision of training for users (table A.17).

4.2 DEPENDENT VARIABLES

4.2.1 BENEFITS

Efficiency index: the extent to which the city has experienced efficiency benefits from computing, consisting of the aggregated city-

Table A.17 DISTRIBUTIONS OF SOCIO-TECHNICAL INTERFACE VARIABLES

	Percent of Cities	(N)
Programmers assigned by EDP to departments		
No	72%	(29)
Yes	28	(11)
	100	(40)
Programmers assigned by departments to EDP		
No	38%	(15)
Yes	62	(25)
	100	(40)
Department-head training provided by EDP		
No	63%	(24)
Yes	37	(14)
	100	(40)
User training provided by EDP		
No	42%	(16)
Yes	58	(22)
	100	(40)

	Mean	Standard Deviation	Range	(N)
User involvement in design	1.7	.8	0–3	(39)

level scores of indicators of improved speed of operations and accuracy of data due to computing use. Speed of operations was measured by two User Core questions: "Computers save me time in looking for information," and "It [it does not] takes too long to get the information I need from the computer." Accuracy of data was measured by one User Core question: "Computerized data is [not] less accurate than data stored on manual files." These indicators were originally 4–point Likert-type items with the response categories: disagree, somewhat disagree, somewhat agree, agree. The responses were dichotomized such that 0 = disagree to somewhat agree, and 1 = agree. To obtain the city-level measure, all section head responses within each city were mean-aggregated to a single city score with scores ranging from 0 to 1.00. The Efficiency Index is the average of these four city-level scores, with a high score indicative of high efficiency impacts from computing. The distribution for this index is in table A.18.

Resource savings index: the extent to which the city has experienced cost and/or staff savings benefits from computing, consisting of the aggregated city-level scores of indicators of cost savings and staff savings. Cost savings was measured by one User Core question: "Where they have been applied, computers have reduced the cost of department operations." Staff savings was measured by one User Core question: "Where they have been applied, computers have reduced the number of people necessary to perform tasks in my department." As with those in the Efficiency Index, these indicators were originally 4-point Likert-type items. The same procedure was followed to produce the index scores. To obtain the city-level measure, all section head responses within each city were mean-aggregated to a single city score with scores ranging from 0 to 1.00. The Resource Savings Index is the average of these two city-level scores, with a high score indicative of high resource savings benefits from computing. The distribution for this variable is in table A.18.

Service delivery effectiveness: the extent to which the city has

Table A.18 DISTRIBUTION OF BENEFIT AND PROBLEMS VARIABLES

Index	Mean	Standard Deviation	Range	(N)
Efficiency	.49	.20	0–1.00	(39)
Resource savings	.19	.21	0–1.00	(39)
Service delivery effectiveness	.56	.26	0–1.00	(39)
Management control over staff	.74	.36	0–2.00	(40)
Management decision making	1.05	.40	0–2.00	(40)
Management planning	.65	.63	0–3.00	(37)
Community planning	1.05	1.01	0–3.00	(38)
EDP staff problems	.36	.18	0–1.00	(40)
EDP technical problems	.22	.14	0–1.00	(40)
EDP responsiveness problems	.29	.15	0–1.00	(40)
EDP resource problems	.30	.17	0–1.00	(40)
EDP support problems	.15	.10	0–1.00	(40)

experienced service delivery improvements from computing, consisting of the aggregated city-level score of one User Core question: "Computers have [not] failed to increase the effectiveness of my department in serving the public." As above, this indicator originally was a 4-point Likert-type item. It was handled in the same manner as the Efficiency and Resource Saving Indices (table A.18).

Management control over staff index: the extent to which the city has experienced staff control benefits from computing, consisting of the aggregated city-level scores of indicators of computing uses for control of staff by management. Staff control was measured by two User Core questions: "How much does computing increase your ability to control staff or units under your responsibility?" and "How useful to you has computer-based information been in identifying abuses or inefficiencies in units you supervise?" These indicators were originally 5-point items with the response categories: no computer-based information, not at all useful, somewhat useful, useful, very useful. These responses were trichotomized such that 0 = no computer-based information or not at all useful, 1 = somewhat useful, and 2 = useful to very useful. To obtain the city-level measure, all department head responses within each city were mean-aggregated to a single city score with scores ranging from 0 to 2.00. The Management Control over Staff Index is the average of these two city-level scores, with a high score indicative of high use of computing for staff control. The distribution for this variable is in table A.18.

Management decision-making index: the extent to which the city has experienced management decision making (both daily and major decisions) benefits from computing, consisting of the aggregated city-level scores of indicators of computing uses for decision making by management. Daily decision making was measured by two User Core questions: "How useful to you has computer-based information been for day-to-day expenditure decisions?" and "How useful has computer-based information been in allocating manpower?" Major decision making was measured by two User Core questions: "How useful has computer-based information been during the annual budget cycle?" and "How useful has computer-based information been for (decision on) salary questions and negotiations?" As with the management control over staff index above, these indicators were originally 5-point items. Scoring was done the same way. The management decision-making index is the average of the four city-level scores on these questions, with a high score indicative of high use of computing for management decision making. The distribution for this variable is in table A.18.

Management planning benefits index: the extent to which managers utilize computing effectively in long-range planning within departments and city-wide, as scored by the investigators based on a composite listing of the responses to various items in the MOC questionnaire, the User Core questionnaire, and the site reports written during the interview stage of URBIS Phase 2. All 40 cities were arrayed and clustered into a 4 category index with 0 = no impact and 3 = high impact. Cities were therefore compared with one another in assigning scores. The distribution for this variable is in table A.18.

Community planning benefits index: the extent to which managers utilize computing effectively in long-range planning with the community, scored by the investigators in a manner similar to management planning benefits index above (table A.18).

4.2.2 PROBLEMS

EDP staff problems index: the extent to which the city has experienced user-EDP staff interaction problems, consisting of the aggregated city-level scores of User Core questions regarding EDP staff. Three items were used for the index: "Data-processing staff are more interested in working on new computer uses than making improvements in ones we now use"; and "Data-processing staff are more intrigued with what the computer can do than with solving the problems of my department"; and "Data-processing staff confuse our conversations with their technical language." These three indicators were selected based on a factor analysis of all "problems" indicators using a principal factoring method with orthogonal rotation. The factor analysis results are in chapter 4 (table 4.1). These indicators were originally 4-point Likert-type items with the following response categories: disagree, somewhat disagree, somewhat agree, agree. The responses were dichotomized such that 0 = disagree, somewhat disagree, and 1 = somewhat agree, agree. To obtain the city-level measure, all CAO, department head, and section head responses within each city were mean-aggregated to a single city score with scores ranging from 0 to 1.00. The EDP staff problems index is the average of these three city-level scores, with a high score indicative of high EDP staff-user interaction problems. The distribution for this variable is in table A.18.

EDP technical problems index: the extent to which the city has experienced technically-based computing problems, consisting of the aggregated city-level scores of User Core questions regarding problems with technology. Two of the three items used were taken from a list of problems presented to the respondent with the following instructions: "Below are listed problems sometimes associated with data processing in local government. Indicate for each whether this has been a problem in your department, agency, or office within the last year." The technology-related problems were: "Foul-ups in day-to-day computer operations," and "Frequent technical and organizational changes in data-processing services." The response categories provided were: not a problem, at times a problem, often a problem, very often a problem. These categories were dichotomized into 0 = not a problem, at times a problem, and 1 = often a problem, very often a problem. The third question used for this index was: "Please rate the quality of the data-processing services provided to your department, agency, or office." The 4-point rating scale was from poor to fair to good to excellent. Responses to this item were dichotomized into 0 = poor, fair and 1 = good, excellent. These three indicators were selected based on a factor analysis of all "problems" indicators using a principal factoring method with orthogonal rotations. The factor analysis results are in chapter 4 (table 4.1). To obtain the city-level measure, all CAO, department head, and section head responses within each city were mean-aggregated to a single city score with scores ranging from 0 to 1.00. The EDP Technical Problems Index is the average of these three city-level scores, with a high score indicative of high EDP technologically based problems. The distribution for this variable is in table A.18.

EDP responsiveness problems index: the extent to which the city has experienced computing responsiveness problems, from the same User Core question used in the technical problems index. The three responsiveness-related problems were: "Slow response of data processing to requests for information"; "Computer-based data not available for the analysis of specific questions or problems"; and "Difficulty in getting priority in using the computer." The same analysis was used for these questions as was used in the responsiveness problems index. The distribution for this variable is in table A.18.

EDP resource problems index: the extent to which the city has experienced computing resource problems, from the same User Core question used to construct the responsiveness problems index. The resource-related problems were: "High cost of computer use"; and "Difficulties in accessing computer-based data gathered or held by other departments and agencies." Analysis was the same as that used in the responsiveness problems index. The distribution for this variable is in table A.18.

EDP support problems index: the extent to which the city has experienced problems with support for computing, consisting of the aggregated city-level scores on two User Core questions: "In general, computers and data processing have failed to live up to my expectations"; and "Within the next five years, computers will [not] greatly improve the operations of this government." These indicators were originally 4-point Likert-type items with the following response categories: disagree, somewhat disagree, somewhat agree, agree. The responses were dichotomized such that $0 =$ disagree, somewhat disagree, and $1 =$ somewhat agree, agree. These two indicators were selected based on a factor analysis of all "problems" indicators using a principal factoring method with orthogonal rotation. The factor analysis results are presented (table 4.1). To obtain the city-level measure, all CAO, department head, and section head responses within each city were mean-aggregated to a single city score with scores ranging from 0 to 1.00. The EDP Support Problems Index is the average of these two city-level scores, with a high score indicative of EDP support problems. The distribution for this variable is in table A.18.

REFERENCES

Ackoff, R. 1967. Management misinformation systems. *Management Science,* 14(4):B147–156.

Ahituv, N. and S. Neumann. 1982. *Principles of Information Systems for Management.* Dubuque, Iowa: W. C. Brown.

Allen, B. R. 1981. Technology is not enough. In C. Ross, ed., *Proceedings of the Second International Conference on Information Systems,* pp. 365–378. Cambridge, Mass.: Society for Management Information Systems.

Alter, S. 1977. A taxonomy of decision support systems. *Sloan Management Review* (Fall).

Alter, S. 1980. *Decision Support Systems: Current Practices and Continuing Challenges.* Reading, Mass.: Addison-Wesley.

Appleton, D. S., K. L. Kraemer, and D. G. Schetter. 1977. *A National Urban Information Systems Resource Center: Assessment of Need and Concept.* Irvine, Calif.: Public Policy Research Organization, University of California, Irvine.

Arrow, K. J. 1970. *Social Choice and Individual Values.* 2d ed. New Haven, Conn.: Yale University Press.

Austrian, G. D. 1982. *Herman Hollerith: Forgotten Giant of Information Processing.* New York: Columbia University Press.

Bassler, R. A. and N. L. Enger. 1976. *Computer Systems and Public Administrators.* Alexandria, Va.: College Readings.

Baumes, G. C. 1961. *Administration of Electronic Data Processing.* NICB BPS #98, New York: National Industrial Conference Board.

Baumol, W. 1959. *Economic Dynamics.* New York: Macmillan.

Bernstein. J. 1963. *The Analytical Engine: Computers—Past, Present, and Future.* New York: Random House.

Blau, P. and R. Schoenherr. 1971. *The Structure of Organizations.* New York: Basic Books.

Boehm, B. W. 1981. *Software Engineering Economics.* Englewood Cliffs, N.J.: Prentice-Hall.

Boguslaw, R. 1965. *The New Utopians.* Englewood Cliffs, N.J.: Prentice-Hall.

Boutell, W. S. 1968. *Computer-Oriented Business Systems.* Englewood Cliffs, N.J.: Prentice-Hall.

Brandon, D. H. 1972. Computer acquisition method analysis. *Datamation* (September), vol. 9.

Braudel, F. 1981. *The Structures of Everyday Life.* London: Collins.

Brooks, F. P. 1975. *The Mythical Man Month.* Reading, Mass.: Addison-Wesley.

Canning, R. G. 1956. *Electronic Data Processing for Business and Industry.* New York: Wiley.

Chapin, N. 1955. *An Introduction to Automatic Computers.* New York: Van Nostrand.

Chartrand, R. L. 1972. *Computers and Political Campaigning.* New York: Spartan Books.

Chartrand, R. L. 1976. Information science in the legislative process. In *Annual Review of Information Science and Technology,* 11:332. Washington, D.C.: American Society for Information Science.

Child, J. 1972. Organization structure and strategies of control: A replication of the Aston Study. *Administrative Science Quarterly,* 17:163–177.

Chrysler, E. 1978. Some basic determinants of computer programmer productivity. *Communications of the ACM,* vol. 21, no. 6.

Churchill, N. C., J. L. Kempster, and M. Uretsky. 1969. *Computer-Based Information Systems for Management: A Survey.* New York: National Association of Accountants.

Colton, K. W. 1978. *Police Computer Technology.* Lexington, Mass.: Lexington Books.

CED (Committee for Economic Development). 1976. *Improving Productivity in State and Local Government.* New York: CED.

Converse, P. E. 1964. The nature of belief systems in mass publics. In D. E. Apter, ed., *Ideology and Discontent.* New York: Free Press.

Council of State Governments. 1974. *State Use of Electronic Data Processing.* Lexington, Ky.: Council of State Governments.

Crecine, J. P. 1967. A computer simulation model of municipal budgeting. *Management Science,* 13:786–815.

Cyert, R. M. and J. G. March. 1956. Organizational factors in the theory of oligopoly. *Quarterly Journal of Economics* (February), pp. 40–51.

Cyert, R. M. and J. G. March. 1963. *A Behavioral Theory of the Firm.* Englewood Cliffs, N.J.: Prentice-Hall.

Dallota, T. A., M. I. Bernstein, R. S. Dickson, Jr., N. A. France, B. A. Rosenblatt, D. M. Smith, and T. B. Steel, Jr. 1980. *Data Processing in 1980–1985.* New York: Wiley.

Daniel, D. R. 1961. "5000-mile check up" for computer installations. *Management Review,* 1(3):21–66.

Danziger, J. N. 1977a. Computers and the frustrated chief executive. *MIS Quarterly,* 1(2):43–53.

Danziger, J. N. 1977b. Computers, local governments, and the litany to EDP. *Public Administration Review,* 37(1):28–37.

Danziger, J. N. 1979. The skill bureaucracy and intra-organizational control. *Sociology of Work and Occupations,* 6(2):204–226.

Danziger, J. N. and W. H. Dutton. 1977. Technological innovation in local government: The case of computing. *Policy and Politics,* 6(1):27–49.

Danziger, J. N., W. H. Dutton, R. Kling, and K. L. Kraemer. 1982. *Computers and Politics: High Technology in American Local Governments.* New York: Columbia University Press.

Danziger, J. N., K. L. Kraemer, and J. L. King. 1977. An assessment of computer technology in U.S. local governments. *Journal of Urban Systems,* vol. 2, no. 2.

Davis, G. B. 1973. *Computer Data Processing.* 2d ed. New York: McGraw-Hill.

Davis, O. A., M. A. Dempster, and A. A. Wildavsky. 1966. A theory of the budgetary process. *American Political Science Review,* 9(3):529–547.

Davis, R. M. 1972. Federal interest in computer utilization by state and local governments. *The Bureaucrat,* 1(4):349–356.

Dearden, J. 1965. How to organize information systems. *Harvard Business Review,* 43(2):65–73.

Dearden, J. 1966. *Computers in Business Management.* Homewood, Ill.: Dow Jones-Irwin.

Dearden, J. 1972. MIS is a mirage. *Harvard Business Review* (January/February), p. 90.

Dearden, J. and R. L. Nolan. 1973. How to control the computer resource. *Harvard Business Review* (November/December), p. 68.

Dial, O. E., ed. 1972. Computers: To dedicate or not to dedicate, that is the question. *The Bureaucrat,* 1(4):305–378.

Dickson, G. W. and R. F. Powers. 1971. *MIS Project Management: Myths, Opinions, and Reality.* Minneapolis: University of Minnesota Management Information Systems Research Center.

Diebold, J. 1962. Bad decisions on computer use. *Harvard Business Review,* 47(1):14–28.

Downs, A. 1967. A realistic look at the final payoffs from urban data systems. *Public Administration Review,* 27(3):204–210.

Downs, G. and L. Mohr. 1976. Conceptual issues in the study of innovation. *Administrative Science Quarterly,* 21:700–702.

Drury, D. H. 1983. An empirical assessment of the stages of EDP growth. *MIS Quarterly,* 7(2):59–70.

Dutton, W. H. 1975. Major policy concerns facing chief executives. *Nation's Cities,* 10(3):28–30.

Dutton, W. H. and S. Pearson. 1975. Executives cite common data systems problems. *Nation's Cities,* 10(3):33–36.

Dutton, W. H. and K. L. Kraemer. 1979. Technology and urban management: The power payoffs of computing. *Administration and Society,* 9(3):305–340.

Dutton, W. H. and K. L. Kraemer. 1983. *Modeling as Negotiating: The Political Dynamics of Computer Models in the Policy Process.* Irvine, Calif.: Public Policy Research Organization, University of California.

Edwards, A. L. 1957. *Techniques of Attitude Scale Construction.* New York: Appleton-Century-Crofts.

Ein-Dor, P. and E. Segev. 1978. *Managing Management Information Systems.* Lexington, Mass.: Lexington Books.

Feigenbaum, E. A. and J. Feldman, eds. 1963. *Computers and Thought.* New York: McGraw Hill.

Fuller, R. B. 1970. *Operating Manual for Spaceship Earth.* New York: Pocket Books.

Gaits, G. 1978. Description of the OECD study on Local Government and Information Technology, and Principal Findings. In OECD, *Local Government and Information Technology,* Informatics Studies #12. Paris: OECD.

Galtung, J. 1967. *Theory and Methods of Social Research.* London: Allen & Unwin.

Garrity, J. T. 1963. Top management and computer profits. *Harvard Business Review,* 41(4):6–12.

Garrity, J. T. and V. L. Barnes. 1964. The payout on computers: What management has learned about planning and control. *Management Review,* 53(12):4–15.

Gibson, C. F. and R. L. Nolan. 1974. Managing the four stages of EDP growth. *Harvard Business Review,* 52(1):76–88.

Gill, S. and P. A. Samet. 1969. Charging for computer time in universities. *Computer Bulletin,* 13(1):499–509.

Glaser, G. 1970. The centralization vs. decentralization issue. *Data Base,* 2(3):3.

Glaser, G., A. L. Torrance, and M. H. Schwartz. 1983. Administrative applications. In A. Ralston and E. D. Reilly, eds., *Encyclopedia of Computer Science and Engineering,* pp. 23–40. New York: Van Nostrand-Reinhold.

Goldstein, R. and I. McCririk. 1981. The stage hypothesis and data administration. In C. Ross, ed., *Proceedings of the Second International Conference on Information Systems,* pp. 309–324. Cambridge, Mass.: Society for Management Information Systems.

Goldstine, H. H. 1972. *The Computer from Pascal to von Neumann.* Princeton, N.J.: Princeton University Press.

Greenberger, M., ed. 1962. *Management and the Computer of the Future.* New York: Wiley.

Gregory, R. H. and R. L. Van Horn. 1960. *Automatic Data Processing Systems.* San Francisco: Wadsworth.

Guthrie, A. 1972. *A Survey of Canadian Middle Manager's Attitudes Towards Management Information Systems.* Ottawa: Carleton University.

Harvard. 1967. Computer Management Series, Part 1. Reprints from the *Harvard Business Review.* Cambridge: Harvard Business Review.

Harvard. 1969. Computer Management Series, Part 2. Reprints from the *Harvard Business Review.* Cambridge: Harvard Business Review.

Harvard. 1976. Management Information Series, Part 3. Reprints from *Harvard Business Review.* Cambridge: Harvard Business Review.

Heany, D. F. 1968. *Development of Information Systems.* New York: Ronald Press.

Heilbroner, R. L. 1979. Reflections. *New Yorker* (October 8), 55:121–123. Reprinted in *Los Angeles Times,* October 21, Opinion Section.

Hicks, J. R. 1939. The foundations of welfare economics. *Economic Journal,* 49:696–712.

Hoos, I. R. 1960. When the computer takes over the office. *Harvard Business Review,* 38(4):102–112.

Hootman, J. T. 1969. The pricing dilemma: It all adds up. *Datamation,* 15(8):61–66.

Horton, F. W. and D. A. Marchand. 1982. *Information Management in Public Administration.* Arlington, Va.: Information Resources Press.

Humphrey, S. and R. Yearsley. 1970. *Computers for Management.* New York: American Elsevier.

Illich, I. 1971. *Deschooling Society.* New York: Harper and Row.

International City Management Association. 1976. *The Municipal Year Book.* Washington, D.C.: ICMA.

Jenkins, J. M. and R. S. Santos. 1982. Centralization vs. decentralization of data processing functions. In R. Goldberg and H. Lorin, eds., *The Economics of Information Processing.* New York: Wiley.

Kanter, J. 1977. *Management-Oriented Management Information Systems.* Englewood Cliffs, N.J.: Prentice-Hall.

Kimbel, D. 1973. *Computers and Telecommunications: Economic, Technical and Organizational Issues.* Paris: OECD.

Kimberly, J. R. 1976. Organizational size and the structuralist perspective: A review, critique and proposal. *Administrative Science Quarterly,* 21:571–597.

King, J. L. 1978. Centralization vs. decentralization of computing. Irvine, Calif.: Public Policy Research Organization, University of California.

King, J. L. 1980. Organizational cost considerations in computing decentralization. Irvine, Calif.: Public Policy Research Organization, University of California.

King, J. L. 1982. Local government use of information technology: The next decade. *Public Administration Review* (January/February).

King, J. L. 1983. Centralized vs. decentralized computing: Organizational considerations and management options. Working paper, Department of Information and Computer Science, University of California, Irvine.

King, J. L. and K. L. Kraemer. 1978. Electronic funds transfer as a subject of study in technology, society and public policy. *Telecommunications Policy,* 2(1):13–21.

King, J. L. and K. L. Kraemer. 1980. Cost as a social impact of information technology. In M. L. Moss, ed., *Telecommunications and Productivity,* pp. 93–130. Reading, Mass.: Addison-Wesley.

King, J. L. and K. L. Kraemer. 1983. Evolution and organizational information systems: An assessment of Nolan's stage model. Irvine, Calif.: Public Policy Research Organization, University of California.

King, J. L. and E. L. Schrems. 1978. Cost-benefit analysis in information systems development and operation. *Computing Surveys,* 10(1):19–34.

Klein, B. H. 1977. *Dynamic Economics.* Cambridge: Harvard University Press.

Kling, R. 1979. Social analyses of computing: Theoretical perspectives in recent empirical research. *Computing Surveys,* 12(1):61–110.

Kling, R. and P. Crabtree. 1978. DP sales ploys and counterploys. *Datamation,* 24(6):194–203.

Kling, R. and W. Scacchi. 1979. Recurrent dilemmas of computer use in complex organizations. In *AFIPS Conference Proceedings,* 48:107–115. Montvale, N.J.: AFIPS Press.

Kling, R. and W. Scacchi. 1982. The web of computing: Computer technology at social organization. In M. Yovits, ed., *Advances in Computers 21.* New York: Academic Press.

Kozmetsky, G. and P. Kircher. 1956. *Electronic Computers and Management Control.* New York: McGraw-Hill.

Kraemer, K. L. 1969. The evolution of information systems for urban administration. *Public Administration Review,* 29(4):389–402.

Kraemer, K. L. 1971. USAC: An evolving intergovernmental mechanism for urban information systems development. *Public Administration Review,* 31:543–551b.

Kraemer, K. L. 1974. Information in urban systems. *International Review of Administrative Sciences,* 15(2). Brussels.

Kraemer, K. L. 1976. Transferring R&D technologies and lessons learned in the United States. In B. S. Wellar, ed., *Information Technology and Urban Governance.* Ottawa: Ministry of State for Urban Affairs.

Kraemer, K. L. 1977. Local government, information systems and technology transfer in the U.S.: Evaluating some common beliefs about transfer of computer applications. *Public Administration Review* (March/April), vol. 37, no. 2.

Kraemer, K. L. 1978. An assessment of federal research and development for state and local government information processing. Paper presented to AAAS Workshop on Priority Problems in State and Local Government Management, Finance, and Personnel. Reston, Va.: September 28–30.

Kraemer, K. L. 1980. Computers, information and power in local governments: A stage theory. In A. Mowshowitz, ed., *Human Choice and Computers,* pp. 213–235. New York: North-Holland.

Kraemer, K. L., J. N. Danziger, W. H. Dutton, and S. Pearson. 1975. Chief executives, local government and computers. *Nation's Cities* 13(10):17–40.

Kraemer, K. L., J. N. Danziger, W. H. Dutton, A. M. Mood, and R. Kling. 1976. A future cities survey research design for policy analysis. *Socio-Economic Planning Sciences,* 10(5):199–211.

Kraemer, K. L., J. N. Danziger, and J. L. King. 1978. Local government and information technology in the United States. In *Local Government and Information Technology.* Paris: OECD.

Kraemer, K. L. and W. H. Dutton. 1979. The interests served by technological reform. *Administration and Society,* 11(1):80–106.

Kraemer, K. L., W. H. Dutton, and J. Matthews. 1975. Municipal computers: Growth, usage and management. *Urban Data Service,* 8(2):1–15.

Kraemer, K. L., W. H. Dutton, and A. Northrop. 1981. *The Management of Information Systems.* New York: Columbia University Press.

Kraemer, K. L. and J. L. King. 1975. The URBIS project: A policy-oriented study of computing in local government. In D. Anochie, ed., *Computers, Local Government and Productivity.* URISA Conference Proceedings, Urban and Regional Information Systems Association, Chicago.

Kraemer, K. L. and J. L. King. 1976. *Computers, Power and Urban Management: What Every Local Executive Should Know.* Beverly Hills, Calif.: Sage Publications.

Kraemer, K. L. and J. L. King. 1977a. An analytical overview of urban information systems in the United States. RM77-22. Laxenburg, Austria: International Institute for Applied Systems Analysis, May.

Kraemer, K. L. and J. L. King. 1977b. *Computers and Local Government, Volume 1: A Review of Research.* New York: Praeger.

Kraemer, K. L. and J. L. King. 1977c. *Computers and Local Government, Volume 2: A Review of Research.* New York: Praeger.

Kraemer, K. L. and J. L. King. 1978a. Development of urban information systems: Status and international relevance of United States experience. *International Review of Administrative Sciences,* vol. 64, no. 3.

Kraemer, K. L. and J. L. King. 1978b. Laissez innover: A critique of federal involvement in development of urban information systems. *The Bureaucrat,* 7(3):23-31.

Kraemer, K. L. and J. L. King. 1979a. A requiem for USAC. *Policy Analysis,* 5(3):313-350.

Kraemer, K. L. and J. L. King. 1979b. Assessing the interaction between computing policies and problems: Toward an empirically-defined stage theory of computing evolution. Irvine, Calif.: Public Policy Research Organization, University of California, Irvine.

Kraemer, K. L. and J. L. King 1979c. New findings on the transfer of computing applications among cities. *Journal of Technology Transfer* (Fall), 4(1):99-110.

Kraemer, K. L. and J. L. King. 1981a. Computing policies and problems—A stage theory approach. *Telecommunications Policy,* 5(3):198-215.

Kraemer, K. L. and J. L. King, eds. 1981b. *Computers in Local Government: Finance and Administration.* Pennsauken, N.J.: Auerbach Publishers.

Kraemer, K. L. and J. L. King, eds. 1981c. *Computers in Local Government: Police and Fire.* Pennsauken, N.J.: Auerbach Publishers.

Kraemer, K. L. and J. L. King, eds. 1981d. *Computers in Local Government: Urban and Regional Planning.* Pennsauken, N.J.: Auerbach Publishers.

Kraemer, K. L. and J. L. Perry. 1979. The federal push to bring computer technology to local governments. *Public Administration Review,* 39(3):260-270.

Kraemer, K. L., J. R. Matthews, W. H. Dutton, and L. D. Hackathorn. 1976. *The Municipal Information Systems Directory.* Lexington, Mass.: Lexington Books.

Kreitzberg, C. B. and J. H. Webb. 1972. An approach to job pricing in a multiprogramming environment. *AFIPS Fall Joint Computer Conference Proceedings,* 41(1):115-122.

Kuznets, S. 1965. *Economic Growth and Structure: Selected Essays.* New York: Norton.

Lambright, W. H. 1976. *Governing Science and Technology.* New York: Oxford University Press.

La Piere, R. T. 1965. *Social Change.* New York: McGraw-Hill.

Laudon, K. C. 1974. *Computers and Bureaucratic Reform.* New York: Wiley.

Lawrence, P. R. and J. W. Lorsch. 1967. *Organization and Environment: Managing Differentiation and Integration.* Cambridge: Harvard University Graduate School of Business Administration.

Leavitt, H. J. and T. L. Whisler. 1958. Management in the 1980's. *Harvard Business Review,* 36(6):41–48.

Leege, D. C. and W. L. Francis. 1974. *Political Research.* New York: Basic Books.

Library of Congress, Congressional Research Service. 1976. *State Legislative Use of Information Technology.* Washington, D.C.: GPO.

Library of Congress, Congressional Research Service. 1977. *State Legislative Use of Information Technology.* Washington, D.C.: GPO.

Lipperman, L. L. 1968. Advanced business systems. *American Management Association Research Study No. 86.* New York: American Management Association.

Lockheed Missiles and Space Company. 1965. California state-wide information system study. Final Report No. Y–82–65–6. Sunnyvale, Calif.: Lockheed Missiles and Space Company.

Lucas, H. C. 1973a. *Why Information Systems Fail.* New York: Columbia University Press.

Lucas, H. C. 1973b. *Computer Based Information Systems in Organizations.* New York: SRA.

Lucas, H. C. 1974a. *Towards Creative Systems Design.* New York: Columbia University Press.

Lucas, H. C. 1974b. An empirical study of a framework for information systems. *Decision Sciences,* 5(1):102–114.

Lucas, H. C. 1982. *Coping with Computing.* New York: Free Press.

Lucas, H. C. and J. Sutton. 1977. The stage hypothesis and the S curve: Some contradictory evidence. *Communications of the ACM,* 20(4):254–259.

Luing, G. A. 1969. Integrated information systems for large and small municipalities. *Municipal Finance,* 41(3):138–144.

Marx, K. 1867, 1962. *Das Kapital.* Berlin: Dietz.

Matthews, J. R., W. H. Dutton, and K. L. Kraemer. 1976. County computers: Growth, usage and management. *Urban Data Service Report* (February), vol. 8, no. 2.

Matthews, J. R., K. L. Kraemer, L. D. Hackathorn, and H. W. Dutton. 1976. *The County Information Systems Directory.* Lexington, Mass.: Lexington Books.

McDonough, A. M. 1963. *Information Economic and Management Systems.* New York: McGraw-Hill.

McFarlan, F. W. 1971. Problems in planning the information systems. *Harvard Business Review* (March/April), p. 78.

McFarlan, F. W., R. L. Nolan, and D. P. Norton. 1973. *Information Systems Administration.* New York: Holt, Rinehart and Winston.

McGuire, M. C. 1982. Normative economics. In D. Greenwald, ed., *Encyclopedia of Economics,* pp. 708–710. New York: McGraw-Hill.

McKenney, J. L. and F. W. McFarlan. 1983. The information archipelago—maps and bridges. *Harvard Business Review,* 60(5):109–119.

McLean, E. R. and J. V. Soden, eds. 1977. *Strategic Planning for MIS.* New York: Wiley.

McRae, T. W. 1970. The evaluation of investment in computers. *Abacus,* 6:56–70.

Meyer, M. W. 1972. Size and structure of organizations: A causal analysis. *American Sociological Review,* 37:434–440.

273   References

Meyers, C. A. 1967. *The Impact of Computers on Management.* Cambridge: MIT Press.

Middleton, C. J. 1967. How to set up a project organization. *Harvard Business Review,* 45(2):73–82.

Minsky, M. 1967. *Computation, Finite and Infinite Machines.* Englewood Cliffs, N.J.: Prentice-Hall.

Moore, W. E. 1967. *Order and Change: Essays in Contemporary Sociology.* New York: Wiley.

Moore, W. E. and R. M. Cook. 1967. *Readings on Social Change.* Englewood Cliffs, N.J.: Prentice-Hall.

Morgan, H. L. and J. V. Soden. 1973. Understanding MIS failures. Proceedings of the Wharton Conference on Research on Computers in Organizations. In *Data Base,* 5(2,3,4):157–171.

Mosely, M. 1964. *Irascible Genius: A Life of Charles Babbage, Inventor.* London: Hutchinson.

Murdick, R. G. and J. E. Ross. 1975. *MIS in Action.* St. Paul: West Publishing.

Nash, J. F. 1950. The bargaining problem. *Econometrica,* 18(2):155–162.

National Academy of Engineering. 1976. *Local Government Information Systems—A Study of USAC and Future Application of Computer Technology.* Washington, D.C.: National Academy of Sciences.

National Commission on Productivity and Work Quality. 1975. Fourth Annual Report. Washington, D.C.: GPO., March.

Nelson, R. A. and S. G. Winter. 1982. *An Evolutionary Theory of Economic Change.* Cambridge, Mass.: Belknap.

Newell, A. and H. A. Simon. 1972. *Human Problem Solving.* New York:McGraw-Hill.

Nielsen, N. R. 1968. Flexible pricing: An approach to the allocation of computer resources. *AFIPS Fall Joint Computer Conference Proceedings,* 31(1):521–531.

Nielsen, N. R. 1970. The allocation of computer resources: Is pricing the answer? *Communications of the ACM,* 13(8):467–474.

Nisbet, R. A. 1969. *Social Change and History: Aspects of the Western Theory of Development.* New York: Oxford University Press.

Nolan, R. L. 1973a. Managing the computer resource: A stage hypothesis. *Communications of the ACM,* 16(7):339–405.

Nolan, R. L. 1973b. Computer data bases: The future is now. *Harvard Business Review* (September/October), p. 98.

Nolan, R. L. 1973c. The plight of the EDP manager. *Harvard Business Review* (May/June), p. 143.

Nolan, R. L. 1977a. Controlling the costs of data services. *Harvard Business Review* (July/August).

Nolan, R. L. 1977b. *Management Accounting and Control of Data Processing.* New York: National Association of Accountants.

Nolan, R. L. 1979. Managing the crisis in data processing. *Harvard Business Review* (March/April), pp. 115–126.

Nolan, R. L. 1982. Managing information systems by committee. *Harvard Business Review,* 60(4):72–80.

OECD (Organization for Economic Cooperation and Development). 1971. *Computerized*

Databanks in Public Administration. OECD Informatics Studies #1. Paris: OECD.

OECD (Organization for Economic Cooperation and Development). 1972. *Digital Information and the Privacy Problem.* OECD Informatics Studies #2. Paris: OECD.

OECD (Organization for Economic Cooperation and Development). 1973a. *Computers and Telecommunications: Economic, Technical and Organizational Issues.* OECD Informatics Studies #3. Paris: OECD.

OECD (Organization for Economic Cooperation and Development). 1973b. *Automated Information Management in Public Administration: Present Developments and Impact.* OECD Informatics Studies #4. Paris: OECD.

OECD (Organization for Economic Cooperation and Development). 1973c. *Towards Central Government Computer Policies: Data Base Developments and International Dimensions.* OECD Informatics Studies #5. Paris: OECD.

OECD (Organization for Economic Cooperation and Development). 1974a. *The Evaluation of the Performance of Computer Systems.* OECD Informatics Studies #6. Paris: OECD.

OECD (Organization for Economic Cooperation and Development). 1974b. *Information Technology in Local Government.* OECD Informatics Studies #7. Paris: OECD.

OECD (Organization for Economic Cooperation and Development). 1975a. *Applications of Computer/Telecommunications Systems.* OECD Informatics Studies #8. Paris: OECD.

OECD (Organization for Economic Cooperation and Development). 1975b. *Training Policies for Computer Manpower and Users.* OECD Informatics Studies #9. Paris: OECD.

OECD (Organization for Economic Cooperation and Development). 1976. *Policy Issues in Data Protection and Privacy.* OECD Informatics Studies #10. Paris: OECD.

OECD (Organization for Economic Cooperation and Development). 1977. *Conference on Computer Telecommunications Policy.* OECD Informatics Studies #11. Paris: OECD.

OECD (Organization for Economic Cooperation and Development). 1978. *Local Government and Information Technology.* OECD Informatics Studies #12. Paris: OECD.

Orlicky, J. 1969. *The Successful Computer System.* New York: McGraw-Hill.

O'Toole, R. J. and E. F. O'Toole. 1966. Top management involvement in the EDP function. *Management Controls,* 13(6):124–132.

Pendleton, J. C. 1971. Integrated information systems. In AFIPS *Conference Proceedings,* pp. 491–500. 1971 Fall Joint Computer Conference. Montvale, N.J.: AFIPS.

Penitzka, C. 1978. General profile of participating cities. In OECD, *Local Government and Information Technology.* Paris: OECD.

Perry, J. L. and K. L. Kraemer. 1979. *Technological Innovation in American Local Governments: The Case of Computing.* New York: Pergamon.

Phister, M., Jr. 1979. *Data Processing Technology and Economics.* Bedford, Mass. Digital Press.

Ponsioen, J. A. 1969. *The Analysis of Social Change Reconsidered.* The Hague: Mouton.

Powers, R. F. 1971. An empirical investigation of selected hypotheses related to the success of management information systems projects. Ph.D. dissertation, University of Michigan. Ann Arbor, Mich.: University Microfilms.

Price, H. 1969. Centralized versus decentralized data processing in municipal government. *Data Processing,* 14:389–402.

Price, K. D. 1965. *The Scientific Estate.* Cambridge: Harvard University Press.

Przeworski, A. and H. Teune. 1970. *The Logic of Comparative Social Inquiry.* New York: Wiley.

PPRO (Public Policy Research Organization). 1974. Evaluation of information technology in the United States. A proposal submitted to the Research Applied to National Needs Division of the National Science Foundation.

PPRO (Public Policy Research Organization). 1977. A national urban information systems resource center: Assessment of need and concept. Final Report, submitted to the Office of Policy Development and Research, Department of Housing and Urban Development. Irvine, Calif.: PPRO.

Roessner, J. D. 1979. Federal technology policy: Innovation and problem solving in state and local governments. *Policy Analysis,* 5:181–200.

Rogers, E. 1975. Innovation in organizations: New research approaches. Paper presented at the conference of the American Political Science Association, San Francisco, September 2–5.

Rogers, E. and F. Shoemaker. 1971. *Communication of Innovation, Organizations.* 2d ed. New York: Free Press.

Rostow, W. W. 1971. *The Stages of Economic Growth.* 2d ed. Cambridge: Cambridge University Press.

Rothernberg, J. 1968. Consumer sovereignty. In D. L. Sills, ed., *International Encyclopedia of Social Sciences,* 13:326–335. New York: Macmillan, Free Press.

Saumier, A. and B. S. Wellar. 1974. *Results Accruing from Information Systems in Urban and Regional Governments: Contexts, Identification and Measurement, Appreciation.* Ottawa: Ministry of State for Urban Affairs.

Scacchi, W. S. 1981. The Process of Innovation in Computing. Irvine: Department of Information and Computer Science, University of California.

Schank, R. C. and K. M. Colby, eds. 1973. *Computer Models of Thought and Language.* San Francisco: Freeman.

Scheuch, E. K. 1968. The cross-cultural use of sample surveys: Problems of comparability. In S. Rokkan, ed., *Comparative Research across Cultures and Nations.* Paris: Mouton.

Schoderbeck, P. P. and J. D. Babcock. 1969a. The practice of computer selection: A survey of users. *Datamation,* 12(5):35–42.

Schoderbeck, P. P. and J. D. Babcock. 1969b. At last, management more active in EDP: Trends in involvement and applications. *Business Horizons,* 12(6):53–68.

Selltiz, C., L. Wrightsman, and S. Cook. 1976. *Research Methods In Social Relations.* New York: Holt, Rinehart and Winston.

Sharpe, W. F. 1969. *The Economics of Computers.* New York: Columbia University Press.

Shult, G. P. and T. L. Whisler, eds. 1960. *Management Organization and the Computer.* Glencoe, Ill.: Free Press.

Simon, H. 1973. Applying information technology to organizational design. *Public Administration Review,* 33(3):268–278.

Simon, H. A. 1960. *The New Science of Management Decision.* New York: Harper.

Simon, H. A. 1965. *The Shape of Automation for Man and Management.* New York: Harper and Row.

Smith, D. M. 1979. Data Processing in the 1980's. In A. E. Westley, ed., *Convergence: Computers, Communications, and Office Automation.* Vol. 2. Maidenhead, England: Infotech International.

Sobczak, J. J. 1974. Pricing computer usage. *Datamation,* 20(2):61–64.

Soloman, M. B. 1970. Economies of scale and computer personnel. *Datamation,* 16(3):107–110.

Sorokin, P. A. 1957. *Social and Cultural Dynamics.* Abridged. Boston: Porter Sargent.

Stewart, F. 1977. *Technology and Underdevelopment.* New York: Macmillan.

Swanson, E. B. 1974. Management information systems: Appreciation and involvement. *Management Science,* 21(2):178–188.

Thomas, U. 1971. *Computerized Data Banks in Public Administration.* Paris: OECD.

Tornatsky, L. G., J. D. Eveland, M. G. Boylan, W. A. Hetzner, E. C. Johnson, D. Roitman, and J. Schneider. 1983. *The Process of Technological Innovation: Reviewing the Literature.* Washington, D.C.: National Science Foundation.

Turing, A. M. 1936. On computable numbers, with an application to the *Entschiedungsproblem. Proceedings of the London Mathematics Society,* November 17, pp. 230–265.

Urban Institute. 1970. *The Struggle to Bring Technology to the Cities.* Washington, D.C.: Urban Institute.

Uretsky, M. 1973. Discussion comments. In *Proceedings of the Wharton Conference on Research on Computers and Organizations, Data Base,* 5(2):65–67.

USAC (Urban Information Systems Inter-Agency Committee). 1976. Support Panel, Committee on Telecommunications, Assembly of Engineering, National Research Council. An information systems resource center for local governments. Washington, D.C.: National Academy of Sciences.

van Parijs, P. 1981. *Evolutionary Explanations in the Social Sciences: An Emerging Paradigm.* Totowa, N.J.: Rowan and Littlefield.

Verba, S. 1969. The uses of survey research in the study of comparative politics: Issues and strategies. In S. Rokkan, S. Verba, J. Viet, and E. Almasy, *Comparative Survey Analysis.* Paris: Mouton.

von Neumann, J. 1958. *The Computer and the Brain.* New Haven: Yale University Press.

Weber, M. 1947. *The Theory of Social and Economic Organization.* New York: Free Press.

Webster, D. 1967. *Third New International Dictionary.* Springfield, Mass.: Merriam.

Weizenbaum, J. 1976. *Computer Power and Human Reason: From Judgment to Calculation.* San Francisco: Freeman.

Whisler, T. L. 1970. *The Impact of Computers on Organizations.* New York: Praeger.

Wildavsky, A. 1974. *The Politics of the Budgetary Process.* Boston: Little, Brown.

Zani, W. 1970. Blueprint for MIS. *Harvard Business Review,* 48(6):95–100.

INDEX

Accuracy, *see* Data

Ad hoc studies: city problems, 84-85

Adoption of computing: meaning, 38

Affective demand, 178; *see also* Demands of change

Aggregation: methods of, 230-31; *see also* URBIS/OECD Projects

Applications: application defined, 48-49; computing use, 48-53; degree of sophistication of, 237; number planned, 237-39, 253-54; number to be modified, 239; user involvement in design of, 242, 257; total in development and total planned, 253-54; board influence in, 256

Automation, degree of, 235, 251

Babbage, Charles, 3

Benefits of computing: data accuracy, 58, 62-63, 128-29; efficiencies realized, 58, 86-87, 128-29; cost savings and avoidance, 59, 63, 66, 86-87, 128-29; staff savings, 59, 63, 128-29; speed of operations, 59-62, 128-29; service delivery effectiveness, 63-66, 73-74, 86-87, 128-29; management control, 67-71, 79-82, 87-88, 128-29; managerial planning, 71-74, 82-83, 88, 128-29; community planning, 75-79, 83-86, 89; how to achieve, 113; policies and environment correlated, 128-38; classified, 129; URBIS cities, 129-34; OECD cities, 134-38; city size related to, 146-55; computing problems related to, 157-61; environments related to, 158; variables described, 243-46, 258-62

Black box, 7

Budgets: decision making in, 71, 83; "time-dependent workflow," 80-81; Nolan stage theory, 174, 177; variable described, 233, 249

CAO, *see* Chief appointed (executive) officer

Census data: described, 84

Centralization/decentralization debate, 7-8; URBIS/OECD cities contrasted, 42-44

Centralized arrangements: benefits realized, 166

Changes over time: method for factoring, 172; *see also* Stage theory

Chargeback systems: problems of, 11-12, 31*n*10; policy for, 112; development charges, 241; operating charges, 241-42, 255

Chief appointed (executive) officer: computing management involvement, 240-41, 256; User Core data base, 247-48

City environment: variables in, 110-11, 134; URBIS cities, 140-42; OECD cities, 145; variables described, 233, 249

City government: research benefits, 13-15; U.S. national policy towards, 20, 40; URBIS/OECD cities contrasted, 26-27, 34-37; computing problems, 27; computing activities, organization, 40-44; size's role in computing, 53-54; "reformed" government structures, 80; *see also* City size; Computing use; OECD cities; OECD Project; Personnel; URBIS cities; URBIS Project

City size: as city environment variable, 110-11;